# CEREMONIES of the HEART

## Celebrating Lesbian Unions

### Edited by Becky Butler

Seal Press

Grateful acknowledgment is made for permission to reprint the following: From "A Force for Families" by the American Home Economics Association, Washington, D.C., reprinted by permission of the American Home Economics Association; "Six Years," copyright © 1978 by Alice Bloch, first appeared in *rara avis*, reprinted by permission of the author; lines from twelfth-century verse-poem translated by John Boswell in *Christianity, Social Tolerance, and Homosexuality* by John Boswell, reprinted by permission of the author and the publisher, the University of Chicago Press, copyright © 1980 by The University of Chicago; "The Ones Who Aren't Here," copyright © 1982 by John Calvi, reprinted by permission of the author; lines from "Twenty-One Love Poems" and the lines from "Transcendental Etude" are reprinted from *The Fact of a Door Frame, Poems Selected and New 1950-1984*, by Adrienne Rich, by permission of the author and W. W. Norton & Co., Inc. Copyright © 1984 by Adrienne Rich. Copyright © 1975, 1978 by W. W. Norton & Co., Inc. Copyright © 1981 by Adrienne Rich; "To Wed at First Sight" by Mary Anne Martin first appeared in *Womyn's Press*, reprinted by permission of the author.

Grateful acknowledgment is also made for the use of excerpts from *The Riverhouse Stories* by Andrea Carlisle (Portland, OR: Eighth Mountain Press, 1988) and *Our Passion for Justice: Images of Power, Sexuality, and Liberation* by Carter Heyward (New York: The Pilgrim Press, 1984).

Cover design by Kate Thompson
Cover photo by Steve McElrath
    Dresses by Cicada, Seattle; flowers by Ilex, Seattle; stylist: Beth Beljon

*Library of Congress Cataloging-in-Publication Data*
Ceremonies of the heart : celebrating lesbian unions / edited by Becky Butler.
    1. Lesbian couples—United States. 2. Weddings—United States.
    3. Lesbianism—History.   I. Butler, Becky, 1958-
    HQ75.6.U5C47   1990
    306.73'8—dc20                                                90-8721
    ISBN 1-878067-87-7

Printed in the United States of America
Second edition printed January 1997
10 9 8 7 6 5 4 3 2 1

Distributed to the trade by Publishers Group West
Foreign Distribution:
    *In Canada:* Publishers Group West Canada
    *In Great Britain and Europe:* Airlift Book Company, London
    *In Australia:* BH Walshe & Son, Victoria

## Acknowledgments

There are a number of people whose support and assistance have been integral in helping this book take form. Faith Conlon, my editor at Seal Press, deserves special thanks for her enthusiasm as well as for her wise guidance. Our almost-daily conversations not only provided valuable direction but were also a source of great encouragement and sustenance for me. My thanks also to the production staff of Seal Press for their part in "birthing" this volume. Working with Seal Press has been a joy — an experience for which I am very grateful.

Thanks is also due to Cathy Johnson for her careful copy-editing and to Coletta Reid for bringing her fine editorial eye to the historical essay. Chris Lahowitch, Gayla Jamison, Nancy Ohlmeyer and Ryn Edwards all read portions of the manuscript and provided invaluable feedback and encouragement. Alfredo Duarte, Marjolein Kars, Marilyn Lavallee and Rene Searles all graciously translated international calls for submissions as well as correspondence and stories. My thanks to all of them. My love and gratitude also go to my dear friends, Maria Papacostaki and Harry Brod, for offering their wise counsel and loving support through every stage of this project.

Bet Power and the New Alexandria Lesbian Library provided wonderful resources for historical research. Yael and Luana Silverberg-Willis, Carol Bellin and Trinity Ordoña all helped to create a volume more nearly representative of the great diversity of lesbian experience. I also want to acknowledge my appreciation of Ruth Weber, Carol Tully and Kathryn Bigham, all of the University of Georgia School of Social Work, for their support of this project and for making it possible for me to complete this volume while working on my master's degree.

My heartfelt thanks go to Barbara Thomason, Suzanne Imes and the Monday night group, all of whom have helped keep me grounded and hopeful and given me at least a few glimpses of sanity while in the final throes of completing this book. I also want to thank my mother, Jean Rouverol Butler, for her unwavering support and love. Thanks also to the rest of my family for their love and encouragement, and to Rusty and Jim Bralley for making me feel so cared for and welcome.

When Patty Bralley and I first fell in love, we both hoped that our relationship would serve as the foundation from which we could create works which brought together heart, soul and mind. I hope that this book is only the first of many such projects. Aside from providing the inspiration for the anthology, Patty has been a constant source of encouragement, love and nurturing. In addition to offering the emotional support which has sustained me during the past three years of working on this book, she has also read and helped edit almost every line. Our partnership is truly the source of this volume, and I thank her for her support, her love, her belief in me and her extraordinary vision. Thanks is also due to Carole Light for accompanying Patty on her journey to me.

Lastly, my thanks go to the women who have contributed to this anthology. Their courage and commitment have been a continual source of inspiration.

# Contents

# Introduction

In 1990, when this book was first published, I felt as though I were witnessing the dawning of a new tradition. Lesbian couples choosing to acknowledge and honor their relationships with ceremonies were doing so not only outside the margins of heterosexual life, but outside the margins of lesbian life as well. Lesbian weddings were new and astonishing. Created out of nothing more than each couple's own hearts and imaginations, the ceremonies reflected a loving insistence on our right to define our own forms of family. The ceremonies also evoked impassioned debate: the dangers of treading so close to a tradition imbued with the patriarchal silencing of women versus the possibility of forever transforming that same tradition.

The debate about same-sex weddings, and same-sex marriage, continues. It is an invaluable one, reflecting a community intent upon both liberation and equal justice, wary of sacrificing ultimate freedom for a short-term vision of equality. But as the dialogue has continued, it has become increasingly evident that hope has outweighed wariness. Legal sanction of same-sex marriage has surged to the head of the lesbian and gay agenda and to the center of public policy debate. Legal recognition of same-sex marriage has become an arena where many important civil rights battles are being waged. Lesbian and gay advocacy groups are creating an ever-expanding coalition of support for allowing lesbian and gay couples to marry. Same-sex marriage has managed to tap the extraordinary energy that lies at the intersection of love and law.

This galvanizing of legal advocacy is not just a response to the confluence of several important judicial and legislative battles. Nor is it solely a practical response to the inequities not remedied by domestic partnership legislation. While these are important factors, I believe the principal factor is the symbolic charge carried by marriage. The hope and imagination of lesbians and gay men has been ignited by their right to full recognition of their unions: recognition by family, society, law and spirit.

While the battle for legal recognition continues, ceremonial acknowledgments of same-sex unions have flourished. Increasingly, lesbian couples are creating ceremonies to celebrate and honor their unions, presenting themselves, proudly and lovingly, before family, friends and spirit, as partners in life. And with all that has changed in the past several years, what remains is the sense of a new dawn.

There is something so uniquely empowering and sacred about creating an event to celebrate and honor a lesbian relationship. Lesbian ceremonies do not involve the sense of inevitability that often accompanies heterosexual weddings. There is a sense of wonder, a sense of something new and evolving. There is never an assumption that if a lesbian relationship is strong enough or committed enough, a wedding will certainly follow. Because of this quality of being somehow unexpected, I believe we approach our decisions to have such ceremonies with particular awareness. Some lesbian couples may decide that their ceremony is, in fact, a wedding, but that definition is not automatically assumed. For lesbians, ceremonies of union are still fluid in meaning and form. With that fluidity comes great freedom, as well as a demand for consideration and definition.

The first question is frequently, What does the ceremony mean? It's a question that is central to the creation of new forms and new traditions. For many couples, the process of answering this question is the most valuable aspect of creating their ceremony. The ceremony itself often begins here, with the discovering, and creating, of meaning. It is a process which involves the subtle interplay of heart and mind and arriving at a shared vision not only of the ceremony but also of the relationship itself. What does it mean for two people to create a life together? What qualities does this union embrace? What hopes and dreams do we bring to one another?

A ceremony can become a way to express a couple's gratitude for what their relationship has already brought them, as well as a way of celebrating what lies ahead. As a backdrop for their ceremony, Patti and Diane embroidered a banner with a quote from Dag Hammarskjöld, "For all that has been—thanks! To all that shall be—yes!" The ceremony was an offering of thanks for what had passed and a sign of their joyful willingness to enter the future together.

Ceremonies are also often born of a couple's desire to express their commitment to sustaining their relationship. For many couples, a ceremony is a way of acknowledging that they intend to spend a lifetime together: the ceremony includes a commitment to nurture the relationship and to continue nurturing it when the path ahead becomes more difficult. It is, in a sense, a way of speaking to the future, a way of embedding in memory a couple's love and hope; so that if the road becomes rocky, the ceremony remains as an experience to which the couple can look back and, perhaps, in that remembrance find again their love and intention.

Present in many ceremonies is a request, either implicit or explicit, for support for that relationship. The frequent absence of social and family sanction has left us with few resources to draw upon in maintaining even the most committed of relationships, and in many instances, even lesbian communities do not particularly support the longevity of relationships. A ceremony can be a statement to friends and, often, to family: "This is a relationship which is of the deepest importance to us. Help us carry it forward." That two individuals are willing to commit themselves to working at a relationship is not always enough. A relationship which rests upon the support of friends, community and family is one which can more easily survive the difficulties inevitable in long-term partnerships.

These ceremonies can also often be ways of being profoundly visible. As lesbians, we can too easily become accustomed to hiding our love. Even for those of us who are completely out as lesbians, the world does not encourage our expressions of love. It can be too easy at times to avoid mentioning our relationships. How many couples deeply in love still refer to each other in public as "roommates"? These ceremonies are ways of affirming the full extent of our relationships. They are public acknowledgments that we have chosen another woman not as our roommate, not as our friend, but as our full partner in life.

Many women in this volume have created ceremonies which involved taking enormous steps out of the closet. Many describe realizing that they had suddenly entered a relationship that was too big, too meaningful, to deny. Relationships which feel like life partnerships demand a wider and more complete acknowledgment. The relationship itself becomes a call to courage and visibility; the ceremony provides a response to this call, and the world is changed by that response. Judy and Rosanne refer to their ceremony as Tikkun Olam, a Hebrew phrase that means "a healing of the world." It is a healing found in every story in this volume.

Ultimately, the healing affects our own self-love. Kilby and Janet explain that in the past they had always found ways of denying their lesbianism; each had been in previous relationships that they had considered "special friendships." But in their love for one another, such diminishing or denial was no longer possible. Their ceremony signified not only a commitment to one another but also a full acknowledgment of their own lesbianism. Such ceremonies blaze with a clarity and pride that burn away internalized homophobia. There seem to be no dry eyes at these ceremonies: not only are two people joining their lives together, but two people are celebrating the wonder of their love in the face of a society which has denied them.

When ceremonies involve biological family or the wider heterosexual community, healing also occurs as the distance between lesbian and straight is bridged. When Rosanne and Judy were preparing for their ceremony, Rosanne sent invitations to sixty members of her extended family. Her invitation was also a coming out letter in which she explained the fears that had prevented her from being open with them in the past. Only four family members did not reply; the other fifty-six are now a reclaimed part of Rosanne and Judy's lives.

One of the most inspiring elements of these ceremonies is the way in which couples interact with the heterosexual community: renting reception halls; printing invitations; arranging for the creation of a lesbian ketubah, or Jewish marriage contract—always being honest about the nature of the ceremony. These acts invoke a profound sense of open-heartedness and the courage that comes with such open-heartedness. Entering the world with full pride can be a supremely transformative act. The willingness to have our love fully and completely visible is, I believe, as powerful a tool of transformation as exists. It touches the miraculous, as all transformations do. It heals ourselves, our communities and, as in Tikkun Olam, the world.

For many couples these ceremonies are also a means of acknowledging the spiritual nature of their bond. Many create ceremonies to celebrate the spiritual element already there and also to ask for the blessings of a spiritual community and for the blessings of God or Goddess(es). This acknowledgment of spirit is present throughout the spectrum of religious and spiritual traditions. It is present in the Wiccan tryst of Noreen and Helen, the Quaker ceremony of Linda and Cindy, the Catholic holy union of Kirby and Janet, the Native American spirituality of Atimah and Aylana, the traditional Jewish ceremony of Rosanne and Judy and the Buddhist celebration of Harper and Kristina.

An extraordinary aspect of the ceremonies is that they can involve any combination of the elements described above. There are no scripts, no rules, no assumed models, no checklists for the mother-of-the-bride. Each ceremony arises directly from the experience of the couple: from each partner's heritage, from their distinct personalities and from their relationship with one another. When a couple does draw on established tradition, they do so with awareness. Certain elements are often altered and many times traditions are interwoven: Yael and Luana draw upon Jewish heritage, interweaving it with African-American tradition; Deborah and Zandra combine Hispanic tradition with New Age philosophy; Atimah and Aylana interweave Native American tradition with images that came to them in dreams; and Harper and Kristina combine elements of Buddhism with singing "Pennies From Heaven," the first song that each of their fathers sang to them.

Symbols are incorporated into these ceremonies with awareness and consciousness. Each symbol has specific meaning for one or both of the partners and, as such, is imbued with great power. The symbols resonate with a significance that is missed when we unquestioningly enter into a tradition that is already fully formed. The result of such conscious creation is a ceremony that is deeply transformative. Perhaps the transformation occurs during the ceremony itself; rituals have long been considered the means by which matter and spirit intermingle. But the process of creating such a ceremony is in itself empowering and healing. It is a process that demands that we listen to ourselves, that we trust our own voices and our own experiences. The accounts in this volume reflect that sense of keen and loving honesty, that commitment to trusting our own deepest selves.

Preceding the accounts of ceremonies in this volume is a chapter tracing the history of lesbian partnerships. When Patty and I were creating our ceremony, I was acutely aware of feeling disconnected from historical tradition, of somehow having fallen out of time. I had bits and pieces of information about the history of women-loving-women, but nothing cohesive. I began research for this essay in order to heal my own sense of disconnection. My hope is that it will be of help to others as well. I think we are starved for images of women's bonding. We need to hear stories of those who came before us. A sense of heritage can only lead to greater wholeness. There is a great similarity in the spirit reflected in the history of women's bonding and in the more current accounts of lesbian ceremonies of union. Both offer images of the proud celebration of women's love for other women. Both offer stories of women joining together to enter the future with love, courage and honesty.

—Becky Butler
August, 1996

*For Patty,*
*my life's blessing*

*Part One*

*A History of Lesbian Partnerships*

# A History of Lesbian Partnerships

Passionate love between women has always existed. In all parts of the world, through all periods of history, women have found ways to be together. Despite the economic and psychic oppression to which they have been subjected, women have devised means to nurture and support each other. Many have even found ways to join with each other as life partners. These lesbian partnerships have taken diverse forms, each a response to the era and culture from which it arose.[1] In tracing the existence of these varied unions, we begin to reclaim a sense of our own history. We begin to recognize and embrace the triumphs and struggles of our predecessors and to find voices in historical record that resonate with our own.

While the concept of lesbianism is actually a late nineteenth-century construct, I use the term here in much the same way as Adrienne Rich has used "lesbian continuum," which includes "a range... of woman-identified experience." The term transcends the question of whether or not a woman has had, or desired, sexual contact with another woman. Rather, it encompasses a broad spectrum of the forms of "primary intensity" between women. The term includes "the sharing of a rich inner life, the bonding against male tyranny, the giving and receiving of practical and political support."[2]

With the exception of the initial discussion of lesbians in tribal cultures, the following includes little historical information that falls outside of white Western culture. In researching this history, I was initially struck by the paucity of resources about lesbian existence. I was struck even more forcefully, however, by the lack of historical information about lesbians of color. Their exclusion from Western written record speaks to the extent to which white patriarchal history "tends to bury what it seeks to reject."[3]

The essay also does not attempt to cover the full spectrum of lesbian existence. It deals solely with those women who, against all odds, devised ways to choose another woman as their partner in life. Some of the relationships were marriages, complete with liturgical ceremony; some were "romantic friendships"; some of the women passed as men; and some retained the accoutrements of an otherwise acceptable female existence. Our history includes them all, and their collective courage is an extraordinary legacy.

## Lesbian Unions in Traditional Tribal Cultures

In traditional Native American cultures, the truest and highest form of power was the power of the Spirit world, the guiding force for all creation. All individual actions were efforts to live in alignment with the forces of Spirit, and human events took their sole value from their relationship with that Spirit.[4] Dreams, visions, spirit guides and sacred objects were the means of communication between worlds, and people's lives were guided by the directives that came through these channels. Power was not defined by ownership or physical strength, but by sensitivity to and relationship with these forces of Spirit.

In many Native American tribes, women were perceived as being profoundly connected to the Spirit world and, as such, held great power within the tribe. They sat on tribal councils, held high office, participated fully in tribal affairs and, most significantly, were accorded spiritual authority. In describing the experience of women's power in traditional American Indian cultures, Paula Gunn Allen explains that power is "a matter of spirit, involvement, and destiny. Woman's power comes automatically, hers by virtue of her femaleness, her natural and necessary fecundity, and her personal acquaintance with blood."[5] Women's menstruation was perceived with awe and wonder, her bleeding a sign of the sacred and an indication of her connection with Spirit.

In the context of a more nearly equal power balance between the sexes, many Native American cultures not only accepted lesbians and gays as part of society but also honored their unique spiritual authority.[6] It was understood that children and adolescents became gay or lesbian by guidance from the Spirit world, guidance made manifest through dreams, omens or direct experience with Spirits.

In stark contrast to Judeo-Christian concepts of "natural" and "unnatural" sexuality, lesbianism among traditional Native Americans was seen as a life choice that one made in order to live in accordance with Spirit. To ignore the guidance offered by the Spirits could bring grave consequences. Allen writes that resisting the direction offered by the Spirits could result in physical or psychological destruction, not because the Spirits were vindictive, but rather because it is the nature of paranormal power to make itself manifest through action. If resisted, the Spirit power would express itself in ways that could be dangerous and damaging both to the chosen individual and to her family.

Cultural emphasis was on listening for guidance and following that guidance. The Spirit world offered directives which would lead one to greater wholeness, and the community encouraged individuals to attend to that guidance. While lesbians and gays were still occasionally ridiculed for their sexual orientation, there nevertheless existed a basic understanding that sexual identity was a response to guidance from higher worlds and was inseparable from one's path to wholeness.

Among one category of lesbians, for whom Allen coins the term "ceremonial lesbians," sexual identity was particularly united with spiritual power. A ceremonial lesbian was a woman who was called to become both lesbian and shaman. Allen explains that an American Indian woman called to become a ceremonial lesbian underwent a rigorous initiation process:

> She will be required to pass grueling physical tests; she will be required to lose her mundane persona and transform her soul and mind into other forms. She will be required to follow the lead of the Spirits and to carry out the tasks they assign her. . . [All accounts of these rites] point to a serious event which results in the death of the protagonist, her visit to the Spirit realms from which she finally returns, transformed and powerful. After such events, she no longer belongs to her tribe or family, but to the Spirit teacher who instructed her.[7]

In her study of lesbians and gays in Native American tribes, Sue-Ellen Jacobs found twelve tribes in which gays and lesbians acted as shamans.[8] Among the Navajo, the lesbian and gay shamans were the tribal leaders, collectively known as the *nadle*. Those within the *nadle* married members of their own sex and, by their participation in tribal leadership, brought great honor upon their family. In one of the Navajo creation myths, lesbians and gays were singled out as having control of the world's wealth. As a result, the members of the *nadle* were also put in charge of tribal property.[9] In 1935, one Navajo elder said, "I believe that when all the *nadle* have passed away, it will be the end of Navaho culture. . . . They are the leaders."[10]

The *hwame*—lesbian cross-dressers among the Mojave—were also considered to be especially powerful shamans. Nahwera, a Mojave singer, was quoted by George Devereux in the 1930s: "From the very beginning of the world it was meant that there should be homosexuals, just as it was instituted that there should be shamans. They were intended for that purpose."[11] Nahwera goes on to make it clear that he means lesbians (*hwame*) as well as gay men (*alyha*). The Mojave creation myths describe initiation ceremonies for these gays and lesbians, and for centuries the Mojave performed such ceremonies. The ceremonies were an acknowledgment that the individuals would be taking on many of the roles traditionally associated with the opposite sex and would be marrying members of their own sex. Each *hwame* or *alyha* would also take on a new name, after which, Devereux explains, she or he greatly resented being called by the "discarded name."[12]

In *Gay American History*, Jonathan Katz includes the story of a Kutenai lesbian cross-dresser who changed her name to Kaúxuma núpika, or "Gone to the spirits." She is described as passing for a man, traveling in the company of her "wife." One European trader writes: "In the account of our voyage I have been silent as to the two strangers who cast up at Storia, and accompanied us from thence; but have noticed already, that instead of being man and wife, as they first gave us to understand, they were in fact both women—and bold adventurous amazons they were."[13]

In addition to being a courier, guide and peace mediator, "Gone to the spirits" also became known as a shaman. It was told that in addition to using her powers to heal, she also used them to make "prophecies subversive to the ruling class of white traders." She was finally killed in an ambush by the Blackfoot tribe. It was said that even after many shots, her wounds healed themselves. It was only when the Blackfoot opened her chest and cut her heart in two that she was unable to heal. After her death, "no animals or birds disturbed her body."[14]

Just as lesbians and gays were often seen as holding spiritual authority, many tribes also perceived lesbian relationships as being informed with the power of Spirit. This spiritual dimension of women's love is reflected in a Lakota ceremony Allen describes, a ceremony uniting two lesbians or *kŏskalala:*

> These women are said to be the daughters (the followers/practitioners) of *wiya numpa,* or Doublewoman. Doublewoman is a Spirit/Divinity who links women together making them one in Her power. They do a dance in which a rope is twined between them and coiled to form a "rope baby." The exact purpose or result of this dance is not mentioned, but its significance is clear. In a culture that values children and women because they bear them, two women who don't want to marry (a man) become united by the power of *wiya numpa* and their union is validated by the creation of the rope baby. That is, the rope baby signifies the potency of their union in terms that are comprehensible to their society, and therefore legitimizes it.[15]

Like many of the unions described in this volume, this ceremony is more than a simple exchange of vows or promises. It is an acknowledgment of the powerful presence of female Spirit which inspires both partners. It is an acknowledgment of the strength of a union born from Spirit, a testament to the transcendent power present in each woman's love for the other. The bond of the *kŏskalala* originates in the divinity of Doublewoman.

In traditional Native American cultures, there were also intimate bonds between women which were unrelated to shamanic tradition. In addition to casual sexual relationships between women, there were women who married other women outside of the shamanic tradition, many of them taking on the traditional male roles of hunting and warriorship. As in other cultures, the bonds that Native American women formed with each other sometimes included elements traditionally associated with heterosexual marriage: one partner would be the cross-dresser, taking on male roles and attire, and the other partner would assume the role of wife. In doing this, they placed their relationship in a context that was comprehensible to the society around them. We can only speculate as to whether such cross-dressers were motivated by love for other women or by the desire to adopt the roles reserved for men, nor can we be sure to what extent their interaction diverged from traditional male/female dynamics. Such relationships may have perpetuated a power imbalance between "husband" and "wife." Nevertheless, woman-marriage such as this played a significant role in the history of women's bonding and appears among many tribal cultures. Among Native American tribes, in addition to the already mentioned Mojave, Navajo, Kutenai and Lakota, there are also accounts of woman-marriage from the Eskimo, Yuma, Cocopa, Quinalt, Klamath, Crow and Blackfoot.[16]

*Gay American History* includes "Biography of Woman Chief" written by Edwin T. Denig in the mid-nineteenth century. The story chronicles the life of the most famous female war leader in the history of the upper Missouri tribes: the Crow "Woman Chief." She had been born among the Gros Ventre of the Prairie, but by age ten had been taken prisoner by the Crow and was raised as one of their tribe. While she always wore female dress, she early on preferred riding and hunting to the more traditional female pursuits.

One year her Crow encampment was attacked by a Blackfoot tribe. After several men had been killed, the Blackfoot demanded to speak with some member of the Crow. She was the only one who ventured out. Seeing her, the Blackfoot thought her an easy target and showered her with gunfire, the entire band charging towards her. Undaunted, she shot one Blackfoot down with a pistol and two more with arrows before she escaped back to safety. This show of courage stamped her as "a brave," and she went on to lead excursions against other tribes. After many successes, she took her place among the tribal chiefs.

At this point Denig notes, "As yet no offer of marriage had been made to her by anyone. Her habits did not suit their taste. Perhaps they thought she would be rather difficult to manage as a wife."[17] In any event, she herself soon married a woman, and during the next few years, as was the tradition for chiefs of her standing, she married three more wives. She lived as a successful chief and family leader until she was killed many years later on a peace mission to the Gros Ventre.

Katz also quotes a brief account of a lesbian marriage among the Klamath written by Leslie Spier in the 1930s: "A woman named Co'pak lived like a man although she retained women's dress. She married a woman who lived with her for a long time and finally died. She observed the usual mourning, wearing a bark belt as a man does at this time to prevent the back from growing bowed."[18]

Tribal cultures other than Native American ones have also acknowledged the bonds between women. Among many African tribes, the tradition of woman-marriage was accepted and, in certain tribes, was relatively common. In most of these cultures, the patriarchal construct of wife as property was the foundation of the marital relationship, including the foundation of woman-marriage. For a woman to marry another woman was often a sign of prestige and power, and usually only women of status were in an economic position to pay the necessary bride-price.

In the 1930s E. E. Evans-Pritchard spent twelve months among the Nuer, a people of the Upper Nile. In writing about his observations, he notes: "What seems to us, but not at all to the Nuer, a somewhat strange union is that in which a woman marries another woman and counts as the pater of the children born to the wife. Such marriages are by no means uncommon in Nuerland, and they must be regarded as a form of simple legal marriage, for the woman-husband marries her wife in exactly the same way as a man marries a woman."[19]

Evans-Pritchard goes on to note that the Nuer "woman-husbands" often practiced as magicians or diviners. In many tribes this was the way women accumulated enough wealth to buy a wife. In other tribes, the bride-price was earned by women who were petty chiefs, medicine women or potters. One chronicle remains of a Kipsigis woman named Mwanaisha Adamu who earned the bride-price through prostitution. Having been a successful prostitute, she earned enough money to buy a piece of property and build a house. As the ethnographer describes, "When she became elderly, she 'married' a young Kipsigis woman. . . . The girl then had four children 'illegitimately': children who were, however, the legitimate offspring of Mwanaisha. When Mwanaisha became ill the girl came to Nairobi to look after her. She took her to the hospital [and] stayed with her until her death."[20]

Among the Lovedu, a society in which women had unusually high status, marriages between women were especially common. The Lovedu were ruled by a queen who traditionally had the power to bring rain. The queen herself always had a number of wives, some of whom were given to her by chiefs supplicating for rain, and others whom she chose herself. While some of her wives were later given to counselors or nobles, the queen's favorite wives remained with her for life and were often given villages of their own to rule. Among the Lovedu, as among other tribes, woman-marriage was ceremonialized with the same ritual that accompanied heterosexual marriage.[21]

In addition to the Lovedu, the Nuer and the Kipsigis, many other African tribes accepted the legitimacy of marriages between women. A few of the tribes for which we have recorded evidence of woman-marriage include the Yoruba, Yagba, Akoko, Nupe, Gana-Gana, Fon, Ibo, Dinka, Venda, Igbo and the Bobo Nieniege of the Ivory Coast.[22] There have also been African societies in which lesbians and gays have been the tribe's medicine people. Among these tribes are the Bantu; the Kwanyama; the Lango of Uganda; the Konso of South Abyssinia; the Cilenge-Humbi of South Quillenges; and the Barea-Kunama, Korongo and Mesakin, all of Northeast Africa.[23]

There have been nonindustrial cultures outside of Africa and North America in which lesbian and gay cross-dressers have also been perceived as holding spiritual authority. In the Kannada-speaking region of South India, those men and women who take on the traditional clothing and roles of the opposite sex are considered to have been "caught" by the goddess Yellamma ("mother of all"). They are called carriers of Yellamma and are taken to the great pilgrimage center known as Yellamma's Hill to be initiated by the temple priest. From then on they are considered to be bearers of divinity and are key figures in religious ceremonies and rites. The women, known as *jogamma*, carry a replica of Yellamma with them at all times and return to Yellamma's Hill at every full moon.[24]

Among the Buryat, who live between the Caspian Sea and the Bering Strait, gay and lesbian cross-dressers hold the positions of shamans, each of whom is "a soul-projector, a spirit master," whose powers can be used to cure illness. Each shaman has undergone a rigorous vision-quest, through which he or she has obtained special powers and a unique relationship with the supernatural.[25]

There are undoubtedly countless other tribal cultures which have accepted and even honored lesbian existence, cultures which have left no written record. Even the few described here, however, give us a glimpse of the depth and breadth of lesbian existence in tribal societies. In many ways, lesbian existence in these cultures can provide a powerful mirror to our own time. We can see the extent to which women's bonds are shaped by, and are responses to, cultural traditions and expectations. In the perception of lesbians and gays as holding spiritual authority, we can also see the extent to which lesbian identity is much more than a mere choice of sexual partner—and how that identity is informed by one's world vision and, often, by a sense of transcendent Spirit.


## Sapphic Spirit and the Ancient Western World

From lesbian and feminist research of the past two decades, it appears that the patriarchal history in which so many of us have been schooled is just one splinter of the history of humanity, resting upon a time when the world was much more woman-guided and woman-inspired. The images from that time shape our collective memories and dreams, and the voice that speaks of that past most clearly is Sappho's.[26] Through the surviving fragments of her work, we forge a link to a distinctly female history.

Sappho lived in the sixth century B.C., a time when a tradition rich with women's spirit and vision was still vibrant and alive, and it is this tradition which inspired her work. It was a time when countless religious rituals and rites were accessible to women only. Numerous young women who wanted to learn the arts of song and dance necessary for participating in these rites journeyed to the island of Lesbos to study with Sappho.

Through the surviving fragments of Sappho's poems, we get glimpses of a lesbian life both sensual and holy, a life among a community of women dedicated to the cultivation of beauty, the invocation of gods and goddesses and the love of one another: "Hither to me from Crete to this holy temple, where is your delightful grove of apple-trees, and altars smoking with incense; therein cold water babbles through apple branches, and the whole place is shadowed by roses, and from the shimmering leaves the sleep of enchantment comes down."[27] Over this tender and dulcet existence watched the goddess Aphrodite, for whom most of the frankincense was burned and most of the libations poured. Worship for the goddess took place in groves, often at dusk: "The moon shone full, and the girls took their places to dance around the altar. . . . So once Cretan women rhythmically danced with delicate feet about the fair altar and trod upon meadow flowers softly sprouting."[28]

It was Aphrodite who was entreated to intervene in the mishaps of love, and she who was thanked for the bestowing of beauty and grace. In what is known as "Ode to Aphrodite," Sappho entreats Aphrodite to be her ally, her "fellow-fighter," in her efforts to win a woman's love. Sappho speaks with the assurance that her love of women is as blessed by the gods and goddesses as is her tending of Aphrodite's altar. For Sappho, the sacred was inseparable from women's bonds. The divine and earthly intersected in every desire and every passion.

the ideal Biblical expression of love, incorporated into traditional heterosexual marriage ceremonies, is a declaration of love spoken by one woman
to another.

After the death of her son—Ruth's husband—Naomi told her
daughter-in-law that she was returning to her own homeland, Bethlehem.
She urged Ruth to return to her ancestral home in Moab, but Ruth refused. She declared that she would rather turn her back on her homeland,
her people and even her God than lose Naomi:

> Intreat me not to leave thee, or to return from following after thee:
> for whither thou goest, I will go; and whither thou lodgest, I will
> lodge; thy people shall be my people, and thy God my God. Where
> thou diest, will I die, and there will I be buried: the Lord do so to
> me, and more also, if aught but death part thee and me.[35]

## The Rise of Intolerance in the Holy Roman Empire

During the late Roman Empire, the tolerance that had existed towards lesbians and gays began to give way to antagonism. By the end of the fourth
century, gay marriages had been pronounced illegal, and harsh condemna-
tions of male homosexuality had been issued. The edicts regarding male
homosexuality didn't carry much force initially, but they were revived in
the sixth century by Emperor Justinian I, one of the principal architects of
the Western legal system. Justinian blamed homosexuality and blasphemy
for the land's "famines, earthquakes, and pestilences," and proclaimed
both punishable by death. His codification of these laws would serve as
the basis for the legal punishment of gays for over thirteen hundred years.[36]

Although many of the edicts prohibiting homosexuality were passed
by the Christianized Roman emperors, historian John Boswell points out
that Christianity had been the official religion of the empire for over two
centuries before this antagonism ever arose. He posits that this
antihomosexual attitude was a result of the increasing absolutism of the
government and the decay of the empire's urban centers. By the fourth
century, the government's rule had become so absolute that some citizens
were not allowed to choose their occupation or their place of residence.[37]

Conditions for gays and lesbians improved somewhat towards the
end of the eighth and the beginning of the ninth centuries. Starting in the
tenth century, Western Europe's economy began a period of dramatic
growth. Urban centers thrived, and along with urbanization came increased personal freedom. The late eleventh and early twelfth centuries especially were periods of great openness. New ideas were encouraged and

embraced, and a fascination with love, in all its forms, began to spread throughout Western Europe. The troubadours glorified relationships based on *amor,* individual romantic love, a concept which had been absent from society for so long that it was seen as the troubadours' invention.[38]

*Amor* was interpreted as the heartfelt connection of love between two individuals, a love arising from personal choice and experience. Mythologist Joseph Campbell points out that the radical nature of this concept can be seen as symbolized by the spelling: *Amor* is the reverse of *Roma,* seat of the Roman Catholic Church, which had long sanctified marriages arranged according to social and political advantage.[39] By the twelfth century, romantic love had become the obsession within the Roman Empire, and given the simultaneous increase of individual freedom, gay and lesbian love was proclaimed as passionately as heterosexual love.

This was also a period during which women held significant influence within the Church. In the twelfth century, Pope Eugene III publicly sanctioned the female mystic and social activist Hildegard von Bingen.[40] Hildegard's mystic visions were filled with images of a great Mother, or Goddess, and the Pope's approval of those visions reflects the extent to which the female spirit still had a place in Catholicism. In addition to this female presence in theology, women also had political power within the Church: in Europe there were almost as many female abbots as male.[41]

While women of this period were still in no position economically to live their lives together, evidence of lesbian passion survives. One twelfth-century manuscript from a Bavarian monastery includes the following verse, written from one woman to another:

> To G., her singular rose,
> From A.—the bonds of precious love.
> What is my strength, that I should bear it,
> That I should have patience in your absence? . . .
> I shed tears as I used to smile,
> And my heart is never glad.
> When I recall the kisses you gave me,
> And how with tender words you caressed my little breasts,
> I want to die
> Because I cannot see you. . . .
> As long as the world stands
> You shall never be removed from the core of my being.
> What more can I say?
> Come home, sweet love!
> Prolong your trip no longer;
> Know that I can bear your absence no longer.

Farewell.
Remember me.[42]

By the thirteenth and fourteenth centuries, this period of openness and enthusiasm came to an end. Personal freedom, which had been so encouraged, was gradually replaced by a rigid commitment to conformity. By the middle of the fourteenth century, minorities of all kinds found themselves the objects of harsh and unyielding oppression: Jews were exiled from England and France; lepers were imprisoned and often executed; vast numbers of women were tortured and burned alive on accusations of witchcraft; and homosexuals were subject to dismemberment, burning and hanging.[43]

The greatest vehicle for the enforcement of conformity was the Office of the Holy Inquisition. Initiated early in the thirteenth century, the Inquisition was created to resolve theological disputes and eradicate heresy. Early in the course of the Inquisition, the association was made between heresy and homosexuality. As the identification between the two became more common, increasing numbers of gays and lesbians were tortured and executed. Finally, the two became so interchangeable that the same French word, *bougre,* was used to describe them both. This identification of heresy and homosexuality also encouraged secular governments to pass more rigid antihomosexual legislation. Boswell points out that between 1150 and 1350, homosexuality went from being the sexual preference of an aristocratic minority to being punishable by death in many European states.[44]

Legislation outlawing homosexuality began at this time to include proscriptions against lesbian sexuality. Previously, antihomosexual legislation had applied only to men. The first secular law with explicit reference to sexual relations between women came out of the district of Orleans in 1260, dictating punishment by mutilation for the first and second offenses, and death by burning for the third offense. While lesbian sexual acts were never prosecuted to the same extent as male homosexual acts, the two were nevertheless legally equivalent in France, Spain, Italy, Germany and Switzerland.[45]

The enactment of legislation prohibiting lesbian sexuality was not only a reflection of antihomosexual hostility but also a sign of the increasing suppression of women. Women's power had been diminishing rapidly since the twelfth century. At the beginning of the thirteenth century, despite the large number of female abbots, women were not allowed to administer sacraments, and later in the century, both the Church hierarchy and secular government instituted rigid requirements which effectively excluded women from both institutions.[46]

Women continued, however, to retain certain status among the peasant culture, a status generally associated with pre-Christian belief systems. As Christianity spread through Europe, it did not fully replace the pagan religions which preceded it. Often the aristocracy converted to Christianity while the peasant class continued to practice their traditional forms of worship. Anthropologist Margaret Murray proposed that what became known as witchcraft had in fact been an organized religion: the Old Religion surviving from the pre-Christian era, complete with specified rituals, symbols and the worship of a deity who could take male, female or animal form. The God/Goddess was believed to "perpetually incarnate on earth," a manifestation of natural energy.[47] In Murray's thesis, worshippers (witches) were organized into covens, with women filling many of the positions of leadership. These witches were well loved within the community, acting as healers, herbalists and offering spiritual guidance; many were the "wise-women" of their villages.[48]

This combination of female power and pagan heresy ignited the wrath of the Christian Church. After two centuries of consolidation of power, the Inquisition was prepared to embark on one of the most effective and appalling purges of women's power in history. In 1484, Pope Innocent VIII made clear the Church's intent to persecute witches.

Citizens were told that pagan religions were the work of the devil, and women the primary practitioners of this satanic worship. A portrait was painted of witches as ugly carnivorous hags who transformed themselves into wolves and devoured young infants. It was told that they rode in the dead of night, sucking the blood of sleeping villagers and fornicating with Satan. They were said to travel in packs, or covens, bringing about sexual impotence, sudden illness and demonic possession.[49]

Any indication of eccentricity, especially among peasant women, was sufficient to warrant the accusation of witchcraft. Like other heretics, women suspected of witchcraft would be tortured to confession, then tortured again until they named other women as accomplices. Estimates regarding the number of women killed vary from several hundred thousand to ten million.[50] The women executed were healers, midwives, oral historians, practitioners of the Old Religion and, above all, single women or widows exhibiting independence or eccentricity: nonconformist women living outside of accepted heterosexual lifestyles.[51]

Present-day lesbians have claimed a positive and profoundly powerful legacy from the time of the Old Religion. During the last two decades, many women have rejected the patriarchal vision of witchcraft, reclaiming it as their own tradition.[52] Witchcraft, also called Wicca, has been revived. It has come to mean the honoring of the Goddess and the acknowledgment of the Goddess as present in all forms of life. Wicca's heritage is seen to extend back through the time of the witchhunts to the ancient period of

Goddess worship. In Wicca, many women have discovered the female spirit long excluded from Judeo-Christian traditions. The re-emergence of this tradition, silent since the witchhunts, has been greeted with joyful celebration.

The return of the Goddess and the embracing of feminist spirituality have also brought an honoring of female bonding and female ritual. Many lesbians have drawn upon Wicca practice and tradition in the creation of commitment ceremonies, known in Wicca as trysts or handfastings, accounts of which are included in this volume. Through the revival of Wicca we have proclaimed our insistence upon defining our own traditions, naming our own experiences. In reclaimed Wicca, we have reached into the flames of patriarchal history and recovered female wisdom and power.

## Cross-Dressing: The Thirteenth through Nineteenth Centuries

Even after the thirteenth century and the increase in the censure of lesbianism, few women were brought to trial for that reason alone. Women loving women, even sexually, was not inherently threatening or distasteful to male power, in part because women were so economically dependent upon men that lesbianism posed little threat to the heterosexual bond. The majority of men viewed life through a veil of phallocentrism: they believed that no sexual encounter was significant without male penetration.[53] Men understood lesbian sex as something women engaged in when no man was available or as a prelude to heterosexual sex. It was a pastime easily dismissed.

The eighteenth-century Compte de Tilly's *Souvenirs* quotes one young man discussing his wife's lesbian activity: "I confess that this is a kind of rivalry which causes me no annoyance; on the contrary I am immoral enough to laugh at it."[54]

Men's dismissal and contempt were also often mixed with an element of titillation. Starting in the eighteenth century, pornography began to include erotic scenes of lesbian lovemaking. The scenes were always followed, of course, by "real" heterosexual sex. Whereas to this day many men find it difficult to believe that a woman can be sexually satisfied without a man, to pre-twentieth-century male society the idea was utterly incomprehensible. Given the absurdity of the concept, there was little reason to actively discourage lesbian activity; at most, men thought, women would find it a temporary diversion.

This tolerance, however, applied only to those women who did not disrupt the social order in other ways, who continued to dress in feminine clothes and respect the appropriate limits of female behavior. Women who not only indulged in same-sex love but also threatened the exclusivity of male privilege and prerogative were an entirely different matter. Those women who wore male clothes and who stepped outside of the traditional female world were deeply disturbing to the social order. They posed a threat similar to that posed by women accused of witchcraft: they were consolidating power outside of patriarchal control.

Society's extinction of lesbian experience is nowhere more evident than in the historical accounts of lesbian marriages involving cross-dressers. In Henri Estienne's sixteenth-century *Apologie pour Herodite*, he mentions a woman from Fontaine who, disguised as a man, worked her way up from stable boy to vineyard master. Still dressed as a man, she fell in love with, and married, another woman. The two lived together for two years before she was identified as a woman, arrested and condemned to death.[55]

A similar story appears later in the sixteenth century, in Montaigne's *Voyage in Italy*, in which he writes of several young women from Chaumont en Bussigni who agreed to dress, and live, as men. One of them became a weaver and, after passing as a man for several years, fell in love with and married another woman. The weaver was hanged six months later, having been recognized by someone from her own village.[56]

The fullest account we have of the collision between lesbian marriage and social order is in the story of Catharina Margaretha Linck and Catharina Margaretha Mühlhahn, two women from Saxony who came to trial in the early eighteenth century. Their trial records were preserved in the Royal Prussian Secret Archives and were translated into English by Brigitte Eriksson in 1980.[57]

According to trial records, Linck early on disguised herself as a man, "in order to lead a life of chastity." After leaving home in search of a holy life, she encountered a group of Inspirants traveling the countryside. They embraced her as a prophet, and for two years she stayed with them, preaching and traveling. When her gift of prophecy began to fail, she left the troop and joined the Hanoverian army as a musketeer. She deserted after three years of service and, upon being apprehended, was sentenced to hang. After it was revealed that she was a woman, her sentence was waived and she was released. Soon after, Linck joined the Prussian troops, serving only a year before being recognized as a woman and sent away. After having similar experiences in both the Polish and the Hessian armies, she left her life of soldiering and, still passing as a man, went to work for a French stockingmaker, at which point she met and fell in love with Catharina Margaretha Mühlhahn.

Linck and Mühlhahn were married shortly thereafter and "lived together as an alleged married couple, and kept the same table and the same bed." The trial records note that after their marriage, the couple started struggling financially and began arguing. Several years later, after one particularly bad argument, Linck returned home to find Mühlhahn's mother there. The mother "attacked [Linck], took her sword, ripped open her pants, examined her and discovered that she was indeed not a man but a woman." Mühlhahn's mother brought Linck to trial, indignantly submitting Linck's leather dildo as evidence. Mühlhahn and Linck were both tried by the court. Mühlhahn, judged to be "a simple-minded person who let herself be seduced into depravity," was condemned to three years imprisonment, followed by banishment. Linck was found guilty of "unnatural lewdness" and, at age twenty-seven, was put to death by the sword.[58]

In tracing the history of lesbian partnerships, especially those involving cross-dressers, much of the historical material available is the result of society's efforts to eradicate those partnerships. The fragments of information that survive, such as trial records or psychiatric case studies, are the documents chronicling the dissolution and condemnation of those partnerships. Many of the accounts thus end in separation, imprisonment or execution. Presumably, many couples survived quite happily, unnoticed by the sentinels of church and state. Of these, however, we have little written record. What we do have are accounts of lesbian partners who managed to spend most of their lives together before having their lesbianism revealed, as well as couples who spent their entire lives passing as heterosexuals, their lesbianism revealed only after death.

In 1863, *Fincher's Trade Review* carried several stories of cross-dressing women, some of whom had married other women. Among these was the story of Mary East and her partner. In the 1730s, after inheriting a large sum of money, Mary East and a friend of "similar mind" decided to move to a village where they were not known and live together as man and wife. Mary took the male role, calling herself James Howe, and her friend became Mrs. Howe. "Mr. and Mrs. Howe" bought a small pub in Epping and lived as upstanding and active members of the community. Finally, many years later, Mary was recognized and blackmailed by someone from her home village. Mary met the blackmailer's demands, and it was only when her partner died, after thirty-four years together, that Mary brought the blackmailer to court. Mary and her "wife" had functioned as such upstanding members of the community that, despite the revelation of her true sex, she was allowed to go free while the blackmailer was imprisoned.[59]

One of the most colorful accounts of cross-dressing is the story of Murray Hall, or Mary Anderson. Born in Goven, Scotland, she immigrated to New York City, where she lived for thirty years as a man. She became somewhat notorious as a Tammany Hall politician and was known for playing poker and pinochle and being "sweet on women." While her first marriage ended in a separation, her second lasted twenty years, ending only when her partner died. Hall, with her wife, also raised an adopted daughter, a daughter who discovered her "father's" true sex only upon Hall's death at the age of seventy.[60]

Similar stories are recounted in both Ellis's *Psychology of Sex,* and Katz's *Gay American History.* Briefly mentioned is Catharine Coome, who lived as a man for forty years and was married to a woman for fourteen of those years. Also mentioned is Fernando Mackenzie, a woman who, disguised as a man, worked for the police in Seville, Spain, for thirty years. For over twenty years she lived with her wife. Two years after her partner's death, Fernando was injured in a street accident and revealed to be a woman. Nicholai de Raylan, secretary to a Russian consul, was discovered to be a woman after her death in 1906. Nicholai had been married twice. While her first marriage had ended in a separation after ten years, she was still married to her second wife when she died.[61]

It is a measure of the entrenchment of male privilege that women today continue to pass as men, both for the economic opportunity and for the freedom to have socially sanctioned partnerships with other women. Early in 1989 an article appeared in a Spokane newspaper regarding the death of Billy Tipton. Billy was a jazz musician who in the 1940s played with many of the greats of jazz. In the 1950s he formed a trio and played in clubs up and down the West Coast of the United States. The Tipton Trio cut two albums, featuring Billy on sax and piano. In the late fifties, Billy met and married Kathleen "Kitty" Flaherty. Billy and Kitty raised several adopted children, and Billy even served as Scoutmaster for his sons' Boy Scout troops. Early in 1989, after refusing to go to the hospital, Billy died of a bleeding ulcer. Shortly thereafter physicians announced that "he" had been a woman. Billy's children were astonished. The oldest son told a reporter, "Now I know why I couldn't get him to a doctor. . . . He had so much to protect, and I think he was just tired of the rat race, tired of keeping the secret."[62] In the end, Billy chose to die rather than disclose her true sexual identity.

Cross-dressing women knew they could not survive without freedom, without self-determination, without those privileges usually reserved for men. Many were also resolute in their commitment to embrace another woman as their partner in life. They took the only option they saw available: they adopted the dress and roles of men. They did so knowing they were risking ridicule, humiliation and legal retribution if found out. Many of them lost their lives in the pursuit of a less restricted life, and we must count them among our most courageous predecessors.

## Romantic Friendship: The Eighteenth and Nineteenth Centuries

The history of women-loving-women encompasses several distinct currents of experience, each current reflecting a unique aspect of female bonding. One of these historical currents is the tradition of passionate love between female friends. In *Surpassing the Love of Men,* Lillian Faderman traces the development of this tradition, which was referred to in the eighteenth century as "romantic friendship."

Originating in the revival of platonic love during the Renaissance, this tradition of passionate love between female friends reached its height in eighteenth-century England and France. The friendships had all the elements of ardent love affairs. Women, while living with husbands, wrote letters declaring their undying and eternal love for their beloved female "friend." They sent each other love poems, describing in evocative detail the depth and fire of their longing. Although we do not know whether these relationships included genital sexuality, they did include expressions of sensual desire and appreciation. As long as they did not wear men's clothes or threaten the exclusivity of male privilege, women could publicly kiss, embrace, walk hand in hand and declare each other the center of their emotional lives. From the Renaissance through the late nineteenth century, women had society's sanction to give voice to their passionate love for other women.

While few women were writing and publishing during the sixteenth and seventeenth centuries, by the eighteenth century women were writing volumes of poetry, prose, letters and journals, many of which gave impassioned expression to their love for other women. Some typical expressions of the love that emanated from these steamy romantic friendships appear in the letters of Elizabeth Carter and Catherine Talbot, both eighteenth-century writers. Neither of them married men, and while the ostensible reason was that Elizabeth was responsible for the care of her widowed father and Catherine was an invalid living with her mother, Faderman finds it unlikely that either would have married men even if circumstances had been different. While they never left their parents' homes to live together, their relationship lasted from their first encounter to Catherine's death in 1770.[63]

Elizabeth was enamored upon first meeting Catherine. In an early letter to the mutual friend who introduced them, Elizabeth wrote, "Miss Talbot is absolutely my passion; I think of her every day, dream of her all night, and one way or another introduce her into every subject I talk of. . . . You will see her tomorrow (a happiness I envy you much more than all your possessions in the skies)."[64]

After an appropriate length of time, Elizabeth started communicating directly with Catherine, openly confessing her love for her:

> People here are not in the least danger of losing their wits about you, but proceed as quietly and as regularly in their affairs as if there was no such person in being. Nobody has been observed to lose their way, run against a door, or sit silent and staring in a room full of company in thinking upon you, except my solitary self, who (as you may perceive in the description) have the advantage of looking half mad when I do not see you, and (as you may know by many ocular proofs) extremely silly when I do."[65]

Such confessions of passion were completely appropriate by eighteenth-century standards. Faderman posits that it was no fear of being accused of unseemly love that stopped the two from moving in together, but rather the concern that Elizabeth would have been accused of deserting her widowed father. Such lapse of filial duty would have been acceptable if Elizabeth had left his household in order to care for a husband, but not in order to set up housekeeping with a romantic friend. Despite their separate residences, Catherine and Elizabeth remained partners in life for thirty years, celebrating every year the anniversary of their meeting.

In the essay "The Female World of Love and Ritual: Relations between Women in Nineteenth-Century America," Carroll Smith-Rosenberg describes the context in which these relationships were accepted as completely normal and appropriate, and although she only discusses nineteenth-century America, her observations are equally applicable to England and Europe. She describes the environment as being almost completely segregated according to gender: throughout their lives, women lived in women's worlds. Young girls moved in a social environment populated almost exclusively with other females: girlfriends; female instructors; mothers, grandmothers and aunts; and their mothers' female friends. The diaries of young girls were filled with exclamations of eternal love for other schoolgirls. Smith-Rosenberg remarks that while men were not perceived antagonistically, they were distant and shadowy figures, never primary in girls' lives. Even after marriage, women moved among other women and children, still having little connection with the lives of men. Even husbands and wives often shared little emotional intimacy. The significant events that filled women's lives occurred in the company of other women, from the more dramatic ones, such as childbirth, to the daily ritual of "taking tea."[66] Women, Smith-Rosenberg explains, held positions of emotional centrality in each other's lives. It was considered that the natural movement of a woman's heart was to love and embrace another woman.

In this context, passionate love between women was not only sanctioned but even encouraged. A woman's love for another woman was seen as pure and ennobling, and as long as women celebrated their love within the parameters of acceptable female behavior, their passions were proclaimed loudly and gladly. This was in part because society had been so inculcated with the Victorian understanding of women as asexual beings. The concept of genital sexuality between non-cross-dressing women was something which was rarely entertained by society at large. In 1885, when the Criminal Law Amendment was passed in England, making public or private homosexual acts a misdemeanor, Queen Victoria refused to sign it until all references to women were removed. Female homosexuality, she said, did not exist, and she refused to tarnish the honorable tradition of women's love.[67]

The most celebrated example of romantic friendship, and the relationship to which other romantic friends looked with longing, was the relationship between Eleanor Butler and Sarah Ponsonby, known as "the Ladies of Llangollen." Both from aristocratic Irish families, Eleanor and Sarah had determined to do what so many romantic friends longed to do: run away together. They tried once and, upon discovery, were returned to their respective families. In 1778, with the help of one of the family servants (known as "Molly the Bruiser"), they tried again. After the second attempt, their families surrendered and provided both of them with a small stipend and the request that they relocate. Together they bought a house in the vale of Llangollen in Wales and in that idyllic spot shared a bed and a home for fifty years.[68]

The two were considered by the community as perfect examples of moral uprightness and virtue, and their home became something of a literary haven for the famous, visited by Wordsworth, Scott and the Duke of Wellington. To other less fortunate romantic friends, Eleanor and Sarah modeled the kind of life to which they too aspired. The journal which Eleanor kept from 1788 until her death in 1829 captures the fabric of their life together. It is filled with accounts of their days of "sweetly enjoyed retirement," with entries about the garden, details of village life and references to Sarah: "my Heart's darling," "my sweet love," and "my beloved."

Unfortunately, few had the economic resources to maintain lives independent of heterosexual bonds. The rest continued to experience and express their love and longing despite heterosexual marriage and geographic separation. One such relationship, described by Smith-Rosenberg, was that of Sarah Butler Wister and Jeannie Field Musgrove, who met as teenagers in 1849. During the following two years, while at the same boarding school, they developed a tender and abiding love. Sarah kept a bouquet of flowers underneath Jeannie's portrait, and the two wrote impassioned notes to one another.

Sarah's marriage after boarding school in no way diminished the intensity of their relationship. In 1864, already married and the mother of a child, Sarah wrote Jeannie, "I shall be entirely alone [this coming week]. I can give you no idea how desperately I shall want you. . . . " After one of their visits together, Jeannie responded, "I want you to tell me in your next letter, to assure me, that I am your dearest. . . . I do not doubt you, & I am not jealous but I long to hear you say it once more & it seems already a long time since your voice fell on my ear. So just fill a quarter of a page with caresses & expressions of endearment."[69]

Smith-Rosenberg explains that when Jeannie finally married, at age thirty-seven, Sarah was filled with anxiety. Two days before the marriage, Sarah wrote, "Oh Jeannie. I have thought & thought & yearned over you these two days. Are you married I wonder? My dearest love to you wherever and *who* ever you are."[70] Despite Sarah's fears, Jeannie's marriage had as little impact on their love as Sarah's had; their passion and yearning for each other remained constant throughout their lives.

Towards the end of the nineteenth century, it became increasingly possible for romantic friends to avoid the torment of physical separation. With the feminist movement came increased social and economic freedom. Finally it had become possible for at least a few women to achieve a certain degree of economic independence. What romantic friends had always longed for—a life together—had become a real possibility.

This was the time of "New Women": women who saw the world from a feminist perspective; women who were determined to take advantage of their own new freedoms to organize for social welfare; women who were committed both to their own work and the improvement of society. They were also women who were unwilling to sacrifice this new freedom for the constraints of traditional heterosexual marriage. They knew that the support and understanding in their lives came, not from men, but from other women. These were women who chose other women as life partners, and together worked towards a feminist vision of social justice.

These partnerships became so common in late nineteenth-century New England that they came to be known as "Boston Marriages." One such "marriage" was that between the novelist Sarah Orne Jewett and Annie Fields, who were together for almost thirty years after meeting in the 1880s. For many of those years, they held to a routine which allowed them both the sustenance of each other's love and company and the freedom to pursue their own work. For most of the year the two lived together in either Boston or Manchester, but several months out of each year Sarah would return by herself to South Berwick, Maine. Sarah would spend the time alone in full-time writing. Annie would spend the time working on her own writing along with pursuing other interests, including sending daily notes to Sarah. Faderman notes that Sarah and Annie knew several other New England couples in similar arrangements, all of whom provided support for one another: Willa Cather and her partner of forty years, Edith Lewis; novelist Vernon Lee (Violet Page) and Kit Anstruther-Thomson; and Elizabeth McCracken and her partner.[71]

Similar traditions existed outside of the United States as well. Two English women, Katherine Bradley and Edith Cooper, had a life-long partnership which began at the end of the nineteenth century. Katherine, who was actually Edith's aunt, had lived in the same house with Edith during Edith's childhood. Both feminists, the two later ended up at University College studying together and soon began a collaboration of love and work that was to last for the rest of their lives: "My love and I took hands and swore/Against the world, to be/Poets and lovers evermore."[72]

The two wrote together under the name of "Michael Field," understanding, perhaps, that women's work would not be particularly well received in the 1880s. For them, their love for each other and their poetry were inextricably linked. In reference to Robert and Elizabeth Browning, they once noted in their journal: "These two poets, man and wife, wrote alone; each wrote, but did not bless and quicken one another at their work; *we are closer married*" (italics theirs).[73]

What their audience perceived as love poems from Michael Field to his beloved were actually poems of love and devotion to one another. Their earlier volumes especially are filled with statements of love to each other. Their work was very successful until it was discovered that "Michael Field" was actually two women, after which it soon disappeared from the shelves of booksellers. The two had enough independent financial resources, however, that they could continue to write and live together. They lived together as partners for over thirty years, dying within six months of each other.[74]

## Turn-of-the-Century: Deviance and Pathology

By the second half of the nineteenth century, increasing numbers of women broke away from their roles tending and maintaining men's households and, instead, embarked on their own careers. The "New Women" became college professors, doctors, social workers and writers. They nurtured and supported one another, and as economic freedom increased, more and more of them chose to spend their lives in partnership with other women.

As Faderman notes, the revolutionary implication of these female partnerships was not immediately perceived. Initially, men treated the unions with benign indifference. While they were mystified by the choices women were making, they did not find them directly threatening. By the end of the nineteenth century, however, and certainly through the beginning of the twentieth century, it became clear that love between women, in conjunction with feminist theory and unprecedented economic freedom, had the potential to undermine the exclusivity of the heterosexual tradition, which in turn put patriarchal authority and male privilege at risk. Women were no longer dependent upon heterosexual marriage to meet their needs, economically or emotionally. Simultaneously, the Church, long the enforcer of social mores, was diminishing in influence. The institution which for centuries had buttressed the oppression of homosexuals and women was now losing its unquestioned authority.

It was at this juncture, just as love between women became a threat to the social structure and the Church began diminishing in authority, that homosexuality came under the aegis of scientific inquiry.[75] In 1869 Carl von Westphal published the first case history of a lesbian. Westphal's client loved women instead of men, preferred wearing slacks instead of skirts and longed to partake in the social privileges and activities long restricted to men.[76] Calling her a "congenital invert," Westphal concluded that her "condition" was a result of hereditary factors.

With that one article, lesbianism, as well as male homosexuality, was moved into the realm of the scientific study of deviance. After the publication of Westphal's paper, medical journals were flooded with case histories of lesbians and gays. From that point on, women's love for women would be seen as a perversion, and women's desire for increased freedom would be seen as a symptom of that perversion.

The most influential of Westphal's disciples in the late nineteenth century was Richard von Krafft-Ebing, whose *Psychopathia Sexualis* (1882) profoundly influenced both professional and popular understanding of homosexuality. Krafft-Ebing described "inversion" as a mental disorder resulting from both congenital and environmental factors. In each of his homosexual case studies, he traced the history of family pathology, establishing a relationship between homosexual orientation and extreme pathology. Krafft-Ebing's abiding contribution was thus the association of gayness and lesbianism with insanity, murder, suicide, epilepsy and alcoholism.[77] This association would be accepted by society for decades to come and would be internalized by gays and lesbians themselves, resulting in almost a century of self-hatred.

In the century following the publication of Westphal's 1869 paper, gays and lesbians were institutionalized, given electro-shock treatment, treated with experimental hormone therapy and, through the 1970s, treated with aversion therapy coupling homosexual images with electric shocks, noxious odors and nausea-inducing medication.[78] Throughout all early experimentation and inquiry, the unquestioned assumption underlying every theory and every approach was that same-sex love and attraction was undesirable and unnatural: a sign of psychopathology, biological disorder or arrested development.

The understanding of same-sex love as pathology was reflected and amplified throughout the literature of the time. While popular American magazines such as *Ladies Home Journal* had once thought nothing of publishing countless stories about the passionate love of romantic friends, by the end of World War I this was no longer possible.[79] For a woman to passionately love another woman was a sign of perversion and sickness and could end only in murder, suicide or madness.

Many romantic friends during this time found themselves in the position of having their relationship fully sanctioned by society in one decade and labeled as perverse the next. Two such women were Jeannette Marks and Mary Woolley. The two had met at Wellesley College in 1895, while Jeannette was a student and Mary a professor. Their partnership lasted until Mary's death in 1937, sustained through Mary's presidency of Mount Holyoke College, where Jeannette taught and wrote. It was acknowledged by all that they were partners in life. Before they moved into the president's house together, Faderman notes that one would visit the other's home every evening for a good-night kiss.

The internalized oppression that began to make itself felt during the course of their relationship is reflected in an unpublished essay by Marks entitled "Unwise College Friendships," written in 1908. In it she describes love between women as an "abominable condition" and writes that the only love that can "fulfill itself and be complete is that between a man and a woman." She attacks not only genital sexuality between women, but even what she calls "sentimental" friendship, thus striking out against the very love and friendship which was the foundation of her own life.[80] The essay signals the beginning of women's heartbreaking efforts to reject one of their most precious emotions, their natural inclination to love and embrace another woman.

Love between women had come to be treated with the same hostility that had previously characterized the treatment of lesbian cross-dressers. As long as heterosexual union had been necessary for women's economic survival, passionate love between non-cross-dressing women had been treated benignly, even sanctioned. Women's economic independence, however, and the feminist articulation of women's oppression, was quickly followed by the pathologizing both of women's bonding and of women's desires for freedom.

## The Twentieth Century: Towards Liberation

Starting in the late nineteenth century, a number of social, cultural and political developments began to weave a pattern which would, by the 1970s, lead to a dramatic and exultant emergence of lesbian love. Ironically, one of the early factors contributing to this emergence was one which accompanied the work of sexologists: in removing the aura of innocence from women's love, sexologists brought into the open the existence of sexual love between non-cross-dressing women. The Victorian myth of the asexual woman was shattered: women were sexual beings, and love between women could find sexual expression.

Increasing numbers of women found a sense of identity in a definition of same-sex love which included sexual expression. Such women began to gather together to form communities of their own, subcultures centered around lesbian experience. In turn-of-the-century Germany, a flourishing sisterhood identified themselves as "inverts." Other communities were less visible, composed of women who hid their lesbianism in public but found support and acceptance from within their own ranks. One such network is known to have existed in Salt Lake City during the 1920s and 1930s:[81] middle-class and working-class lesbians, unobserved by the heterosexual mainstream, gathering together to nurture and encourage one another.[82]

Lesbianism was also very much in vogue among early twentieth-century literary and bohemian circles. In France, during the early 1900s, there gathered a group of unconventional women, all of whom were financially independent and many of whom were lesbian. Colette, herself part of this community, described the enclave as including "Baronesses of the Empire, canonesses, lady cousins of the Czar, illegitimate daughters of grand Dukes, exquisites of the Parisian bourgeoisie, and also some aged horsewomen of the Austrian aristocracy."[83] Also in the community were wealthy American and British expatriates who had fled the restraints of their own cultures. It was the period known as the "Belle Epoque," an era of elegance and playfulness, an era known for its poetry, entertaining and lesbian love affairs.

The most prominent figure in this coterie was Natalie Barney, who, in many ways, exemplified the powerful support lesbians could provide one another. After opening a salon in Paris in 1905, Barney became known both as an exuberant lover of women and as the hostess of gatherings which, for the next seventy years, were the central social events of the lesbian community. Not only did Barney provide lesbians with a haven away from the heterosexual mainstream, but she also provided an arena for lesbian writers and artists to exhibit their work. Faderman notes that Barney offered lesbians an environment in which to cultivate the positive self-image denied to them by popular literature and society.

Early communities such as Barney's provided lesbians with their first opportunities for self-definition. From the unobserved Salt Lake City enclave to the flamboyant Parisian gathering, they provided lesbians with images beyond the evil and madness perpetuated by popular media. Denied positive images by heterosexual society, lesbians came together to create models of healthy and loving lesbian existence. Communities such as these laid the foundation for what half a century later would emerge as lesbian liberation.

Another development that had significant impact on the struggle towards lesbian visibility and liberation was the 1928 publication of Radclyffe Hall's *The Well of Loneliness*. Hall typified what was called at the time the "mannish lesbian." While not attempting to pass as a man, she wore suits and ties and cropped her hair. A significant departure from the innocent image of the nineteenth-century "romantic friends," these lesbians adopted a much more shocking and revolutionary stance. While in previous centuries, some lesbians had worn male clothing in order to pass as men, these "mannish lesbians" of the early twentieth century adopted this stance as a symbol of their increased freedom. The discarding of traditionally feminine attire and deportment signified a rejection of the patriarchal definition of womanhood. In casting off women's traditional roles and clothes, the "mannish lesbians" were reclaiming their freedom of self-definition.

This new stance was also a means of shattering the Victorian image of asexuality. Masculine appearance had come to symbolize not only social freedom but sexual freedom as well. Unlike romantic friendships, these lesbian relationships clearly included overt sexual expression. Given the absence of models of sexual love between women, lesbians adopted the only model available—the male image.[84] The stance of the "mannish lesbian" reflected, in part, the extent to which women had been denied images of passionate, sexual love between women.

Hall and her lover, Lady Una Troubridge, had been together for twelve years when *The Well of Loneliness* was published. According to

Troubridge, Hall had thought for some time of writing a novel about "female inversion."[85] Lesbianism had been dealt with in novels before, but the accounts had always ended either with ridicule or condemnation. Hall wanted to produce a work which would encourage understanding and acceptance. While she had anticipated that the book might encounter criticism, she was not prepared for the furor that followed its publication.

Published in England, the book was initially received with relatively favorable reviews. Then, a few weeks after publication, London's *Sunday Express* carried a photograph of Hall wearing a man's suit and a bow tie and holding a burning cigarette. Next to the photograph was the headline, "A BOOK THAT MUST BE SUPPRESSED," followed by a scathing attack on the book as "moral poison."[86]

The rest followed quickly. The book was withdrawn by the publishers, and Hall soon found herself in London's Bow Street Police Court listening to Chief Magistrate Sir Chartres Biron condemn the book as obscene, not on the grounds that it dealt with any "unnatural offences" between women, but on the grounds that it presented lesbians as "attractive people" and described them as not "in the least degree blameworthy." When Hall protested, the magistrate threatened to have her removed from court. Hall glanced over at Una Troubridge in the visitors' section; then, looking back at the magistrate, she called out her last word to him, "Shame!" The next morning the first 247 confiscated copies of *The Well of Loneliness* were burned in a cellar furnace of Scotland Yard.[87]

Although *The Well* was banned in England for thirty-one years, it became an international bestseller and eventually was published in fourteen countries. It became known as the lesbian classic, often the first book women read upon recognizing their own lesbianism. While some lesbians object to the novel on the grounds that it perpetuates the image of the suffering, tragic lesbian, for decades it was the only piece of literature in which lesbians could find some noncondemning portrayal of their emotions. Its sympathetic representation of lesbians was enough to create a furor in newspapers and journals worldwide; lesbianism had taken a giant step into social visibility.

While the Roaring Twenties offered increased tolerance for the unconventional in the United States, circumstances for both lesbians and gays worsened with the Great Depression. With economic strain came increased discrimination of all kinds.[88] Conditions for lesbians and gays deteriorated outside the United States as well. In the early 1930s the Soviet Union reversed its previous accepting stance towards homosexuality. Stalinists declared that homosexuality was a product of bourgeois decadence, and by 1934 mass arrests had been carried out. Soon after, Hitler brutally exterminated the entire leadership of the Scientific Humanitarian Association, the German gay liberation organization active since the 1890s. Homosexuals were grouped with Jews and other "undesirables" for execution, and tens of thousands of gay men were put to death in concentration camps.[89]

Ironically, the onset of World War II improved some circumstances for American lesbians. While working-class women, especially women of color, had long worked outside of the home, this had not been the case for the majority of middle-class women. With America's entry into the war, both the military and industry needed women to aid the war effort. More than ever before, women were allowed, even encouraged, to perform jobs that had previously been restricted to men. With husbands, fathers and brothers overseas, women traveled alone with relative independence, and since many lived away from their families, women increasingly sought each other out for companionship and group living arrangements. Lesbian bars sprang up, gathering places of the growing lesbian communities. Given economic independence, social freedom and predominantly female environments, it was an era when many women discovered their own lesbian orientation. It was, in all, a time of great "coming out."

In the military itself, there were thousands of new women enlistees, and given the intensity of the war effort, there was little time for homophobia. On the occasions when homophobia did make itself felt, it was quickly overcome by pragmatism. In the film, *Before Stonewall*, Andrea Weiss and Greta Schiller interview Sergeant Johnnie Phelps, a woman who enlisted after Pearl Harbor. Phelps describes an occasion on which General Eisenhower, her commanding officer, ordered her to conduct an investigation to discover which women among her WAC battalion were lesbian. She replied,

> Sir, I'll be happy to do this investigation for you but you'll have to know that the first name on the list will be mine... I think the General should be aware that among those women are the most highly decorated women in the war. There have been no cases of illegal pregnancies, there have been no cases of AWOL, there have been no cases of misconduct, and as a matter of fact, every six months the General has awarded us a commendation for meritorious service.

Eisenhower replied, "Forget the order."[90]

At the war's end, there was a tremendous effort to return America to pre-war norms. Public Service Announcements urged women to give their jobs to returning veterans and go back to tending their homes. By the late forties, a conservative political tide had begun sweeping the country; the McCarthy era was just beginning, and the fear of homosexuality was second only to the fear of communism. Newspapers repeatedly announced the firing of federal employees discovered to be "perverts"; homosexuals were assumed to be Soviet agents, blackmailed into spying because of their sexual orientation.

The military, previously tolerant of gays and lesbians, did a dramatic about-face. Military personnel suspected of being lesbian or gay were given undesirable discharges, often after extreme harassment. One servicewoman, Pat Bond, traces the beginning of the lesbian purges to the instructions given by commanding general Douglas MacArthur as he watched American women soldiers disembark: "I don't care how you do it, but get those dikes [sic] out of here."[91] The parents of women accused of lesbianism were notified of the charges against their daughters, and once discharged, lesbian servicewomen were left without benefits, without jobs and often without family support.

Accusations and threats pervaded society, and acceptable American lifestyle became increasingly narrowly defined. Faced with the harsh oppression of the 1950s, many women who had discovered their lesbianism during the war retreated into the safety of heterosexual marriage. Other lesbians simply went underground, staying in large cities, far from the watchful eyes of home-town families.

Despite the blanket of invisibility which descended upon homosexuality, certain changes the war had brought were irreversible. Beneath the fifties' facade of unblemished heterosexuality, the foundation of future liberation was being laid: gays and lesbians were beginning to organize. In the early fifties, the first two American "homophile" organizations for men were formed: One, Inc. and the Mattachine Society.

In 1955, a lesbian couple in San Francisco, Del Martin and Phyllis Lyon, started the first lesbian organization: Daughters of Bilitis (DOB), named for a book by Pierre Louys which had offered a positive portrayal of lesbianism. Shortly after it was organized, the DOB began publishing a journal known as *The Ladder*. From 1956 to 1972, *The Ladder* was mailed in plain brown envelopes to lesbians all over the country, providing the nation with the first lesbian network.

By the 1960s, several elements combined to refute the assumption of homosexual pathology in contemporary psychological theory and to infuse the fledgling gay liberation movement with new force. Among them were three studies released in the late forties and early fifties, studies that would serve as the scientific foundation for gay and lesbian liberation. Although the studies concentrated on men, they greatly affected the view of lesbianism as well.

In 1948, Kinsey published the dramatic results of his study of American male sexuality. To those who assumed that homosexuality was confined only to the "fringe" portion of the population, the results were staggering. Kinsey announced that thirty-seven percent of the male population had had sexual contact to the point of orgasm with another male, and ten percent of the male population considered themselves primarily homosexual.[92]

Three years later, in 1951, Ford and Beach published their cross-cultural studies of sexual behavior in *Patterns of Sexual Behavior*. They found that in forty-nine of the seventy-six societies for which data were available, some form of homosexuality was not only considered normal but was even socially sanctioned. In seventeen of the seventy-six, female homosexuality was either accepted or encouraged.[93]

Finally, Dr. Evelyn Hooker's research showed that the psychological tests of nonclinical samples of male homosexuals were indistinguishable from the tests of heterosexuals.[94] While Kinsey, Ford and Beach revealed the scope of homosexual activity, Hooker's study challenged the essential assumption of pathology. In the late sixties, these studies were brought to the forefront as the gay liberation movement disputed common perceptions of homosexuality.

Another significant influence on the 1960s gay liberation movement was the civil rights movement, which profoundly influenced the attitudes of all those who were disenfranchised. The civil rights movement, with its conviction that all individuals had inalienable rights, inspired a more militant attitude in the traditional homophile organizations. The traditional organizations assimilated these new attitudes to the extent they were able; when they could move no further, more militant groups broke off and acted independently.

With all of these forces converging, the "formal" launching of the gay liberation movement occurred in Greenwich Village one evening in June of 1969. As elsewhere, gay bars in the Village had become accustomed to fairly regular police harassment; it was never a great surprise to see the paddy wagon pull up in front of a bar. There was rarely any violence or active resistance; gays and lesbians, humiliated and subdued, usually filed out of the bar into police custody.

By the night of June 27, 1969, however, gays and lesbians at the Stonewall Inn had acquiesced long enough. As they were being taken into custody, many of the drag queens began jeering at the police. Then one lesbian performed a profoundly revolutionary act: she resisted. Her refusal to passively cooperate with the police ignited the crowd, and rioting began. Once begun, the rioting continued for several nights, the accumulated rage and indignation finally finding expression. The nation was stunned both by the intensity of the reaction and by the numbers involved. That night at the Stonewall Inn, and the evenings that followed, marked the beginning of the modern gay liberation movement.

Paralleling the dramatic growth of gay liberation was the women's movement. Feminism, relatively dormant since the turn of the century, re-emerged in the sixties. As this second wave of feminism gained momentum, many lesbians came to realize that they had more in common with feminists than with gay men, and lesbianism was redefined not as a purely sexual identity, but as a political one as well: a bond forged between women in the midst of an oppressive patriarchal society. In 1965 the following letter was published in *The Ladder:*

> Many women who prefer commitment to a career without the responsibilities of wifehood and motherhood would also like to find the kind of emotional satisfaction that is possible only on a sustained basis between equal partners. In today's world this kind of life is open only to the lesbian.[95]

Two years later *The Ladder* implemented a policy of using the word lesbian instead of variant or homosexual, reflecting the important distinction between lesbians and gay men and implying an understanding of lesbianism as a feminist stance.

The final obstacle to the full-blown emergence of lesbian-feminism was overcome when Del Martin and Phyllis Lyon helped lead the way for lesbians into the National Organization for Women, fighting the homophobia of founder Betty Friedan and others who did not want NOW identified with lesbians. After much internal struggle, in 1971 NOW passed a resolution in support of homosexual rights, and lesbian-feminists went on to become a central component of the women's movement.

Another important step was taken in 1973 when, in response to militant lobbying by lesbians and gays, the American Psychiatric Association reversed the trend of the previous century and removed homosexuality from its list of mental disorders.[96] The mental health community's official buttressing of discrimination against lesbians and gays was coming to an end.

Since these events over two decades ago, gay liberation activists and lesbian-feminists have brought the struggle for lesbian and gay rights into the forefront of public policy debate. Gay and lesbian advocacy organizations have matured into strong and effective lobbying groups, wielding far more power than would have been conceivable twenty years ago. Both local and national activists loudly and persistently hold businesses and politicians accountable for homophobic stands and actions. In reaction to much of this triumphant increase in visibility and political presence, the country has also seen a backlash aimed at bringing such progress to a halt. The condemnation of gays and lesbians has become a rallying cry for right-wing extremists. Many municipalities have passed ordinances condemning the "homosexual lifestyle." Organized efforts have been made to pass legislation prohibiting civil rights protection for lesbians and gays. Such efforts are usually driven by hostile and alarmist pedagogy. While the political turbulence continues, and the pitch of the debate rises, public consensus seems to be inexorably moving towards increased protection of the rights of lesbians and gays. The number of states offering civil rights protection for lesbians and gays is slowly increasing, and a Supreme Court ruling in 1996 determined that no state could specifically disallow civil rights protection for lesbians and gays.

Meanwhile, lesbian networks have flourished. The last twenty-five years have seen the growth of strong and supportive centers of lesbian life. Communities have witnessed the emergence of countless lesbian-owned businesses, newspapers, advocacy organizations, arts and entertainment centers, travel networks, spiritual retreats and legal resources. Both feminist and mainstream presses publish ever-increasing numbers of journals and books about gay and lesbian life. The Internet has provided an additional, and powerful, avenue for the dissemination of information related to lesbian and gay issues, offering opportunities for connection and communication unimaginable even five years ago. In these ways, lesbians have created a worldwide community of women-identified women. Although coming out still requires great courage, lesbians today can emerge into communities of women who have reclaimed their right to self-definition, women who have embraced their lesbianism as the proud and powerful expression of women's love for other women.

## Lesbian Unions: Legal Issues

During the last twenty-five years, as lesbians have gained a growing sense of pride and entitlement, they have begun to insist on social and legal recognition of the significance of their unions. Legal marriage grants certain important rights that have long been denied to gay and lesbian couples: social security survivors' benefits, hospital visiting privileges, tax benefits, spousal health insurance, the granting of inheritance to the surviving partner when a spouse dies intestate, crime victim benefits, contractual rights, and many more. One avenue many activists have pursued in order to grant lesbian and gay couples some of these benefits has been the effort to gain legal rights for unmarried "domestic partners."

This is an area which has been invested with additional urgency as a result of the AIDS epidemic. In addition to dealing with the illness itself, couples in which one or both partners have AIDS have been harshly confronted by their lack of spousal rights: gays have been denied the right to visit their ill or dying partners in the hospital; surviving partners have been evicted from apartments because their names were not listed on the lease and they were not considered "family"; and gay partners have often been left with no claims to their deceased lover's property when that partner has died without drafting a will.

The struggle for spousal rights has also been inspired by the work of Karen Thompson. In 1983, Karen's lover, Sharon Kowalski, was seriously injured in an automobile accident. Despite the fact that Karen and Sharon had been together for four years and owned a home together, Sharon's father was appointed guardian and, within twenty-four hours, had denied Karen visitation rights. Karen spent the next six years in and out of court, trying to gain guardianship, visitation rights and a court order to have Sharon relocated from a nursing home to an environment where she could get rehabilitative care. Karen did finally win the right to care for her lover, but only after many legal losses and at extraordinary personal and financial cost.

Through the course of her struggle, Karen became a vocal presence in the lesbian community, drawing upon the community for support and insisting that we address our lack of inherent legal rights as lesbian couples. Her story provided additional incentive for lesbian and gay couples to complete durable powers of attorney: legal agreements which authorize a specified individual to handle one's financial affairs and, if noted, also to make medical decisions in the event that one becomes incapacitated.

In addition to durable power of attorney, there are a number of other documents that lesbian and gay couples rely on in order to achieve some of the rights automatically granted to heterosexual married couples. Some of these documents include wills; living wills; and if one of the partners is the legal guardian of a child, travel authorizations and emergency health care authorizations which grant the non-relative partner the right to transport the child across state lines and to have the child medically treated in case of emergency. [97]

As increasing numbers of lesbian and gay couples have taken individual steps to protect their legal rights as families, activists have continued to advocate for domestic partnership benefits. During the last ten years, there has been a steady increase in the number of both private employers and governmental entities that recognize domestic partnerships. In the case of employers, this usually means offering some form of spousal insurance coverage to domestic partners. In the case of certain municipalities, this means permitting a couple who live together and meet certain requirements to publicly register as "domestic partners." This serves primarily as a symbolic recognition of their union, sometimes accompanied by the extension of health care benefits to the domestic partners of municipal employees.

While there has been a general appreciation in the lesbian and gay community regarding the importance of legal rights for unmarried domestic partners, a more galvanizing issue and national strategy has recently emerged: the effort to gain legal sanction for same-sex marriage. Actually, the first steps in this effort came several decades ago. As early as 1957, Daughters of Bilitis sponsored a public discussion entitled "Is a Homophile Marriage Possible?" The keynote speaker for the evening, a psychotherapist, answered yes: "Any marriage is possible between any two people if they want to grow up."[98]

In the late 1960s and early 1970s, lesbians began to test the limits of what the state would sanction as legal marriage. On June 12, 1970, the first marriage designed to legally unite two women was performed in Los Angeles. The Reverend Troy Perry presided as Neva Joy Heckman and Judith Ann Belew exchanged rings and vows. Rev. Perry issued a church marriage certificate under a California statute that exempts a common-law couple from having to obtain a state marriage license. The legality of the union was struck down, however, when it became clear that the statute read "man and wife."[99]

Meanwhile, a similar struggle was being waged in Louisville, Kentucky. There, Marjorie Ruth Jones and Tracy Knight took their case to the circuit court after being denied a marriage license by the county clerk. The two women contended that the Kentucky marriage statute did not specify that a marriage had to be between a heterosexual couple. The court was not receptive: the county attorney argued that the state legislature had never intended to sanction homosexuality in any form. In addition to striking down the women's case, the county attorney referred Marjorie Jones, a mother of three, to officials of Juvenile Court and Metropolitan Social Services. The attorney asked officials to investigate whether Jones, as a result of her actions, had contributed to the delinquency of her children.[100]

The case of Jones and Knight, along with a similar case involving two men, created a flurry of activity in the national media. The *San Francisco Chronicle* ran a series of articles debating the merits of homosexual marriage. On July 16, 1970, the final editorial concluded:

> Marriage is the public announcement of a civil contract between two people showing binding intent to share their lives. It is also a personal contract between two people showing intent to share their

mental and emotional resources. Members of the heterosexual majority derive great security, pride and social acceptance from this 'rendering public' of an honest social commitment in the eyes of 'God and Man.' It would seem only in keeping with the times that consideration be given to allowing the homosexual minority the same rights to this sense of fulfillment.[101]

Soon after the *Chronicle*'s editorial, Ruth E. Hauser, U.S. Representative to the U.N. Commission on Human Rights, delivered a speech to the American Bar Association questioning the constitutionality of denying gays and lesbians the right to marry.[102]

As the issue gained increased attention nationally, individual efforts to achieve legal sanction of lesbian partnerships continued. In 1971, Donna Burkett and Manonia Evans, two African-American lesbians in Wisconsin, filed a class action suit against the Milwaukee county clerk for refusing to issue them a marriage license.[103] Two lesbians in Chicago, Nancy Davis and Toby Schneiter, were arrested four times in 1975 and 1976 for staging sit-ins at the marriage license bureau, insisting upon their right to a marriage license. The two spent a year in the state penitentiary for their final conviction.[104]

Throughout the 1970s and 1980s, the discussion of legally sanctioned same-sex marriage created considerable controversy in the lesbian and gay community. Many lesbian-feminists saw efforts to create "lesbian marriages" as inimical to feminist theory. Marriage is an institution which was for centuries rooted in an understanding of women as male property. Many lesbians and gays believed that to participate in such an institution was essentially seeking approval from the very tradition which had helped ensure women's subjugation.

In a 1989 essay arguing against efforts to gain legal approval of same-sex marriage, Paula Ettelbrick of Lambda Legal Defense and Education Fund urged the lesbian and gay community to recognize the traps inherent in seeking such approval. She viewed such efforts as undermining some of the most significant goals of the lesbian and gay movement. Same-sex marriage would be a dramatic form of assimilation which would render invisible the unique qualities of lesbian and gay identity. She also argued that while legalizing same-sex marriage would inevitably alter the institution of marriage in a positive direction, we would be sacrificing a much larger goal: the transformation of our society into one which could acknowledge the validity of many forms of relationships, not just marriage.[105]

In a companion essay, Thomas Stoddard, also of Lambda, defended the choice of gay and lesbian couples who would enter into same-sex marriages. He argued that until lesbians and gays had exactly the same legal rights as heterosexuals, they would always be accorded secondary status. As such, he saw the legalizing of same-sex marriage as the final recognition of the validity of lesbian and gay relationships. He also wrote that by broadening the definition of marriage to include same-sex couples, the institution of marriage itself would be transformed in a powerful and positive direction: without an institutionalized power imbalance based on gender, marriage itself would break from patriarchal tradition.[106]

While some lesbian and gay advocacy organizations supported same-sex marriage in principle, many felt that it was not a significant enough issue, or realistic enough goal, to warrant the expenditure of financial resources and political influence. Whether the debate has focused on principle or priority, discussion of this issue within the lesbian and gay community has been heated and passionate. That it has sparked so much impassioned debate speaks of a community struggling to find the most meaningful expression of their relationships and the most powerful route to liberation.

Before this debate had reached resolution, or any semblance of consensus had been achieved, the issue of legalized same-sex marriage suddenly emerged at the center of national policy debate. In large part, this was due to certain key judicial and legislative battles. The Hawaii Supreme Court had ruled that discrimination against same-sex couples violated Hawaii's Equal Rights Amendment. By 1996, despite a few judicial hurdles, it appeared it was only a matter of time before lesbian and gay couples could legally marry in the state of Hawaii.

Representatives from other states began to scramble, aware that their states would be required to honor marriages from Hawaii. In the summer of 1996, in a vote of 342-67, the U.S. House of Representatives passed the "Defense of Marriage Act," which defines marriage as a commitment between one man and one woman, thus ensuring that same-sex couples cannot receive federal spousal benefits. Under the bill, states are free to legalize same-sex marriage within their own boundaries, but other states are not required to honor them. Rep. John Lewis of Georgia, who had marched beside Martin Luther King, Jr., argued against passage of the bill, saying, "I have known racism. I have known bigotry. This bill stinks of the same fear, hatred and intolerance."[107]

Despite the passage of the bill, the issue of same-sex marriage continues to spur advocacy and action. Lambda Legal Defense and Education Fund has established The Marriage Project, coordinating efforts to promote the legalization of same-sex marriage. The National Gay and Lesbian Task Force has begun working with activists throughout the country in battling measures hostile to same-sex marriage. Numerous other advocacy groups have evolved, focused specifically on the issue of same-sex marriage.

While there are undoubtedly more judicial and legislative battles ahead, what seems assured is that the right of gay and lesbian couples to legally marry has a place at the head of the lesbian and gay agenda. It is an issue which, in a spontaneous and self-organizing manner, has captured the hope and imagination of lesbian and gay couples insistent upon the full legal recognition of their unions.

## Ceremonies Celebrating Lesbian Unions

In addition to struggling for legal recognition, during the last twenty-five years lesbian couples have increasingly focused attention on the ceremonial acknowledgment of their relationships. Initially, lesbian couples turned to traditional religious organizations, looking for the few members of the clergy willing to bless a same-sex union. In 1968, in response to the need he saw within the gay and lesbian communities, the Reverend Troy Perry founded the Universal Fellowship of Metropolitan Community Churches (MCC). The MCC not only welcomed gays and lesbians but also recognized the sanctity of a same-sex union. By the end of 1972, the MCC had forty-three congregations and an international membership of fifteen thousand, and Perry himself had performed two hundred and fifty services of holy union for same-sex couples.[108]

Many lesbian-feminists viewed this development with distrust. As with efforts to gain legal sanction for same-sex marriage, many lesbians believed that those participating in holy unions were being assimilated into a historically patriarchal tradition. They saw those choosing holy unions as mimicking heterosexual marriage and seeking approval from religious traditions which had long been oppressive to women.

The lesbian couples choosing these ceremonies, however, saw their participation in these ceremonies as a way of insisting on the validity and sanctity of their partnerships. Having found a loving and committed relationship, they wanted the same public acknowledgment and spiritual blessing that was offered to heterosexual couples. They sought the means to fully and proudly acknowledge the depth of their commitment to another woman. To them, performing a rite of holy union was a means of affirming lesbian existence, not diminishing it.

The opposition from the lesbian-feminist community to ceremonies of commitment began to soften with the emergence of women's spiritual-

ity in the feminist movement. Beginning in the early 1970s with the publication of Mary Daly's *Beyond God the Father*, women started to articulate
a spiritual orientation compatible with feminism, a vision combining the
political and the spiritual. For some, like Rosemary Ruether and Elisabeth
Schussler Fiorenza, this meant a feminist re-visioning of the Judeo-
Christian tradition. Others followed the lead of Merlin Stone in separating
themselves from patriarchal religion, re-establishing a connection to the
Goddess and celebrating the sacred unity of all life. Many women of color,
such as Luisah Teish, found their spirituality interwoven with their cultural heritage. Yet others, like Zsuzsanna Budapest and Starhawk, found
Goddess religion expressed most clearly through the feminist reclaiming of
Wicca, or witchcraft. Feminist psyches stirred with spiritual awareness, and
what emerged was a spirituality based on a reverence for the intrinsic sanctity of life and a sense of awe for its mysteries.

With the rise of the women's spirituality movement there also grew
an appreciation of women's rituals. Rituals have come to be understood as
essential modes of revitalizing, sanctifying and empowering, representing
both celebration and transformation. The creation of women's rituals has
come to be seen as a way of affirming our own identity, a way of creating
our own symbols and traditions. For centuries, the only organized form of
spirituality available to women was patriarchal religion, a tradition in stark
opposition to lesbian-feminism. With the emergence of women's spirituality, the division between the political and spiritual has begun to be bridged,
and with the healing of this rift, the lesbian community has increasingly
come to honor and embrace the ritual affirmation of lesbian partnerships.

In the last few years, lesbian ceremonies of commitment, holy
unions, trysts, handfastings and lesbian weddings have burst into visibility.
Today, wedding ceremonies for same-sex couples are conducted not only
by the MCC, but also by an increasing number of clergy from traditional
denominations. Lesbians are also creating their own ceremonies, interweaving what is meaningful for them from various traditions with words
and images from their own imaginings. Lesbians are manifesting their own
loving and powerful visions of relationships, and creating out of their own
hearts and minds the ceremonies to acknowledge and celebrate those relationships.

---

1. This essay is intended to illustrate various currents within the history of lesbian partnerships. For more comprehensive presentations of lesbian history, readers are encouraged to
refer to the principal sources for this work: John Boswell, *Christianity, Social Tolerance, and
Homosexuality: Gay People in Western Europe from the Beginning of the Christian Era to the
Fourteenth Century* (Chicago: University of Chicago Press, 1980); Lillian Faderman,

*Surpassing the Love of Men: Romantic Friendship and Love Between Women from the Renaissance to the Present* (New York: William Morrow and Company, 1981); Judy Grahn, *Another Mother Tongue: Gay Words, Gay Worlds* (Boston: Beacon Press, 1984); Dolores Klaich, *Woman + Woman: Attitudes Toward Lesbianism* (New York, Simon and Schuster, 1974; reprinted Tallahassee: Naiad Press, 1989); and Carroll Smith-Rosenberg, "The Female World of Love and Ritual: Relations between Women in Nineteenth-Century America," *Signs: Journal of Women in Culture and Society* 1 (1975): 1-29.

2. Adrienne Rich, "Compulsory Heterosexuality and Lesbian Existence," *Signs: Journal of Women in Culture and Society* 5 (1980): 648.

3. Blanche, Wiesen Cook, "'Women Alone Stir My Imagination': Lesbianism and the Cultural Tradition," *Signs: Journal of Women in Culture and Society* 4 (1979): 720.

4. Paul Gunn Allen, "Lesbians in American Indian Cultures," *Conditions: Seven* (1981): 70.

5. Allen, 76.

6. See Arthur Evans, *Witchcraft and the Gay Counterculture* (Boston: Fag Rag Books, 1978), 101-104; and Judy Grahn, *Another Mother Tongue: Gay Words, Gay Worlds* (Boston: Beacon Press, 1984), 49-72.

7. Allen, 82.

8. Sue-Ellen Jacobs, "Berdache: A Brief Review of the Literature," *Colorado Anthropologist* 1 (1968): 25-40. Cited in Grahn, *Another Mother Tongue*, 55.

9. Grahn, *Another Mother Tongue*, 60; and Carolyn Niethammer, *Daughers of the Earth* (New York: Macmillan, 1977), 229.

10. Hermann Baumann, *Das Doppelte Geschlecht* (Berlin: Dietrich Reimer, 1955). Cited in Evans, 102.

11. George Devereux, "Institutionalized Homosexuality of the Mohave Indians," *Human Biology* 9 (1937): 501.

12. Devereux, 509.

13. Claude E. Schaeffer, "The Kutenai Female Berdache," in Jonathan Katz, *Gay American History: Lesbians and Gay Men in the U.S.A.* (New York: Thomas Crowell, 1976), 297.

14. Schaeffer, in Katz, 298.

15. Allen, 82.

16. Susan Cavin, *Lesbian Origins* (San Francisco: Ism Press, 1985), 131-133; Katz, 293-311; and Niethammer, 229-32.

17. Edwin T. Denig, "Biography of Woman Chief," in Katz, 310.

18. Leslie Spier, "Transvestites or berdaches," in Katz, 322-23.

19. E.E. Evans-Pritchard, *Kinship and Marriage Among the Nuer* (Oxford: Clarendon Press, 1964), 108-9.

20. Janet M. Bujra, "Women Entrepreneurs of Early Nairobi," *Canadian Journal of African Studies* 9.2 (1975): 231.

21. Eileen Jensen Krige, "The Place of North-Eastern Transvaal Sotho in the South Bantu Complex," *Africa* 11 (1938): 272; J.D. Krige and Eileen Jensen Krige, "The Lovedu of the Transvaal," *African Worlds: Studies in the Cosmological Ideas and Social Values of African Peoples,* ed. Daryll Forde (London: Oxford Univ. Press, 1954), 57; Eileen Jensen Krige, "Property, Cross-Cousin Marriage, and the Family Life Cycle among the Lobedu," *The Family Estate in Africa: Studies in the Role of Property in Family Structure and Lineage Continuity,* eds. Robert F. Gray and P.H. Gulliver (Boston: Boston Univ. Press, 1964), 144, 160, 173-5; Eileen Jensen Krige and J.D. Krige, *The Realm of a Rain Queen: A Study of the Pattern of Lovedu Society* (London: Oxford Univ. Press, 1943), 156.

22. Cavin, 129-33; Melville J. Herskovits, "A Note on 'Woman Marriage' in Dahomey," *Africa* 10 (1937): 335-341; Northcote W. Thomas, "Anthropological Report on Ibo-Speaking People of Nigeria," Part IV, *Law and Custom of the Asaba District, S. Nigeria* (London: Harrison and Sons, 1914), 58, 83; Unokanma Okonjo, *The Impact of Urbanization on the Ibo Family Structure* (Gottingen: Verlag Udo Breger, 1970), 149; Charles Kingsley Meek, *Law and Authority in a Nigerian Tribe: A Study of Indirect Rule* (New York: Barnes and

Noble, 1970), 275-6; Victor Chikezie Uchendo, *The Igbo of Southeast Nigeria* (New York: Holt, Rinehart and Winston, 1965), 50.

23. Baumann, cited in Evans, 106.

24. Nicholas J. Bradford, "Transgenderism and the Cult of Yellama: Heat, Sex, and Sickness in South Indian Ritual," *Journal of Anthropological Research* 39 (1983): 307-322.

25. Lawrence Krader, "Buryat Religion and Society," *Gods and Rituals,* ed. John Middleton (New York: Natural History Press, 1967), 112.

26. In this discussion of Sappho, I draw heavily upon Judy Grahn, *The Highest Apple* (San Franciso: Spinster Ink, 1985).

27. Sappho, *Greek Lyric,* vol. 1, trans. David Campbell (Cambridge: Harvard Univ. Press, 1982), 57.

28. Sappho, *Early Greek Poetry and Philosophy,* Hermann Frankel, trans. Moses Hadas and James Willis (1962; reprinted New York: Harcourt Brace Jovanovich, 1973), 183.

29. Sappho, *Sappho and the Greek Lyric Poets,* trans. Willis Barnstone (New York: Schoken Books, 1988), 95.

30. John Boswell, *Christianity, Social Tolerance, and Homosexuality: Gay People in Western Europe from the Beginning of the Christian Era to the Fourteenth Century* (Chicago: University of Chicago Press, 1980), 82-4.

31. See Boswell, 83-4.

32. Plato, *Dialogues of Plato,* ed. G. Kaplan (New York: Washington Square Press, 1950), 192.

33. Vern L. Bullough, *Sexual Variance in Society and History* (New York: John Wiley and Sons, 1976), 229-31, 299.

34. Babylonian Talmud, *Shabbath,* 65a. Cited in Derrick Sherwin Bailey, *Homosexuality and the Western Christian Tradition* (1955; reprinted Hamden, Conn.: Archon Books, 1974), 61.

35. Ruth, 1: 16-17

36. Terry Calvani, "Homosexuality and the Law—An Overview," *New York Law Forum* xvii (1971): 273-275.

37. See Boswell, 119-136 and 169-206.

38. Joseph Campbell with Bill Moyers, *The Power of Myth* (New York: Doubleday, 1988), 185-205.

39. Campbell, 190.

40. Ralph Metzner, "The Mystical Symbolic Psychology of Hildegard von Bingen," *Revision* 11.2 (1988): 3-4.

41. Grahn, *The Highest Apple,* 13.

42. Quoted in Boswell, 220-21.

43. Boswell, 269-302.

44. Boswell, 295.

45. Louis Crompton, "The Myth of Lesbian Impunity," *Journal of Homosexuality* 6.1-2 (1980/81): 11.

46. Grahn, *The Highest Apple,* 13; Boswell, 271.

47. Margaret Murray, *The God of the Witches* (1931; reprinted New York, Doubleday, 1960); Margaret Murray, *The Witch-Cult in Western Europe: A Study in Anthropology* (1921; reprinted Oxford: Clarendon Press, 1966), cited and discussed in Carol P. Christ, *Laughter of Aphrodite: Reflections on a Journey to the Goddess* (San Francisco: Harper and Row, 1987): 45-6.

48. See Barbara Ehrenreich and Deirdre English, *Witches, Midwives, and Nurses: A History of Women Healers* (SUNY: The Feminist Press, 1973).

49. Alan C. Kors and Edward Peters, *Witchcraft in Europe 1100-1700: A Documentary History* (Philadelphia: Univ. of Pennsylvania Press, 1972), 9.

50. Evans, 99.

51. For more on this see Mary Daly, *Gyn/Ecology* (Boston: Beacon Press, 1978), 178-222.

52. See especially Starhawk, *The Spiral Dance* (San Francisco: Harper and Row, 1979) and

Zsuzsanna Budapest, *The Holy Book of Women's Mysteries* (1980; reprinted Berkeley: Wingbow Press, 1989).

53. For the sections on cross-dressing and romantic friendship, I have drawn heavily on Lillian Faderman, *Surpassing the Love of Men: Romantic Friendship and Love Between Women from the Renaissance to the Present* (New York: William Morrow and Company, 1981). I urge readers to refer to her work for more complete discussions of either subject.

54. Havelock Ellis, *Studies in the Psychology of Sex,* vol. 1 (1905; reprinted New York: Random House, 1942), 204n.

55. Crompton, 17; and Faderman, 51.

56. Crompton, 17; Faderman, 51; and Foster, 44.

57. "A Lesbian Execution in Germany, 1721: The Trial Records," trans. Brigitte Erikkson, *Journal of Homosexuality* 6.1-2 (1980/81): 27-40.

58. Erikkson, 31-40.

59. Faderman, 55-6; and Fincher's Trade Review, "A Curious Married Couple" and "Thirty-four years of pretended matrimony," in Katz, 225-6.

60. Ellis, 246-7; and Katz, 232-238.

61. See Ellis, 247-8.

62. Quoted in Doug Clark, "Jazz musician spent life concealing fantastic secret," *Spokesman-Review,* 31 Jan. 1989, B1.

63. Faderman, 125-132.

64. *A Series of Letters Betwen Mrs. Elizabeth Carter and Miss Catherine Talbot,* vol. 1, 23. Quoted in Faderman, 126-7. Faderman notes that in the eighteenth century "Mrs." was a title of respect unrelated to marital status.

65. Carter and Talbot, 9. Quoted in Faderman, 127.

66. Caroll Smith-Rosenberg, "The Female World of Love and Ritual: Relations between Women in Nineteenth-Century America," *Signs: Journal of Women in Culture and Society* 1 (1975): 1-29.

67. Dolores Klaich, *Woman + Woman: Attitudes Toward Lesbianism* (New York: Simon and Schuster, 1974), 227.

68. Mary Gordon, *Chase of the Wild Goose* (1936; reprinted New York: Arno Press, 1975), 11-14; *Life with the Ladies of Llangollen,* ed. Elizabeth Mavor (New York: Viking, 1984), 11-13; Faderman, 120-25; and Foster, 122-25.

69. Quoted in Smith-Rosenberg, 4-5.

70. Sarah Butler Wister, London, to Jeannie Field Musgrove, New York, June 19 and August 3, 1870. Quoted in Smith-Rosenberg, 5.

71. Faderman, 197-203. Faderman does not mention the name of McCracken's partner.

72. Michael Field, *Underneath the Bow,* 3d ed. (1893; Portland, Me.: Thomas B. Mosher, 1898), 50. Quoted in Faderman, 209.

73. T. and D.C. Sturge Moore, *Works and Days: From the Journal of Michael Field* (London: Murray, 1933), 16. Quoted in Faderman, 209.

74. Faderman, 212.

75. See Ronald Bayer, *Homosexuality and American Psychiatry: The Politics of Diagnosis* (1981; Princeton: Princeton Univ. Press, 1987); also see Faderman, 239-53.

76. Faderman, 239.

77. Bayer, 19-20.

78. Council on Scientific Affairs, "Aversion Therapy," *Journal of the American Medical Association* 258.18 (1987): 2562-66.

79. Faderman, 297-8.

80. Faderman, 228-230.

81. Vern Bullough and Bonnie Bullough, "Lesbianism in the 1920s and 1930s: Newfound Study," *Signs: Journal of Women in Culture and Society* 2.4 (1977): 895-904.

82. The communities referred to here were communities of white lesbians. Little information survives regarding lesbians of color during this period.

83. Colette, *The Pure and the Impure*, trans. Herma Briffault (New York: Farrar, Straus and Giroux, 1967), 69. Quoted in Klaich, 162.

84. See Esther Newton, "The Mythic Mannish Lesbian: Radclyffe Hall and the New Woman," *Signs: Journal of Women in Culture and Society* 9 (1984): 557-575.

85. Klaich, 183.

86. Klaich, 185.

87. Klaich, 184.

88. Andrea Weiss and Greta Schiller, *Before Stonewall: The Making of a Gay and Lesbian Community* (Tallahassee, Fl.: Naiad Press, 1988), 12-30. See this for a more in-depth discussion of gay and lesbian life from 1900 through the Stonewall Riots.

89. John Lauritsen and David Thorstad, *The Early Homosexual Rights Movement (1864-1935)* (New York: Times Change Press, 1974), 44-5.

90. Quoted in Weiss and Schiller, 35.

91. See Grahn, *Another Mother Tongue*, 175-176.

92. Alfred Kinsey et al., *Sexual Behavior in the Human Male* (Philadelphia: Saunders, 1948), 625.

93. Cleland S. Ford and Frank A. Beach, *Patterns of Sexual Behavior* (New York: Harper and Brothers, 1951), 130-133.

94. Evelyn Hooker, "The Adjustment of the Male Overt Homosexual," *Journal of Projective Techniques* 21 (1957): 23.

95. "Readers Respond," *The Ladder,* vol. 9, no. 9 (June 1965), 25-6. Quoted in Faderman, 381.

96. This was eroded with the inclusion of "ego-dystonic homosexuality" in the 1980 edition of the *Diagnostic and Statistical Manual of Psychiatric Disorders (DSM)*. Ego-dystonic homosexuality was dropped from the *DSM* in 1986.

97. My thanks to Kathleen Stoll of HRCF for information about documents protecting partnership rights. While none of these tools to protect the rights of lesbian and gay families can be guaranteed to be enforced, we stand a much better chance of having our partnership rights respected if we have made provisions such as these well in advance of any emergency. For samples of many of these documents, see Hayden Curry and Denis Clifford, *A Legal Guide for Lesbian and Gay Couples* (Berkeley: Nolo Press, 1986).

98. "Is Homophile Marriage Possible," *The Ladder*, vol. 1, no. 10 (1957): 17-23.

99. Del Martin and Phyllis Lyon, *Lesbian/Woman* (San Francisco: Glide Publications, 1972), 99-100.

100. Martin and Lyon, 100-101.

101. *San Francisco Chronicle*, 16 July 1970. Quoted in Martin and Lyon, 101.

102. *The New York Times*, 11 Aug. 1970, 23.

103. "Black Women Exchange Vows During Holidays," *Proud Woman* (March/April 1972): 8; "Marriage Fight Due," *Mother*, vol. 1, no. 7 (Dec. 1971): 1; "Gay Women United in Public Ceremony," *Focus* (March/April 1972): 12; and "Two Women Plan to be Married," *Jet*, 4 Nov. 1971, 21-25.

104. Lynn Sweet, "Prison can't crush lesbians' marriage crusade," *Chicago Sun Times*, 1976.

105. Paula L. Ettelbrick, "Since When Is Marriage a Path to Liberation," *Out-Look*, no. 6 (Fall, 1989): 9, 14-17.

106. Thomas B. Stoddard, "Why Gay People Should Seek the Right to Marry," *Out-Look*, no. 6 (Fall, 1989): 9-13.

107. *The Atlanta Journal/The Atlanta Constitution*, 13, July 1996, A3.

108. "Churches Expand for Homosexuals," *The New York Times*, 1 Jan. 1973.

# Part Two

## The Ceremonies

*The rules break like a thermometer;*
*quicksilver spills across the charted systems,*
*we're out in a country that has no language*
*no laws, we're chasing the raven and the wren*
*through gorges unexplored since dawn*
*whatever we do together is pure invention*
*the maps they gave us were out of date*
*by years . . .*

From "Twenty-One Love Poems: XIII" by Adrienne Rich

# Diane Benjamin

## &    Patti Christensen

Patti (left) & Diane (right)
photographer: Sher Stoneman

## June 11, 1988 ❧ Minnesota

# "To All That Shall Be—Yes!"

A friend of ours jokingly called it our "uncommitment ceremony." Another called us up excitedly wondering when he could give us our wedding present. A number of friends said they'd be glad to come, but what exactly was it that we were doing?

We thought the invitations were clear enough: "Diane Marie Benjamin and Patti Jo Christensen joyfully invite you to join with their family of friends in celebrating their relationship." We weren't having a wedding, tryst, handfasting, commitment ceremony or blessing. We were doing something that we'd never seen or heard of before. We were creating our own form to celebrate six years of living and loving together, first as friends and then as lovers.

Months of agonizing planning preceded those simple invitations. After a year of tentative "what would you think about maybe someday doing some kind of ceremony" discussions, the time felt right. We didn't want to do a traditional wedding, substituting two brides for a bride and a groom. A "commitment ceremony" didn't feel right either. We had already made many commitments to each other: when we chose to live together, when we struggled through couples therapy, when we made joint purchases, put each other in our wills and took out powers of attorney. These seemed much more real than standing up and making promises to each other, such as "I will always be with you and always stay in this relationship even if it becomes unhealthy for me. Amen." We finally decided that a celebration was what we wanted, and we took a quote from Dag Hammarskjöld as our theme: "For all that has been—thanks! To all that shall be—yes!"

We settled on a remote county park location and a potluck picnic, with an invitation for friends to camp with us the night before the ceremony. We also decided to pay a local lesbian photographer to record the event. Even keeping things this simple required much more planning and preparation than we had imagined. We also had to make a number of difficult decisions, everything from "do we use our middle names on the invitations" (we did) to "do we invite our friend's husband whom we don't know very well" (we didn't).

We made a conscious decision not to invite our families of origin but rather to gather our "family of friends." This was primarily because we were doing something that would have been so foreign to our parents—gathering with twenty lesbians, three gay men, three straight friends and a couple of children on lawn chairs in a circle in the woods, calling the four directions and wrapping ourselves in ribbons. While our families have been fairly accepting of our relationship, we felt they wouldn't understand and would restrict the choices we made for the celebration. Finally, the decisions were all made, for better or worse, and the day arrived.

Diane wore a simple white shirt she had made; Patti wore a brightly colored shirt scavenged from her favorite second-hand shop. A friend gave us a surprise gift of garlands for our hair; another group of friends brought flowers. Our backdrop was a handmade banner of the Dag Hammarskjöld quote. People managed to follow the complicated directions to the park fairly well, and finally Diane's best friend from college began the prelude on his viola.

Patti led the group in calling on the spirits of the four directions to join the circle. Diane sang a love song, and a friend led the group in a centering meditation. Then various people shared readings and poems that had significance to us. Next came one of the highlights of the celebration. This was a time for our friends to share stories and memories about us and our lives with them. Several people told the exact same story about watching us prepare a tempura dinner for them; we were fighting in the kitchen throughout the elaborate preparation and our not so cooperative cooking styles. Another two friends related how they had borrowed our copy of *Lesbian Sex*—only to find the margin notes we had written much more interesting than the book. Yet another friend told of a wager she had made with her partner on a fateful evening three and a half years ago as to whether we were already lovers or were about to be. She won: we became lovers that night. She likes to think she was the first to know. This part of the celebration brought blushes, laughs and memories flooding to the surface.

The next segment we termed our "vaguely vowlike statements." We each simply wrote out what the other had meant to us and what she had brought to our life. We did these separately and didn't read them to each other until that day. We both ended in tears and smiles and felt the power of declaring out loud and in the presence of our community what we share together.

The last part of our ceremony, and one of the most unique, was to have each person bring a long ribbon with them and then individually (or in couples) come up to us and offer a blessing or wish for us. They then gave us one end of the ribbon and kept the other, moving back into a circle with us in the center like the hub of a wheel. After all had come forward, they walked around us, wrapping us up in their blessings and then let go, leaving us totally surrounded by ribbons and love. It was extremely moving to have a visible symbol of our connection with these people and of their love and care for us. We closed with a spirited rendition of "Song of the Soul" and a very delicious meal.

Doing this celebration did not make a sudden change in our relationship, but rather, it felt like a very integrated part of our ongoing growth together. Our friends were very pleased and honored to have been a part of our ceremony, and a few of them are now thinking about doing a similar sort of ritual themselves. We feel very glad that we dared to gather up all of the love and affection of our friends and community and let ourselves really feel their joy in our relationship. It's our hope and wish that more lesbian and gay couples find ways to do the same.

*—Diane Benjamin & Patti Christensen*

## The Readings

The definition of family as it appears in the pamphlet, "A Force for Families," published by the American Home Economics Association:

> AHEA defines the family unit as two or more persons who share resources, share responsibility for decisions, share values and goals, and have commitment to one another over time. The family is that climate that one "comes home to," and it is this network of sharing and commitments that most accurately describes the family unit, regardless of blood, legalities, adoption or marriage.

"Six Years" by Alice Bloch:

> A friend calls us
> an old married couple
>
> I flinch
> you don't mind
> On the way home
> you ask why I got upset
> We are something
> like what she said
> you say    I say
> No
>
> We aren't married
> No one has blessed
> this union    no one
> gave us kitchen gadgets

We bought our own blender
We build our common life
in the space between the laws

Six years
What drew us together
a cartographer        a magnetic force
our bodies        our speech
the wind        a hunger

Listeners both
we talked

I wanted: your lean wired energy
control        decisiveness
honesty        your past
as an athlete
You wanted:
my "culture"
gentleness        warmth

Of course that was doomed
You brought out
my anger        I resist
your control        your energy
exhausts me        my hands
are too hot for you        you gained
the weight I lost        my gentleness
is dishonest        your honesty
is cruel        you hate
my reading        I hate
your motorcycle

Yet something has changed
You have become gentler
I more decisive
We walk easily
around our house
into each other's language
There is nothing
we cannot say together

Solid ground
under our feet
we know this landscape

We have no choice
of destination      only the route
is a mystery      every day
a new map of the same terrain

From "Sexuality, Love, and Justice," in *Our Passion for Justice: Images of Power, Sexuality, and Liberation* by Carter Heyward:

To say I love you is to say that you are not mine, but rather your own.

To love you is to advocate your rights, your space, your self, and to struggle with you, rather than against you, in our learning to claim our power in the world.

To love you is to make love to you, and with you, whether in an exchange of glances heavy with existence, in the passing of a peace we mean, in common work or play, in our struggle for social justice, or in the ecstasy and tenderness of intimate embrace that we believe is just and right for us—and for others in the world.

To love you is to be pushed by a power/God both terrifying and comforting, to touch and be touched by you. To love you is to sing with you, cry with you, pray with you, and act with you to re-create the world.

To say "I love you" means—let the revolution begin!

ॐ

*Diane Benjamin: I'm twenty-six years old and in graduate school working on my master's degree in community health education. I'm a musician, karate student, gardener, activist and a homebody at heart.*

*Patti Christensen: I just turned thirty and am listening to my biological clock tick. I'm a counselor with battered women and kids, and I enjoy writing, secondhand shops, gossip and being a foster parent with Diane.*

# Luana Silverberg-Willis

## & Yael Silverberg-Willis

Yael (left) & Luana (right)
photographer: H. L. Keller

*August 9, 1987* ❧ *California*

# Gospel under the Chuppah

*On August 9, 1987, in a ritual of love and extreme passion*
*Yael Lee Silverberg and Luana Lynette Willis*
*will become*
*Yael Lee Silverberg-Willis*
*and*
*Luana Lynette Silverberg-Willis*

Luana Silverberg-Willis is my wife and soul mate. She is a creative, intelligent and powerful woman of thirty-four years whose herstory is vastly different from my own. Luana grew up in Minneapolis as a Black woman with a mother and two brothers. Her economic level while growing up was working class, and she attended Catholic schools through college. She danced and taught dance for nineteen years and, in 1983, came to California to get her master's degree in dance education at Mills College in Oakland. It was at this point that she and I met.

My name is Yael Silverberg-Willis. I am twenty-nine-years old, studying to be a nurse-midwife, and I am also a powerful woman. I grew up in an upper-middle-class home in New York. My family is culturally very Jewish, with a large and active extended family. My nuclear family consists of a father, mother and four sisters. We were very close until, at age eighteen, I came out to them. At that point, the family went through major changes. In 1981, I left the East Coast to find: myself, lesbian role models, and support for my life choices, since I had received little of that from my family. In 1983, I was facilitating a lesbian support group at the Pacific Center for Human Growth, and Luana joined the group.

We courted. I had never done that before. Many women "fall in love" so quickly, but Luana and I romanced. Each date ended with my walking her to her car and kissing her on the hand. We were both nervous and felt like teenagers. Somehow, though, it seemed worth it. Months later, I felt it was time to express some of the overpowering feelings inside of me. I invited her over to my apartment. I sang her the Holly Near song, "Sit With Me," and we kissed.

Our relationship has always stressed communication and humor. We play like kids and have a talent for being able to change things that are hard by merely mentioning them. Our brand of love is also a passionate one; we never take the other person for granted. People often think that we are in the first months of our relationship because flowers, poems and gifts are such mainstays for us. Actually, we have been together for over five years; our secret is romance, passion and change.

On December 29, 1986, during the Afro-American holiday of Kwanzaa, I asked Luana for an even deeper statement of our commitment and love for each other. Kwanzaa is a beautiful seven-day holiday which stresses seven principles for maintaining and thriving as a Black community. The twenty-ninth of December is dedicated to familyhood, so the date felt very appropriate. I prepared a beautiful meal and had champagne, roses and a ring with my Hebrew name engraved on it. By dessert I hadn't said a word; I was terrified! Finally, I asked her to create with me a ceremony of love, a commitment of time and dedication to each other. I told her to take her time in deciding. Five minutes later she had said yes! I almost died... Now what? We wanted to call people—but whom? We weren't in the mood to call people who would need convincing that we weren't mad; this isn't an easy issue for either the straight or lesbian communities. Thank God for one of our friends, Carol Charlot, who knew the exact script we needed to hear.

So how do we set the date? Who will perform it? What is it we want to say? And to whom? In what style? And what about our families? We decided to do it in the summer; that was far enough away not to feel so threatening. For reasons that were both practical and romantic, August 9, 1987, became the date. We are family members in a gay synagogue called Sha'ar Zahav, so we decided to have our synagogue's rabbi, Yoel Kahn, perform the ceremony. After we talked to him, we knew that he would meet our needs perfectly. While understanding my desire for a Jewish ceremony, he also voiced the concern that we create a ceremony in which Luana's needs would be fully met as well. We loved him from that point on. We met with him once a month for six months as he led us through lessons of personal growth, dream sharing and conflict resolution. Later we would understand that this process was, in fact, the wedding.

As extravagant women, we decided to have a formal event. We each wanted to wear dresses, and we decided that our attendants would wear black tuxedos. As we moved into gear, it became evident that we would each have to deal with our emotions around not having our families there to help with the process. There was no emotional and, of course, no financial support. It was through putting together this enormous event that we gradually changed our definition of "family." Every need that arose was answered by a core group of friends. One embroidered our chuppah (the canopy under which we were married), another planted all the flowers, another arranged all the bouquets, another baked a three-tier carrot cake and ran our reception. There was also a bridal shower and a bachelorette party; the community was getting ready for a much needed public statement of powerful love and commitment.

I had decided not to tell my family until two months prior to the ceremony. Luana and I had had little luck in getting any positive responses from them, and we didn't want six full months of negative feelings. Why did I tell them at all? Because I wasn't going to hide my passages. The only members of either family who were supportive were Luana's youngest brother, Robert, and my Aunt Terry. Luana decided to have her brother walk her down the aisle, and I chose to go it alone.

The writing of the ceremony was the most difficult part. We worked hard to create a ceremony which integrated our individual cultures as well as our beliefs as a couple. Linda Tillery sang gospel under the chuppah, we drank wine from a kiddush cup and a kikombe (unity) cup from Kwanzaa, and we wrote our own interpretation of the Jewish seven blessings which spoke of our eight most important values. We created a ketubah (a Jewish marriage license) and called our ceremony a kiddushin (a sanctification ceremony), not a wedding. We put together a pamphlet which explained the ritual objects we were using as well as our beliefs. This was important, because our friends' cultures are as diverse as ours.

Ritual is integral to the survival of a people. Support and love are integral to making that survival healthy. We learned, as did our friends, that we must look beyond the limited definitions that exist in both the gay and straight communities. Our ceremony left all one hundred and fifty guests changed. There was such an extraordinary feeling of love filling the synagogue; there wasn't a dry eye left, and everyone's perspective was broadened.

When we entered the local women's bar several days after the wedding, we received a standing ovation. People are proud of those who are willing to take a chance towards love, the chance to build a structure that can withstand the hostilities of this society. Luana and I are a part of that new structure, and we continue to grow as well as to fall more and more in love. Hopefully our children will experience the openness of our love, and they will feel able to be a part of changing this society into a more loving and nonjudgmental place.

—*Yael Silverberg-Willis*

## A Letter to Yael's Parents

You have always taught me to question that which is given, to respect both the complexity and the simplicity of life, and to live each day as a celebration.

You told me to be thoughtful. Not to be a doormat to be trod upon, but to be aware of other people and their needs; to be able to meet them halfway and, on occasion, go the other half joyfully.

You told me to live the courtesy born of caring and to express this caring through the small formalities and customs born of the years.

You told me to be bold and not to be afraid of the unknown, to live life to its fullest and meet each new experience with joy and anticipation.

And you told me of the joy and challenge of being a woman. The joy of having a child... knowing and sharing a life. The joy of making a home... the center but not the limit for the lives of those we love. The joy of exploring a world of my own. The joy of discovering and fulfilling my own capabilities.

You told me of these things as I went along the way, and for all my lessons I am humbly grateful. And as for the things that you did not teach, I have chosen those for myself. I have decided what has meaning and made that my own. For ultimately, I must live my own life; it is mine to build as I choose.

And I told Yael: laugh and dance and sing. There is a lot in life that is hard, but take it as it comes and find the good... and make time to dance! Be creative and explore the seed within you. Find your creative spirit and let it grow.

So now I must tell you about my life, for you know so little of what my life is like.

I am truly happy, and in many ways that is the most important thing that I want you to know. I cannot remember ever being as happy in my adult life, and I hope that you can be happy for my joy. Much of my happiness has its basis in my love for Luana and my love of who I am as a human being. Because we have spent so little time together in the past few years, you have little knowledge of the depth and complexity of either area. That, of course, is not any one person's fault, and in fact, fault is irrelevant. We are different individuals who have chosen similar yet different paths.

Because I love and respect both of you tremendously, and because you and my entire family play a central role in my life, I have something to share with you.

On August 9, 1987, Luana and I will be having a ceremony that will speak to our love for each other. The ceremony will take place in our synagogue and is formally called a kiddushin or sanctification.

The decision to create a ceremony came quite naturally. We are people who believe in the importance of ritual, and we each know that the other person is the one with whom we want to build a family.

I know that this is not easy information for you to hear, for you do not understand my life choices, yet I believe that you do understand a desire to celebrate, through ritual, the love between two people.

You may wonder why I am telling you of our plans. My decision to have you know was a painstaking one. While I wanted you to know, I also knew that the information could possibly do two things: it could be painful for you, and it could potentially cause what would feel like a family assault on me. I did not want either to happen. Our decision to have a ceremony is not meant to hurt anyone—only to celebrate our happiness. And I do not want to be bombarded by my family's inability to deal with me.

But I have told you, and I will tell the rest of the family. Why? Because this will be my sole kiddushin, and I will not make the decision for you that you want no part. I have no expectations regarding my family's participation in the ceremony, but I will not hide my life transitions from you.

This letter is a difficult one to write. It is a hard one to read. I am sharing my life's joys with you only because I love you all. There is little space in your lives for my life and my life choices. You each have made up your own minds about the degree to which you will be involved in my life. While that has not been an easy thing for me, I have come to accept it. One day I may come to realize that you do not want to share even this small amount. Maybe you will have your own realizations. Either way . . . I love you.

Love, Yael

(My parents chose not to participate in our kiddushin.)


## A Letter to Luana's Mother

Mom,

I found my dress for the "wedding." Actually we are calling it a kiddushin. Kiddushin is a Hebrew word meaning sanctification. The ritual on August 9 will sanctify the relationship between Yael and myself. On August 9 Yael and I will stop time for one hour and tell each other and the world that we have chosen each other to love, and that we are committed to developing and cultivating our relationship until "death do us part."

The support from our friends has been wonderful. They are working very hard to make the day special for us. But despite all the friends' support and despite love from Yael, I miss you in this process. I went to the fabric store to look for the material for my dress, and I started crying because in my childhood and young adult dreams you were there to help me. I envisioned Saturdays spent together, looking for things I would need, stopping to have lunch or a beer. I didn't realize how much I wanted you to be part of my "wedding" until I started shopping and planning. You have been there for me for every rite of passage. You have been my friend and mentor. It would be great to have you here now.

I spoke earlier of friends' support. It has been interesting to see the varied responses we get when we tell our friends of our ritual plans. Most of our more recent friends (who are coupled and average forty-two years in age) are very excited and helpful. Unfortunately, most of our long-term friends have been shitty in their response. They say nothing, or they are not excited at all, or they ask why we are following a "heterosexual, male-suppressive ritual." Yael and I look at each other shrugging our shoulders, wondering if our long-term friends are acquainted with the couple, Luana and Yael.

Ritual has always been part of our relationship. We celebrate birthdays to the hilt and anniversaries of every significant event in our lives. We bring flowers to each other for little or big achievements. We attend religious services, and we acknowledge the rituals of others. We are also the most romantic couple we know. The synagogue and rabbi have played a strong role in developing our religious community. So has the Christian church, Church of Divine Man. The synagogue and the church have guided us in our spiritual, familial and personal paths.

So between the religious aspect of our lives, our love of ritual and our romance, it seems natural to take the time to recommit to each other. To us, it's very exciting! Maybe our friends do not understand our values, so it becomes difficult for them to be excited that we are fulfilling one of our dreams. Maybe they are jealous. Maybe they don't believe in ceremonies. Maybe their religious upbringing prohibits them from seeing a wedding type of ceremony in the context of a gay relationship. Whatever the reason... it hurts.

Not only do I miss you being here, but I miss having my history at the wedding. I know that these are all old fantasies, but I guess I still have them and regret that they are not being fulfilled. I want my childhood friends there. I want your friends there. I want you to be proud. I want my brothers there. I want all of the significant people in my present life there to celebrate with me. I know that one of my fantasies is coming true, but the others...

I know I gave up certain benefits when I moved to California. I gave up another set when I chose to be with a woman. These were decisions I made, and I wouldn't change any of them. I love where I live and the woman I am with. But it doesn't stop me from missing the benefits of the other choices in this world. I am trying to obtain most of my fantasies and have a good time. For the most part I am happy and satisfied; I just miss the history and am surprised by the reactions of my long-term friends.

Much, much, much more to say, but I will stop here,

Love you very much, Luana

(Unfortunately, my mother chose not to play any role in our kiddushin.)

## After the Ceremony—Yael's Parents

The kiddushin has aided the growth of our families and ourselves in ways more far-reaching than anyone could have imagined. To begin with, my family—the Silverberg parents—ended up taking the wedding very seriously. My family sees such commitments as life choices, and they applied their beliefs to our wedding as well. I went back to see them in May following the wedding, after the death of my grandfather. My mother didn't even let me get settled before she asked to see the wedding photos I had brought. She and I went through them together. With tears in her eyes, she said that after the ceremony she had called my Aunt Terry and talked for hours, asking about every detail. She needed me to know how much she cared and needed me to know that there were many reasons she could not be there, the biggest one being that my father couldn't handle it. She said that nothing was more important to her than my father and their relationship together. While it was hard for me to hear, some part of me understood, for I hold that same dedication to Luana.

Since then my parents and I have inched closer to understanding each other. Luana and I have now been back to visit them several times. The first breakthrough was when they rented a double futon for us. Then, this last time, we had the first family—"all the daughters and their mates"—dinner. When Mom referred to her daughter-in-law, everyone including Luana looked around to see whom she was referring to. Finally we realized she was talking about Luana. It floored us.

Of course, it hasn't all been easy. My younger sister is getting married this summer, and the family's excitement has been difficult for both me and Luana. The contrast between their wonderful planning for this wedding and their absence from our own is often too much to bear. But we know everyone has made great progress, and we have all moved closer together. We just try to take one step at a time.

The thought Luana's mom has put into all this can probably best be captured by the following letter, which she sent after the wedding.

## *After the Ceremony—A Letter from Luana's Mother*

October 3, 1988

Luana and Yael,

I think I'll give this letter a title:

"By the Way, Mom, I'm Gay"

I know that you didn't say it that way, nor did you take it that casually yourself. But, somehow, it seemed to be told as an afterthought to a perfectly normal conversation about clothes or diet or boyfriends.

My first response (or feeling) was nothing. Sort of a "That's nice, honey, don't fight." Of course, I didn't hear you right. There was nothing in my thoughts and dreams for you that included gayness. I had hoped you would be a dancer or a teacher or a housewife or a career woman or whatever would make you happy (all parents say that, don't we), but none of these things included gayness. I had never thought—I mean never—to say to you, "If you don't like boys, why don't you try girls."

It wasn't that I saw anything wrong with gayness, it was just that I hadn't thought of *you* as gay. Remember when you were in high school and you gave the speech about being kind to gay girls? I advised you that they were having a hard enough time without you joining the group that would make fun of them or isolate them. I knew that since you were going to an all-girls' school and would be going on to a women's college, that you couldn't help but run into it, and I wanted you to be kind. But those were other people's daughters. At that time I had no idea about what their mothers were thinking, and, frankly, I didn't care much. After all, their daughters had a right to choose their own lives.

All of that is still true. You do have a right to choose your own life.

I think at first, I expected you to "outgrow" it. After all, when you first told me about it, you were living with Scott. So I didn't have to give it too much thought. Later when you and Yael moved in together, it still seemed experimental to me, until you came here to visit me in Minneapolis.

When you and Yael ate your first meal out of the same plate, I thought I would die. I had never seen anyone do that in all my life. I couldn't figure out why the two of you (neither one of you said to the other one, "Isn't that kind of strong? Let's not do that.") would make such a strong statement within hours of entering my home. I had to recoup quick, because I certainly wanted both of you to enjoy your visit. But it was hard, because I was constantly bombarded with the sound of "Honey," "Sweetheart," "Darling." I felt like I was on a roller coaster that wouldn't stop. You see, I didn't really have it together yet. Hadn't really given it any serious thought. Didn't know how hard it was going to be to say, "My daughter's gay."

Finally on that trip, I had to ask to see you alone. I didn't want anything in particular, I just wanted to know if you were still you, if we could still talk about the things that we had always talked about or if you would talk to me differently. Well, you were the same, and after you left, I began the adjustment. My daughter is gay. My daughter is gay. Get that through your head, old woman.

Then came the wedding. My daughter was getting married, and I couldn't tell a soul. Well, that isn't quite true, I could tell some people. But no one said, "That's wonderful," so I stopped telling people. I couldn't tell anyone at work. I mean when Rob got married I told everyone including the bus driver (you know how I am). But when you got married, I had to keep it a secret, because people ask questions and want to see the pictures. When I say questions, I mean details. Who was the best man? Did the groom's family attend? If you start to lie (and I couldn't tell the truth), you get so mixed up that you break out in a cold sweat.

Once at work, I did slip up. You see, they ask about you all the time. Mainly because I talked about you so much—like every day. I told them everything you were doing, and they got to know you pretty good. One day Bill asked me if you were still riding your bike. I said, "No, they bought a car." Silence. "They?" The entire department was looking at me. I tried to stay calm as I said, "Yes, she and her roommate bought a car together." "She bought a car with her roommate? I've never heard of that." Well, I mumbled something, and then the phone rang and I got out of it. I'm always afraid that I'll slip up again and say "they." So I try not to talk about you. That's the hard part. I've talked and bragged and commented about you all of your life, and now I'm afraid to say the simplest thing because I may slip up. I don't want to say to fifteen or sixteen people, "My daughter's gay." I can hear the questions. Everyone will be polite, but as the oldest member of the department, the knowledgeable senior, I would be the instant expert on gayness and would have to answer a million questions not only about gayness in general, but my gay daughter in particular.

I'm near the end now, mainly because it's about nine P.M. and I'm tired now. I haven't rounded this out, mainly because I'm still working on it. But there are some suggestions I would like to make to your friends: 1) When you have been invited to visit with your family, *don't* pick that time to be the most loving, nor to have an argument. Your family has accepted your life, but give them time to adjust—after all, it took you a while to adjust to the situation yourself. 2) Know how hard it is for them not to be able to talk about you all the time for fear of "slipping." I'm learning. I can now say roommate without feeling that I have given your life away. Did you notice how I said that? "Give your life away." The fact is that everyone that isn't gay thinks that there is something wrong with being gay, and I don't want anyone to think that there is anything wrong with my daughter, my loving, giving, beautiful, talented daughter. The interesting thing is that my gay friends are the most fearful for you. They have lived the way that they had to live, but they know it's a hard row to hoe. They say to me, "Evelyn, I'm sorry. I would have wanted an easier life for your daughter."

There it is, not well written. Neither cruel nor gentle, just how it is for me. Of course, now there is the threat of AIDS. But this one is not just for you and Yael, but for all three of my children. AIDS makes parents of young people *very* uneasy. So little is known about it, and it's a little more serious than the chicken pox.

The paper is gone and I'm hungry—So I'll say good night, and Love, of course,

Evelyn

## The Ceremony

*Welcoming Pamphlet—Page One*

We have chosen each other because we feel that our union is the best thing we can do for each other and that our united strength can be a model for the world in which we live.

Our free decision to create this ceremony which joins us is prompted by the love that we have for each other. This love provides us with the determination to be ourselves, the capacity to surrender and the push to live life to its fullest. It gives us the courage to hope and the ability to make our dreams a reality. Our purpose in joining together is to nurture that love in each other and, as best we can, give it to others.

We affirm our desire and obligation to work towards the creation of a just social order and the promotion of a more fruitful life for all. We hope that during our life together we shall be able to make contributions towards these ideals.

Together we will share in life's successes and challenges. We ask you, as family and friends, to help us realize our love together. And we invite you to share in its fruits.

Luana and Yael

*Welcoming Pamphlet—Page Two*

The following page has been included because our friends' cultures are as diverse as ours. We hope that you enjoy and participate in today's celebration, for you have been integral in making it possible. The ceremony has integrated both Jewish tradition and Black-American customs. The holiday Kwanzaa is a Black-American holiday celebrated from December 26 to January 1. It celebrates seven principles: unity, self-definition, collective work and responsibility, cooperative economics, purpose, creativity and faith. We have added humor as an eighth principle. We hope that the following descriptions of the ritual objects used will give fuller understanding to the ceremony.

*The Chuppah:* The chuppah, or canopy, is a symbol of our home. It is the paragon of hospitality since it is open on all four sides. It is held by our friends; they are the faces surrounding us as a couple and represent the community that will help us establish our home together. According to custom, the chuppah is understood as a sign of G-d's presence at the ceremony and in the home being established under the canopy. Chuppah means "that which covers or floats above." It is said that the space beneath the canopy is spiritually charged because G-d is floating above it.

*Kiddush and Kikombe Cups:* In the Jewish culture, wine is associated with celebrations. Kiddush, blessing over the wine, is a part of virtually all Jewish observances as a prayer of sanctification. The kikombe cup is part of the Kwanzaa celebration and represents unity. Since two cups of wine are drunk during the ceremony, the first will be the kikombe cup which will be shared with others in our community, and the second, the kiddush cup, will be reserved for ourselves.

*Mazao:* The ear of corn or mazao is a Kwanzaa symbol which represents the rewards of collective productive labor, the gathering-in of the community and a celebration and reinforcement of the kinship and unity among peoples.

*The Mkeka:* The ritual objects are placed on the Mkeka. The Mkeka is a Kwanzaa ritual item symbolizing tradition and history, the foundation for all our actions.

*Rings:* The rings are placed on the index finger during the ceremony because of an ancient Jewish belief that this finger is directly connected by a special artery to one's heart. The rings, therefore, symbolically connect both hearts.

*Seven Blessings Times Three—Hebrew, English and Our Interpretation Using Kwanzaa Principles:* The traditional Jewish Seven Blessings are all in praise of G-d's gifts. Our interpretation stresses the eight values listed in the introduction above, all of which are central in our lives.

*The Ketubah:* The ketubah is a document used as a marriage license in the traditional Jewish wedding. We have chosen to create one as an expression that acknowledges our individuality as well as the mutuality of our agreement to this kiddushin.

*Broken Glass:* The breaking of a glass as the completion of the ceremony is an ancient custom encrusted with generations of interpretations. To us, the breaking of the glass is a statement: "For anyone who wants to come between us and our love, you must first put the glass back together."

*Tzedakah:* It is a Jewish custom for the bride and the groom to give charity before their wedding. We have incorporated that custom into the creation of our ceremony. In doing so we are affirming that in our happiness we will remember our community. We have given three times eighteen dollars (eighteen is the number which symbolizes life): eighteen for Luana, eighteen for Yael, eighteen for our first child!

*Challah:* The challah is the traditional braided bread eaten on the Jewish Sabbath and during various holidays. For us, the challah represents the harvest from which we all reap and share in its nourishments.

*Sequence of Events*

1. Rabbi's Invocation: Introduction to what the ceremony and objects used in the ceremony mean.

2. Processional:
   Linda sings
   Chuppah
   Maria and Carol
   Tamara—rings
   Yael
   Luana with Robert Willis

3. Rabbi speaks of the meaning of the ceremony to Yael and Luana.
4. First glass of wine using the kikombe cup as explained by Rabbi Kahn.
5. Exchange of vows:

Yael: We have chosen each other, and the choice seems obvious to all who know us. We have given the gift that has made this the most powerful love and most exceptional sharing two people can be blessed to hold.

It is not that our ears hear better the words, but that we listen to each other's silences and explore each other's process. We do not always agree but rarely do we not understand.

It is not that our eyes can see beauty unseen by others, but that we strive towards reaching our fullest potentials, a place where we are each strikingly beautiful.

We know each other in ways only time and sensitivity can allow.

There is a sense of limitlessness to our love and to our growth.

Together, nothing seems impossible; we need only to decide what it is that we want and create it.

It is with such a woman that I want to raise my children and create my family. It is with such a woman that I want to continue my growth. It is with you—mind, body and soul—for I love you passionately.

Luana: Passion, romantic drama, strong communication and our ability to laugh is the warp which our relationship is woven around. When I look back over the past three and a half years, our time together has been astonishing.

You've shown me my beauty when my skin broke out and all I could see was my ugliness, and I've shown you your grace when you thought you were awkward.

Education, spirituality, familyhood, having fun, creativity, friendship, loving, and you and I have been our priorities, and we have encouraged each other's growth in these areas.

We have supported each other in difficult and, God only knows, very trying times!

We have respected, had patience with, and delighted in our cultural, spiritual and personal differences... (pause) And to this very day your beauty takes my breath away when you walk into the room.

My vow to you is that I promise to maintain to the best of my abilities the glorious relationship we have, and to embellish when and wherever possible... until death do us part.

6. Exchange of rings.

7. Linda sings "G-d Will Take Care of You."

8. Seven Blessings: 1) Hebrew
                    2) English
                    3) Our interpretation (Rusty reads our interpretation of the Seven Blessings. Linda reads "I Am A Black Woman" by Mari Evans and sings "Lift Every Voice and Sing.")

9. Rabbi reads the ketubah:

> On the first day of the week the ninth day of August nineteen hundred and eighty-seven years, Luana, daughter of Evelyn Fairbanks, and Yael, daughter of Gittel and Mervin Silverberg, say: This ring symbolizes our free decision to create this ceremony which joins us and is prompted by the love that we have for each other. This love provides us with the determination to be ourselves, the capacity to surrender and the push to live life to its fullest. It gives us the courage to hope and the ability to make our dreams a reality. Our purpose in joining together is to nurture that love in each other and as best we can, give it to others.
>
> We promise to try to be ever open to one another while cherishing each other's uniqueness, to comfort and challenge each other through life's sorrow and joy, to share our intuition and insight with one another, and above all to do everything within our power to permit each other to become the person we are yet to be.
>
> We also pledge to establish a home open to the spiritual potential in all life. A home wherein the flow of the seasons and the passages of life are celebrated through the symbols of our heritages. A home filled with reverence for learning, loving and generosity. A home wherein ancient melody, candles and wine sanctify the table. A home joined ever more closely to the communities of the world.

10. Rabbi speaks to Yael and Luana.

11. Priestly benediction by Leslie.

12. Glass breaking.

13. Recessional.

૨**

*Luana Silverberg-Willis: I don't want to just "show up" for my life. I am a Black woman, dancer, teacher, lesbian, creative spirit who demands to be attentive to and participate in my own development. Presently I am searching for a doctoral program which will allow me to combine arts and spirituality.*

*Yael Silverberg-Willis: I am the fourth of five sisters. We grew up in New York in a family strongly influenced by our Jewish heritage and culture. Committed to reaching my own personal excellence, I strive to be a powerful healer, creative teacher and responsive partner in love. I have spent much of my life learning how best to communicate with and care for others and have found my greatest happiness in working with pregnant women. I am currently studying to obtain my master's degree in midwifery.*

# Kristina Breidenbach

## &    Harper Leah

Harper (left) & Kristina (right)
photographer: Maureen Fishleigh

*May 1, 1988* ❧ *Arizona*

# Splendiferous Buddhist Beltane, Full Moon, Eclectic Celebration

When someone asks me these days what my profession is, my answer is a bit more involved than it was a year ago, when I moved to the Southwest from San Francisco. I have always been an artist, but I haven't always been able to make my living as such. I used to say, with a certain amount of regret which I could feel in my body, "Chef. I am a chef." The regret? I wanted to do other things besides cook. The truth is that I do lots of things for a living and for a life. Years of Buddhist training, twelve-step programs, individual therapy and cooking have enabled me to feel more free about my self-definitions. I am an artist and I do many things, including cooking, to make my way.

Last fall I left San Francisco where I had been living, and cooking, for twelve years. I moved to the Sonoran desert in Arizona to help caretake some property. I did a minimal amount of cooking to cover my expenses, and Kristina and I started working with clay. The ritual figures we make, fetishlike in spirit, are now in galleries in the Southwest and on the East and West Coasts. Our dream is that they will provide us with a substantial part of our income, and that cooking for me will become an enjoyable hobby.

I am the only child of two alcoholics. My mother died of cancer two years ago. I have engaged in a long recovery process: recovery from the shame and guilt I had with my parents and the problems I experienced as a result of their addictions. Without this recovery process, I do not feel that I would have been ready for the commitment that Kristina and I have made to each other and to ourselves. To me, getting married has meant that I finally felt ready and able to find and fall in love with a woman I consider my peer. This ceremony was a way to be proud of my life, to acknowledge myself as a person and to marry with the people I hold closest and dearest in my life.

Friendship is very important to me, and I constantly turn over what it means to be a good friend and how I can participate successfully in my friendships. This ceremony was a personal tribute to the joys and struggles of building long-term passionate friendships. In the Buddhist wedding ceremony, the people who are marrying are also marrying all of those attending the ceremony. These people, the other practicing Buddhists, friends and family, are known as the Sangha, or community. This way, one receives full support for her marriage, and I truly think it takes a lot of support from the outside world to make a marriage work.

The Buddhist ceremony asks everyone to take refuge in the Buddha, to have compassion for the person you are marrying and to continually look for the Buddha nature which is present in everyone. The ceremony states that marriage is something that takes time, time to develop and time to ripen.

Although Buddhism is certainly based on a patriarchal system, the ceremony makes no distinction between male and female; in that sense, it is androgynous in nature. Androgyny interests me greatly. There is a movement in gay and straight female societies to rediscover the Goddess: to acknowledge her role in other cultures and in history as a powerful presence and to objectify her through actual worship. I believe that this resurgence of the Goddess is the stepping stone to androgyny in our society. We lesbians are and always have been New Agers, forerunners bringing about new ways of being. By marrying we are paving the way for the recognition of equality in all relationships: male-male, female-male and female-female.

I believe in balanced partnership, and this belief is the basis of my marriage with Kristina. Everyone who attended—gay partners, single gay and straight men and women, married het folks and kids of all ages—supported our form of union. I married for love, and in a larger context, I married in order to make a meaningful statement to our universe that my choices are equally as valid as those made in mainstream heterosexual society; I hope to perpetuate a more equal sense of partnership for all people.

Neither Kristina's parents nor my father attended our May Day matrimonial. On the morning of the ceremony, I summoned my strength and called my dad, who had been ill and was just out of the hospital. He said, "So, today's the big day, huh? I am happy for you if you are happy." Kristina's mother asked for more time to respond to Kristina's decision and didn't feel comfortable enough to attend. Both her parents continue to be outwardly disappointed at the lifestyle she has chosen.

Several of our relatives responded with long letters affirming their love, faith and support for us. Kristina's Aunt Ida, seventy-six and a devout Episcopalian, wrote, "If God wanted us all to be the same, he would have created us that way.... Uncle Til and I will love you forever." My Aunt Martha and Uncle Paul telephoned, welcoming Kristina into their family. Aunt Martha also wrote: "We read and reread your letter and looked and relooked at the pictures you included. We were able to sense the great happiness in your life... and we were glad. It was wonderful... to know that you have found someone worthy of the goodness that you represent. We all need someone to share the best and the worst of our lives with; someone to make the best better and even more memorable as well as to lessen the disappointments and tragedies that inevitably come our way."

We started a photo album/scrapbook before the ceremony. The beginning included old photos of friends who would be attending the ceremony interspersed with our childhood family photos and my dog Wilma's puppy pictures (neither of us has any children). After the ceremony, five people sent their camera eyes' perspectives on the big event.

—*Harper Leah*

ã

I am also an artist, as well as a bodyworker/health educator. I make my living through these ways. I have many friends, a truck, a house full of stuff and many interests. My life is rich and full. My heart and mind are full. I also have many memories if I want to consider them.

It strikes me as ironic that I am well into the middle of my life and yet just beginning what most of my old friends, and indeed most folks in this society, have entered into probably twenty to twenty-five years ago (and of course they most commonly enter into a male-female version). Two years ago I saw some magazine articles about women's diminishing chances of marriage as we got older. I would guess that practices in the lesbian community reflect a less rigid age bias for partnerships and marriages. It is my hope that with years of experience in relationships, and a growing respect for older women and our aging processes, we have developed within our subculture more ease to engage in vital partnerships in our middle and old age. Ageism is relative; we can reinvent our relationships to suit our needs.

There's a certain astonishment I can still feel, seven months after the ceremony: I have actually participated in my own matrimonial ceremony! As individualized as my life has been, this marriage has meant a great leap of faith that continues to take me into the less mapped places of my psyche, offering me rich possibilities for understanding how to humanize and evolve my relationships and integrate otherwise lost and disparate parts of myself. I feel a deep gratitude to myself and my partner for taking this leap of consciousness.

Writing about this most special event adds yet another dimension. It gives me a chance to reimagine it, to give it yet more substance, to view it with perspective (seemingly a Capricorn imperative) and hopefully to cheer on the souls of other women for whom this is also a bright dream. Creating a lesbian wedding was a way to ritually and publicly proclaim the profound love, appreciation and connection I have with Harper and she with me. Furthermore, it has strengthened my desire to develop an even deeper purpose to having a long-term relationship. As simplistic as it sounds, my commitment has committed me, as I hoped it would.

I have approached marriage and similar committed relationships with a great deal of skepticism. I have seen only a couple of people survive being together for years. Survive and thrive, that is, without guilt, denial, various degrees of violence or insult, or the assistance of alcohol and drugs.

When I was thirteen years old, I arbitrarily and adamantly informed my mother, "I will never swear, smoke cigarettes or marry a man with a moustache." I thought all three distasteful; I grew up to embrace the first, periodically drag on the second and stay clear of the third. I had sensed, but not yet articulated, that marriage for me might mean a life dedicated to family, house and, most scary, to having to behave within certain socially prescribed limits. At that time it angered me and struck me as ludicrous.

When I left the homestable, I wanted to run. I needed to figure out for myself who I was and what worked for me. Though I still maintain an explorer's curiosity about myself and the world, there are definite advantages to being in a stable relationship. It makes it easier for me to manifest the desires of the second half of my lifetime: staying healthy, sitting zazen, writing, sculpting, raising a child, recovering from co-dependency and feeling rooted to myself through giving and receiving love and acceptance.

I still maintain a small linen closet full of anxieties about real intimacy, anxieties I can display on occasion: slipcovers and samplers embroidered "Roped and Hogtied," "Souvenirs of Habitland," "Gave Up Her Freedom, 1988." I can be belligerent in demanding "my space," proclaiming my uniqueness apart from anyone, but I have grown to realize that coming from a dysfunctional family system, I had to fight hard to establish an inner security and external limits. I've also learned that being an adept fighter is really necessary only in specific circumstances. I don't want to live all the time with a defensive stance, which can create antagonists out of allies. I've been doing renovations with my linen closet, and although it's still there, it now resembles a screened-in porch, open for fresh breezes and scrutiny.

I have taken forty-four years to shuffle and lurch to the edge of the precipice of Commitment. I have had mostly serial relationships, lovers lasting one to five years. I think I always kept one foot turned away, one bag packed. I would always move a little too fast and far, and then pull back. I now can say that I had difficulty with merging and separating. I am, as I mentioned, seven months into this falling and landing, and I am still in wonder at what can grow in this Garden of Paradox.

Harper and I decided in January 1988 to have a May 1 ceremony. I did the proposing. A Blue Moon Month. We had an established friendship and a happy lovership and had already processed different difficulties while living together for four months. I perceived us as well matched, true peers, equally weird, strange and artistic in the right combinations. For instance, her double decades of practicing meditation as a Zen Buddhist, including three years in a monastery in Maine, give her a great and well-exploited edge in maintaining equanimity against my more reactive and jump-to-conclusions style. My ability to be self-centered and direct gives her permission to express disapproval and disappointment and to hold more firmly to what she feels and needs. We both feel we have chosen grown-up partners, whose wounded children are recognized and nourished but don't get to run the show for long. We are both survivors, artists and humorists, and we blend our talents easily. When we don't, we struggle passionately to find a way.

We started ceremony preparations in January. First we talked about who we wanted to be there: the proverbial guest list. We wanted to be careful in our choices. What our facilities could accommodate was one factor. Another was that though there are a number of very special people in our lives, we wanted to be discriminating and not ask someone to be there with whom we were not current and clear. We wanted to do our best to create an easy emotional climate. Most of our friends had not met each other, and most everyone would be staying over at least three days. Only four women friends lived nearby and didn't need to fly to get here. We lived forty miles north of Phoenix, in the boondocks, on ten acres of land.

It was very exciting to make each and every plan and to have time to pay attention to each detail. We wanted to create everything ourselves, from announcements, to menu, presents, food, music. And we wanted to invite everyone to participate in whatever way felt appropriate in order to integrate our personal experience with the communal experience.

What to call what was happening was one of the sticky glitches for me. I had difficulty letting the words *marriage* or *wedding* be said. I preferred to use and hear the term *matrimonial*, because it contained "matrix," which for me felt closer to our dream: "From the source, woman-centered, womb created. The natural material in which something else, like a gem, is embedded." I especially like the use of matrix because, as a connective tissue therapist, it represents the ground substance or base whose relationship proportionate to cells determines the nature of tissue, that is, blood, bone, loose connective tissue. I have often equated this word, matrix, with others which try to explain the ultimate: void, god, ultimate being, source. Matrix feminizes this for me and introduces spirit into matter in my mind. Also, and more personally, I was about to become a matron which, according to definition, is "a married woman usually marked by maturity or social distinction." I qualified for both, I thought.

We also referred to the event as a Beltane, a Celtic May Day festival. Our invitation read "We invite you to the very merry Matrimonial union of Harper Leah and Kristina Breidenbach. This Splendiferous Beltane, Full Moon, Eclectic Celebration will be held May 1, 1988, at 3:00 P.M. at See Spirit Ranch, New River, Arizona."

Our friends know us well. No one expected tuxes, white gowns or a drunken reception party. We offered an easy weekend full of plans and promises. We offered, in Buddhist tradition, that everyone marry each other and honor her and his vows to love and keep compassion for self, others and all sentient beings.

Five of the women attending had recently lost their mothers. Our friend Rosemary, whose mother, like Harper's, had died of cancer, requested that we call our mothers' names out loud. Everyone did so, allowing his or her mother's name to be carried by the wind. Morgan and Caer, from Santa Fe, smudged each person while standing under willow arches entwined with honeysuckle. They used sweetgrass and sage which our friend Sioux had harvested near her cabin. They then called in the six directions, and the wind came stronger through the rose garden.

Barbara, a New River guest, wrote us a song which she played on her portable electric piano: "All That Really Matters Is the Heart." We then began the Buddhist part of the ceremony. Van, a San Francisco zen student and Harper's friend for years, chanted the heart sutra, a chant to a female Buddhist deity, Avolokiteshvara. We lit candles from the one main candle on our altar, a joyful fruitless endeavour because the wind would not allow it.

Harper read a Marge Piercy poem to me, and I said words expressing my thankfulness to her for her kindness to me and for being so completely satisfying. I asked her sincerely to accompany me on many, many more travels. Our anja (usually the best friend to those marrying, who assists the priest and the couple) was Sioux, who handed each of us the bracelet she had beaded (partly in the Grand Canyon) per our design—symbols of snakes and sea stars, our favorites—which we then encircled on the other's wrist.

At this time, we asked our friends to offer anything in the form of a blessing, acknowledgment or observation about us, or about us and them. That was one of the sweetest parts for me, but I was so high by that point that later I had to ask several friends to repeat what they had said. Sheila, a poet, read us a poem she had written for us called "Marrying," and Thomas read us something Rilke wrote on preserving one's solitude in partnership.

Harper sprinkled rosewater on everyone's crown chakra, and I let rose petals fly and flutter about on the wind. Neon passed around a basket full of pennies, and while each person held a handful, my oldest friend there, Bob, and his wife, Diane, delivered prosperity blessings. We then scattered the coppers in all directions in the garden. Harper and I had wanted to close on a high note, so we all joined hands and sang the first song we had each heard from our dads as kids: "Pennies from Heaven."

I had goosebumps on goosebumps at this point, from nerves, the wind and temperatures that had dropped fifteen degrees in a few hours. We went inside the little ranchhouse and toasted with grape juice and hot sake (a Buddhist custom usually done on New Year's), opened presents and ate pound cake, guacamole, rice and chicken, homemade strawberry ice cream and chocolate cake. One of the three teenagers there was May Day, who was celebrating her fourteenth birthday so... more love... more joy... more presents... more chocolate... more candles...

A community evolved over the course of this unique weekend that nearly everyone describes as unexpectedly beneficial and profoundly nourishing. Our mutual feeling is that without consciously having it as a goal, we had, all of us, created a community, a tribe. We had connected in an inner sense. It was as if we had healed the wound of our separateness, our alienation from each other and the earth. The wedding process had provided security, supportive kin, conscious and kind sisters and brothers who moved in and about our lives as if we shared a similar dream. We ate together, played water volleyball together, chanted, sang, drummed and told stories.

One pivotal and important communion was the sweat lodge Saturday night. Harper and I had built the lodge from river willows in the fall and used it through the winter. We did two sweats that night to accommodate everyone. For many, it was their first sweat lodge. We had rocks heating for hours while we drummed, played pennywhistles, rattled and sang. Our intention was to purify, to give blessings, to honor the earth and sky and to deepen all our connections. For me, the sitting silently, totally unadorned, in the pitchblack womblike steaming hot turtle-shell of a cave enabled me to be very close to my original self. I could feel clearly that my human and spiritual selves were one.

"Primitive," "intense," "holy," "beyond description," were some of the words folks said afterwards. Carolyn said she had bonded in a new way with her daughter Jesse, who was about to leave home and enter college. (Carolyn and her two daughters had slept in a teepee platform while javelina, docile desert animals, paid nocturnal visits to the land.)

This state of grace, this joy, stayed with us, and when Monday morning came and the many one-hundred-mile trips to the airport were about to get under way, we were very sad to have to separate. Many were not ready for the experience to be over, to fly off in different directions (Washington D.C., New Hampshire, San Francisco, New Mexico, Philadelphia, Canada) and begin the regular work week. For some it also meant a return to living alone.

Our ritual had evoked memories of the deep connection we have with the earth, and the entire weekend had fulfilled an inner need for unconditional love, human bonding, spiritual communion, meaningful ritual and creative play. We had all been deeply touched by sharing these wonderful May days.

*—Kristina Breidenbach*

ॐ

*Kristina Breidenbach: Kristina is doing body therapy, painting, performing and flea marketeering in the Southwest, land of faith and exquisite light.*

*Harper Leah: Harper is a volunteer for New Mexico AIDS Service and for a local hospice. She has a private counseling practice, and she is currently sewing her robes for her ordination as a Buddhist priest.*

# Trinity Ordoña

## & *Desirée Thompson*

Trinity (left) & Desirée (center) & Mistress of Ceremonies, Syl (right)
photographer: M. Shu

*June 25, 1988* ❧ *California*

# A Thousand Cranes

*Desirée:* We fell in love in July, 1985, while Trinity was visiting her sister in Hawai'i. Trinity says she fell in love with me within the first twenty minutes. It took me a little longer, since I was in a relationship at the time. Though we had these feelings for each other, we didn't act on them; mainly because I wasn't ready to leave my relationship of three and a half years. During the month after we met, we wrote a few letters and talked about how we felt about each other. Then we stopped all communication and didn't see each other until December of 1986, when Trinity returned to Hawai'i and we started our relationship.

*Trinity:* In May of 1987, five months after we began our relationship, Desirée moved from Hawai'i to San Francisco. The following month, the San Francisco Women's Building offered a four-week seminar called "Lesbians Choosing Children." By this time, I had already had very strong feelings of wanting to have a family. I had never had those feelings until Desirée and I were together. In fact, after our third day together, I had this overwhelming sense of desiring a family, though I didn't realize at the time that it meant having children. To me, the concept of family was associated with meeting somebody who was compatible with my personality, my cultural background, my politics, and whom I just liked being with. That feeling hit a very familiar place in me; it reminded me of my own family, having parents who were together for almost fifty years. Because of that, I had a very strong sense of bonding and commitment, and when Desirée moved to the Bay Area, I wanted us to check out these family issues. We sat through the seminar and found ourselves in a great deal of agreement, both about the desire to have children and also about how we would raise children. We had to work out a few differences, like who would be the donor and the relationship of the donor to the children, but we came to agreement pretty quickly.

Once I realized that we both wanted to have children, I said very bluntly to Des, "We're just going to have to get married." In my mind, if you're going to have a family, and if your family is arising out of a commitment to another person, why not formalize that commitment in marriage? That's how I had been raised as a Filipino, and I didn't see that it should be any different because I was with Desirée. I knew that our marriage in the legal sense was not going to be recognized by the state, but I had long before come to the conclusion that marriage is really a commitment between the two people involved, and everybody else is just a witness. I talked to Desirée about this idea, and she had some reluctance.

*Desirée:* In the beginning, I was strongly against marriage. The word alone sparked my feminist revulsion for the hold that patriarchy has on women. I had viewed my coming out as a political decision, and marriage was not at all a comforting thought. But slowly I began to think of marriage as an expression of my love and commitment to Trinity. She was not going to be "keeping me in my place" as a woman, the way a man would. I was not going to lose my identity by changing my name or having "her" children. We were simply deciding to make this journey through life, with all of its ups and downs, together. I have no regrets about that decision. Going through the ceremony has brought respect for our relationship from our friends, and when we have what seem to be insurmountable differences, neither of us gives up or threatens to leave the relationship, the way we would have before we were married. We're going to be together for a long time, and we are committed to working our differences out together.

*Trinity:* The day after we got married, I was driving the car, and Desirée proceeded to talk to me about how to improve my driving habits. I turned to her and said, smiling, "Well, honey, you've got about forty years to get used to it, so you can start now." With a chuckle, we both realized that in time I would change and she would change. That is, she would get used to the way I drive, and I would get used to the way she criticizes me, and somewhere in between we would both make some adjustments. But we had a long time ahead of us; there was no need to rush.

*Desirée:* Once we had decided to get married, we said, "Well, how do we do it?" We realized that someone had to propose. Trinity had been talking so much about marriage, but it didn't seem that she was going to do the proposing. So, surprising even myself, I proposed to her. I don't remember exactly how I did it. I know it was a quiet moment at home, and I asked her to marry me. And then she became coy and was very reluctant to say yes.

*Trinity:* I just said I needed to think about it for a little bit.

*Desirée:* Which seemed absurd to me, since she was the one who had felt it was so important to be married.

*Trinity:* Anyway, I accepted soon thereafter, and we called our friends, Carmen and Karla, and they invited us over for dinner. We celebrated with a nice dinner and toasted each other with champagne. Then, a few weeks later, we got our rings: very simple gold rings which we managed to get for a reasonable price and which we started showing off as our engagement rings. That was December of 1987. The next question was how to go about telling our friends and family, and how to plan the ceremony.

*Desirée:* We went out and bought a bridal planning book. It was a *Brides Magazine* bridal book with a white heterosexual couple on the cover, but it helped us think about a lot of things that you have to think about in terms of having a somewhat traditional wedding ceremony.

*Trinity:* We figured out our wedding invitations, which we did on a Macintosh. We fought with each other over how to put the invitation together, but we more or less agreed on what to say. Then we put together our wedding list.

*Desirée:* Trinity kept inviting everyone who walked by.

*Trinity:* No, honestly, since December I had been telling all of our friends that we were getting married. And, of course, I would extend invitations even though we had no idea how many people we were really going to invite. So when it finally came down to sending out the invitations, I had to sit down and remember how many people I had already invited. It turned out to be quite a number; we had a hundred and twenty people at the wedding.

Then came the issues of family, wedding dresses and how we were going to put the ceremony together. The first thing we did was set the date. We knew that we wanted our good friend and matchmaker, Ku'umeaaloha, to bless the ceremony with a Hawaiian wedding chant. If we had it on the San Francisco Gay Day Parade weekend, it would be a great opportunity for her to come to San Francisco, be at the ceremony and also be here for that weekend. Her lover, Pianohea, was a member of a Hawaiian band, and soon after we had asked the two of them to come, the band volunteered to come and play for the wedding. So we had the person to officiate, a Hawaiian wedding band and the date.

Then we had to talk about wedding gowns, and that was where my family came in. My mother is a seamstress, which had been a very big plus for me while I was growing up. I had seven sisters, and you can imagine the situation with all of us fighting with each other over shoes, skirts and blouses. We came from a poor family, and we had to make sure that everything had multiple purposes. Anyway, I told my mom in January that we were engaged, and the first thing she said to me was, "Why are you going to do that?" Then she said, "She's going to leave you, anyway." I realized that in the past she had seen me in relationships that lasted for two or three years and then broke up. She had never seen me with anybody for more than a few years; from her perspective, it never worked out. The next thing she said was, "Besides, you're too bossy. You're too domineering." I said, "Gee, Mom, you're a great help." I chuckled, and she laughed, and I realized that she was trying to decide whether she thought this was a good idea or a terrible idea.

It was very important for me, though, to know where my mom stood, so a month later I called her and asked her if she would make me my wedding dress. She said, "Why don't you wear your sister's?" (My sister had just gotten married the year before.) I said to her, "No, Mom. I want a Filipino dress, one with Maria Clara sleeves." Those are the butterfly sleeves on the traditional Filipino woman's blouse or folk gown. It's a very distinctive style. When I told her that I wanted a Filipino dresss, she started changing her tune. Of all the girls in my family, I was the only one who had ever asked her for a Filipino dress, and I think she was really very touched by that. So, without making any commitments one way or the other, we continued to talk, and I said I would be down in April.

In the meantime, I told Des that I didn't want to send out our wedding invitations until I knew where my parents stood; if they weren't going to come, I wouldn't even bother sending them an invitation, but if they were, I would like them to be the first to receive an invitation. So Desirée and I flew down to San Diego in April. I think Des was quite anxious because I kept hinting to her that in our family, whenever the girls get married, the boys always have to ask my parents' permission. It's considered customary and respectful in Filipino culture. Des kept wondering if that meant she had to ask my mom for my hand in marriage. I said, "No. That's not exactly it," though I knew that I had to have some way for them to approve or not.

So in the middle of April, there I was standing in the dining room trying on the dress that Mom had agreed to make. I had also brought down a picture of Desirée when she graduated from Kamehameha Schools in Honolulu, which are for Hawaiian and part-Hawaiian children. In the picture, she was wearing a formal gown called a holokū, which is a traditional Hawaiian dress. We wanted Mom to take Desirée's measurements so we could send the measurements over to Hawai'i and have the dress made. Mom took the picture. She looked at Des and looked at the picture and looked at Des again, and after a minute or two, she said, "Gee, I can make that." So in that weekend, Mom made both of our wedding dresses. With Mom making the dresses, I knew she approved and that I didn't have to worry anymore. We went ahead and sent our wedding invitations to the family. My parents and many of my twelve sisters and brothers came. Altogether, seventeen members of my family were there.

*Desirée:* I, on the other hand, had a hard time with my family. I wasn't out to them, even though I had been a lesbian and they had known all my past lovers; it was something that we didn't talk about. I thought that the best way to do it would be to talk to my brother. I felt that he would probably be more understanding, and if it he wasn't understanding, then my parents definitely would not understand at all. At the time, my brother was working in Washington, D.C. It was kind of strange when I called him because we don't really keep in contact; I guess he thought something might be wrong when I called out of the blue. I asked him if he would come to my wedding, and he said, "Sure." I said, "Well, it's not a regular wedding," and he said, "I know." I said that I would be getting married to Trinity, and he said, "I know," and that he would be there.

I was quite surprised that he knew. When I moved to San Francisco the year before, I had given him my computer. Occasionally, I had written letters to Trinity on the computer—love letters, intimate love letters. I thought that I had erased them from the computer completely, but the letters remained in the computer memory. He said that he had read them and discussed them with my mom. I thought, "Well, then she knows." I asked him whether he thought my parents would come to the wedding. He wasn't really sure, but we both agreed that he would be the one to ask them.

He called my mom the next day, and they had a three-hour conversation. She was upset, very upset. She felt that as a mother she had done something wrong, and that there was something wrong with our generation that we couldn't all be "normal." There was no way that she was going to come to the wedding. My brother called my dad the next day. Apparently, Mom hadn't said anything to him, and my dad had a similar reaction. He wasn't very happy about it, and he couldn't see coming to the wedding.

It wasn't really a surprise to me. I had never come out to them because I couldn't face those kind of statements, that kind of rejection. I was pretty devastated to actually have that fear confirmed. To this day, we do not talk about me being a lesbian. I get cute acknowledgments of our relationship from my dad, but my mom has never said anything.

*Trinity:* In terms of work, I'm out to my boss and a few select friends there, but I didn't know whether to invite my co-workers to the wedding. I asked a good friend at work what to do. I went over the list with her, and we talked about it. I asked her what I should do about the co-workers' husbands, and she said, "Well, let them decide what to do." I said, "Okay. I'll just invite the people I want, and if they want to bring their husbands, I'll tell them that's okay." And that's exactly what happened: I invited my three co-workers and my boss, and they all brought their husbands or wives. They even threw me a little surprise wedding shower, which was really nice.

Our friends were also a big help during the wedding. We asked them to do a lot of different things. We paid for all the expenses, but we asked our friend, MeiBeck, to take responsibility for the wedding car. She got a red mustang convertible and decorated it, including "double happiness" in Chinese on both sides of the car. Friends tied cans to the back of the car so well that we couldn't get them off for a couple of days.

*Desirée:* People also helped us make a thousand gold paper cranes. In Hawaiian-Japanese tradition, when you get married, the bride is supposed to make a thousand paper cranes, origami style. This is important for good luck, and a thousand cranes would bring us lots of good luck. I had never made a crane before, so I bought the paper and the instructions and figured out how to make them. I even made out little step-by-step instructions, so that people could see how to make them when they came over to help. Twenty-six friends helped us make the cranes. We went to one party where a friend was celebrating her birthday, and we took some paper to make cranes with us so as not to waste any time. People started joining in and learning how to make the cranes, and by the end of the party we had made a hundred cranes.

As the wedding approached, we had to be sure that we made a minimum number of cranes per day. In June, when they were all done, Dafna and Barbara strung them up, and we ended up with fifty strands of twenty cranes each. Transporting them to the restaurant was no small feat, but it turned out very nice. Each crane takes about five minutes, and we figured out that it took us a hundred and fifty hours to make all one thousand cranes.

*Trinity:* Including the ceremony, we had four hectic but wonderful days of getting married and celebrating. On Thursday, our friends flew in from Hawai'i. There were three musicians and Ku'umeaaloha, plus instruments (including a stand-up bass), plus three huge boxes of flowers from Hawai'i, which included our wedding leis and and na leipo'o, which are head leis. Thus began the partying, which carried on for three days after that. On Friday, my parents arrived, and my sisters began to fly in from San Diego, Reno and New Jersey. Desirée's brother flew in from Washington D.C., and another friend came in from Boston. By late afternoon, we gathered everybody together for our wedding rehearsal at Golden Gate Park. By the time we came back to the house, my mother had already prepared the traditional wedding party dinner, during which both sides of the family meet. We socialized, and at the end of the evening we took out the two thousand orchids and made leis for the family members who were to arrive later.

Following tradition, Desirée and I separated that night. She went with Belle, her Best Woman and friend from Hawai'i, to a good friend's house. I stayed at our apartment with my parents and my sister Katherine from New Jersey. The next day, Desirée called, but I was not allowed to speak to her; we talked to each other through Katherine. My other sister, Dolores, who had flown in from San Diego, came over to do my makeup. My hairdresser also came over to put my hair up. And Mom helped by packing my honeymoon bag, like she had for all my other sisters. Desirée went through the same process. Karla did her makeup, and Veronica, who had driven up from Los Angeles, did Desirée's hair after having only a few hours of sleep. It was really very hectic, and a lot of people were involved.

The wedding started at three o'clock. Since we weren't supposed to see each other until we walked up the aisle, so to speak, Desirée stood on one side of the park and I stood on the other. We both hid behind bushes until the music started. When the music started, we came from opposite points in the park and met in the middle. Then we began our ceremony.

*Desirée:* The ceremony was pretty traditional. I was the one who created the ceremony itself, having been to so many weddings. We started out by exchanging leis. We had a pikake lei and a maile lei which we exchanged with each other. Since our fathers weren't walking us down the aisle, we decided we would include our families in the ceremony by giving them leis, also. My brother was late, so he missed this part of the ceremony. Then we proceeded to exchange vows. That was really cute because we had been practicing and telling everyone exactly what they were supposed to do, when it came to our part, we'd never clearly stated even to each other what we were going to do. When it came time, I went ahead and talked about my commitment and my love for Trinity, and about working through the ups and downs together. Then I waited for Trin to give her vows. But she was waiting for me to give her the ring—in my mind the rings came later, after the vows. So there was this long pause.

*Trinity:* In the meantime, Des started crying. Fortunately for me, my Best Woman had brought Kleenex, so she gave me one and I dabbed Desirée's eyes. But I continued to wait—for my ring. Finally, Des whispered to me, "What are you waiting for?" I said, "Our rings." And she whispered, "Later." So I turned to the audience with a smile and, as if nothing was amiss, proceeded to give my vows. Since I had the ring exchange as part of my vows, I had to toss that part out and fill in the gaps in a very impromptu fashion. Finally, we exchanged rings, and then after that came the Hawaiian wedding chant. After chanting, Ku'umeaaloha said to everyone in English, "The signs have been good. The gods are with us. The celebration can begin—they are one now." I felt that we were married. We both turned around and smiled at everybody, after which we were pelted with bird seed.

*Desirée:* Then the fanfare began with a procession of cars through the park. It was really fun to get all the double-takes: people would look and say, "It's a wedding," and then they would look again because there were two women and no man. We also decided to drive down Castro Street. In the Castro, people cheered us as we passed—two women, sitting on the back of a convertible, at the front of a row of cars blasting their horns.

*Trinity:* We got to the restaurant and had a really sumptuous meal of Thai food. Then the program began, during which we proceeded to get roasted in public by our best friends. They told very personal and intimate things—very lesbian kinds of things—and periodically I would remember that we were in mixed company, and that my mother and father were listening. But it was really a very special, very happy occasion.

Our good friend, Syl, was the Mistress of Ceremonies and ran the wedding reception program for us. Several friends of ours also performed. Ku'umeaaloha danced a couple of hulas and got Desirée up to dance one with her, to everyone's enjoyment. Carmen sang a Mexican love song for us. Desirée and I had taken ballroom dancing, so we did a cha-cha to Anita Baker's "Rapture." Soon after that, we began a Filipino tradition called the dollar dance, during which everyone who dances with the newleyweds pins money on them, which the couple keeps for the honeymoon.

Then my brother, who had brought his three-piece band with him, started playing, and we had dance music for the rest of the evening. We had the smashing of the cake in each other's faces, and we laughed together over that. Then we drank champagne and got toasts from everyone. A very surprising toast came from my mother, who welcomed Desirée into the Ordoña family, not only as a daughter-in-law, but as another daughter. I swelled with pride, knowing that Mom really accepted us. A number of my friends have commented on how important it was for them to see such support coming from a family.

Finally, we closed up the party and moved to our honeymoon suite. The next morning, we rode in our car for the Gay Day Parade. We waved to everybody from our wedding car, with cans clanging down the street and a sign saying "Just Married." That was our big wedding celebration; it was a very memorable one.

*Desirée:* We have been married for two years now, and we have been continuing in the plans we had talked about even before we got married. We have bought a house here in San Francisco.

*Trinity:* We bought a two-unit flat, with my sister and brother-in-law upstairs and Desirée and myself downstairs.

*Desirée:* And we're currently making plans to have a baby. The timing will be determined by whether Trinity goes back to school or not. We need to get our finances together before we can go ahead with that.

*Trinity:* We want to have a child and raise her/him here until she/he is about five, then move back to Hawai'i. I feel that there is a better climate there for people of color, for ethnic people. We want our child to be raised in a place where she/he would be proud to be a person of color and not have to fight to be included and to be recognized as a normal person.

We are very happy we got married. Desirée and I are very committed to each other and very committed to starting a family with one another. Desirée still teases me when I do this, but every time the occasion comes up, I bring out the wedding pictures, play the wedding video, or drag out the wedding dresses. People love to hear about it. I think they love to hear about it because love and commitment are such natural things.

*This account is based on audio recordings made by Trinity Ordoña and Desirée Thompson.*

ខ

*Trinity Ordoña: I am thirty-nine, and I've been a lesbian for seventeen years. I'm Filipino-American and come from a family of thirteen children. Both my parents immigrated from the Philippines to the U.S. in 1946, and I grew up in San Diego. My adult life, however, has been centered in the Bay Area, where I have lived since 1972. I work at the University of California, San Francisco, and am also very active in the Asian-Pacific lesbian community. The ceremony that we describe, and the love that we honored through that ceremony, was and continues to be very private.*

*Desirée Thompson: I am a blend of Asian-Pacific people. I am of Japanese, Chinese, Native Hawaiian and German ancestry. I'm thirty-four and have been a lesbian since 1977. I'm a letter-carrier. I tell my story to dispel the myth that Americans are just white people. Asian-Pacific people have been a part of nearly two hundred years of U.S. history, and we still are not seen as part of this country. To tell my story is to say that Asian-Pacific lesbians and gays exist; we fall in love, we make commitments and we get married.*

# Helen Heliotrope

## &    Noreen Penny

Noreen (left) & Helen (right)
photographer: Nicholas Young

## March 21, 1986   ❧   New Zealand

# The Tryst of the Slothwoman Coven

In March 1986, after having lived together for three years, Noreen and I had a trysting ceremony at Noreen's beach property. This ceremony was, in Noreen's view, about two and half long years overdue, but for me it was an experience involving considerable conflict. On the one hand, the ceremony felt like an insult to our relationship (our commitment to each other did not require "proper validation" through social ceremonies—it was already valid); like a return to quasipatriarchal institutions (trysting = wedding = overtones of patriarchy); and even like something of a hollow game, because I had no real commitment to Goddess ritual at that time. But on the other hand, I felt as though I was a dreadful heel for having denied Noreen her trysting for so long, especially as it was obviously so important to her.

The interesting thing is that the trysting ceremony means much more to me in retrospect than it did at the time; this because I now feel part of the spiritual tradition in the context of which the ceremony took place. Prior to the trysting, I had been attending group rituals, but feeling rather out of place and quite mystified by many of the goings-on. It seemed to me that I was witnessing a group of mainly middle-aged women who liked lighting candles and incense, who loved dressing up and playing games and dancing about, and who were forever talking about, or to, this Goddess, or that Goddess, or some other Goddess (all of whom seemed to go back to antiquity). It was all so weird! Then one of the group members wrote a master's thesis on the local Goddess groups, and suddenly it all fell into place.

All this is not to say that I was a reluctant group member, but only that I couldn't come to grips with it all. Ever since my university days in the early 1960s, I had had a strong interest in the psychology of religion, and one of the things that drew me to Noreen was her deep involvement with spirituality. But nothing in my background had prepared me for Goddesses, witches and born-again pagans! So for several years I was both attracted to, and highly skeptical of, Goddess ritual and Wicca tradition. My problems in coming to terms with it were exaggerated throughout by my having entered into a lesbian relationship for the first time: I simply did not have enough psychic energy to cope simultaneously with a new sexual orientation and a new religion!

But in retrospect, the trysting ceremony has considerable significance for me. Noreen's beach property consists of a quarter-acre rectangle bordered on all sides by pine, poplar and fruit trees. At one end of the rectangle is a small hill on which sits an old wooden cottage with a veranda that overlooks a grassy expanse. A short distance from the property is a river, a backwater, a lagoon and the beach. Along the banks of the backwater (where Noreen and I often go rowing), there are lots of tamarisk trees. I am very fond of tamarisks, so before the trysting Noreen and I went and collected an armful of tamarisk branches each and spread them round in a circle where we intended to have the ritual. Then we lit a fire in the middle of the circle. The other group members brought flowers and branches of leaves which they also spread around the tamarisk circle. They also brought candles and incense, as well as food, and after the ceremony everyone sat around on the veranda, eating, drinking, talking and watching the fire die down.

I remember feeling particularly touched when one of the newer group members (whom I had been feeling somewhat nervous around) came over and kissed me on the cheek and made some positive remark about Noreen's and my relationship. Somehow her obvious sincerity broke through my uptightness about Goddess religion and enabled me to appreciate the comradeship and the emotional depth of the rituals, especially the trysting.

My family was not invited to the trysting because I felt that they would not have wanted to be there and also because I did not feel up to having them there. My marriage had not officially ended until the day that Noreen and I started living together, and my family members had not been happy about it at all. My son was fourteen and my daughter was eleven at the time of our tryst, and though they had adjusted to the situation, I felt that expecting them to accept feminist Wicca on top of accepting my lesbian relationship with Noreen was a bit much for them to cope with. And if I couldn't have my children there, then there was no way that I was interested in having any other family member present. Besides, at the time the trysting was more than enough for me to cope with!

—Helen Heliotrope

ॐ

I came to Goddess ritual after having been the wife of a Methodist minister. I had been following Zsuzsanna Budapest's books about women's rituals since about 1980, and I think it was because I had previously been involved in the church that I felt it was so important to have a group doing rituals; doing rituals on my own wouldn't satisfy me. Several other women and I organized a weekend conference in 1981, and after that conference, a number of women mentioned that they would like to start having rituals together. We began on Hallowmas 1981, which is the witches' new year, and we've continued meeting ever since. Shortly before my tryst with Helen, the group chose the name of Slothwoman Coven. Zsuzsanna Budapest had written about Slothwoman, a representation of the instinctive side of our minds. We felt it was a suitable name for us, because what we try to do is listen to the instinctive, feeling-oriented side of our brains.

We meet about every six weeks and hold rituals for the seasons of the year. For instance, we've just come through the winter with its celebrations of the solstice and the candlemas ceremonies. We're an all women's community, and there are quite a number of us that are lesbians, though not all of us are. We have come together in order to find a new tradition for women: a tradition different from the patriarchal tradition. And so we invoke the Goddess, although we still have discussions about how we see the Goddess: whether she is an individual entity or whether she is the group energy.

I have a grown-up family of four daughters, all of whom are married and three of whom have children. The oldest one, who's a doctor, is very sympathetic towards the idea of women's rituals, although at the moment she still goes to church. The others don't really understand quite what I'm talking about, and there is a certain tension about the changes that I have made in my life.

It was because of this tension that our biological families were told about the trysting but were not invited. We're still not sure how they felt about that: whether they felt hurt and excluded, or whether they would, in truth, have felt it was too strange. At the time we thought that it would seem too strange to them, and the idea of having them present at our rituals also seemed too strange to us.

We decided to have a ceremony because we felt the need for a public statement of some kind about our commitment to one another. I think that lesbians in New Zealand are quite open to ceremonies of commitment. In Auckland and in Christchurch, there are a large number of groups like ours who celebrate women's religious rituals outside the church, all of them finding new ways of operating outside of the patriarchal tradition. Much of this has spilled over into the lesbian community, and I think more and more of us are realizing that we do need these rites of passage, and that we don't have to draw them from patriarchal tradition.

The trysting ceremony that Helen and I had was adapted from one in Zsuzsanna Budapest's *Holy Book of Women's Mysteries, Part II.** The actual

---

*Zsuzsanna Budapest, *Holy Book of Women's Mysteries* (1980; reprint, Berkeley: Wingbow Press, 1989).

ceremony took place on March 21, 1986, which was autumn equinox here
in New Zealand. We had it at a beach cottage that I own not far away from
Christchurch. I haven't owned property for very long, so it was very important for me that it was on property that I owned. Helen and I were
both wearing long robes. I also had on a girdle that was sent to me by
Zsuzsanna Budapest and the Susan B. Anthony Coven Number One in
Oakland, California.

There were thirteen women there, which is the size of a coven. It was
a lovely fine night, and we sat around a fire. We had two chalices on our altar. Zsuzsanna Budapest suggests giving these as gifts instead of giving
rings; chalices go back a lot further. Ours were both made from pottery.
Also on the altar was a tray of food. We had food from roots (carrots and
celery), food from stems (cauliflower), from leaves (salad vegetables) and
from flowers (dates, almonds and pieces of orange). We had lots of flowers, all of them white or yellow, as those are sacred colors.

We also had a "broomstick" ready. The reason for using a broomstick
is that they were often made of myrtle, and myrtle is the tree of love. In
New Zealand the native myrtle is called manuka. It's a very common small
bush or tree that you can find all over the country, and so we used a piece
of manuka rather than just a broomstick. The tradition of jumping over
the broomstick is one that goes a long way back in many cultures.

The three friends who played the parts of leaders in the ceremony
were all people who have been in my life for a long time. Joy, who called in
the four corners, is one of my partners in a bookshop that we own together, called the Kate Sheppard Bookshop. Erin, who did the anointing
with oil, is another of our partners and is also the one who originally introduced me to Helen. The third leader, Pam, who brought the foods, was at
the conference where I was first given Zsuzsanna Budapest's book. So all
three women are very important to me and, to a large extent, also to
Helen.

We started by following our usual pattern of forming a circle and
then turning to the four corners and asking for the blessings of the Goddess spirits from each corner of the universe. Joy walked around the circle
with incense and said:

> Hail Goddess of the East, bringer of new life and feelings. Come
> into this circle where lovers await your blessings.

> Come fiery Goddess of the North. Bring your energy to fuel this
> bond to be formed here today. Come bring your excitement and joy
> and ecstasy. Blessed be.

> Hail to thee Goddess of the West, love Goddess, water Goddess.

Come to us in this circle and bless the lovers who ask for blessing in your name. Come and bless this union with love.

Come oh beautiful Earth Goddess of the South. Come and nourish us with your love and presence. Blessed be.

We then all put our arms around one another and hummed, raising energy. Then Erin anointed us with oil:

Forehead: I purify you from all anxieties and fears.
Eyes and mouth: I purify your eyes to see, your lips to speak.
Breasts: I anoint your breasts formed in strength and beauty.
Genitals: Your genitals I bless for strength and pleasure.
Hands and feet: I bless your hands to work for women and your feet to walk in good paths.

Then Pam used the foods to invoke the Goddess of life. This seemed very appropriate for Pam, who is a wonderful gardener and grows great vegetables.

I invoke you, Goddess of all life, by the foods here present—the roots to make a strong foundation for this relationship, stems for standing firm and proud to grow and prosper together, by flowers for joy and laughter, and fruits for a long and enduring time together.

We then said the vows that we had adapted ourselves:

I _____ take this woman _____ for my friend and lover for this lifetime. I promise to care for and love her and fight with her from time to time.

The extra piece we added, "and fight with her from time to time," was requested by Helen, because she thinks that people too often paste over the cracks of relationships, and it was better to say up front that we would sometimes fight.

Pam handed us the tray of food, and Helen and I offered it to one another, saying, "May you never hunger." Joy handed us the chalices of wine. Again, we offered wine to one another, saying, "May you never thirst." Erin handed us crowns of flowers. We placed the crowns on one another's heads, saying, "Thou art Goddess." Then Erin held the myrtle branch for us as we jumped over. As we jumped, we said, "To mark this moment of commitment, we jump over the myrtle branch, sacred to the Goddess of love." We jumped east to west, and then said, "We are now lovers in trust." In this, the true meaning of the word *tryst* was exemplified in the word *trust*.

Lastly, we announced, "Let the feasting begin." We felt it was very important that we had the feasting at the end; it's similar to what the Maori people do. They always have food after they've had any ceremony or any meeting, so as to allow the energy that's been raised to be gently dispersed. That way nobody goes away still feeling quite high and uptight and not having had a chance to let that energy go slowly and gradually.

We usually end our rituals by passing around a chalice with wine for giving thanks and for asking for any help that might be needed by anyone in the group. So, after the eating, drinking, congratulations and merriment, we ended with the passing of the chalice.

—*Noreen Penny*

ஃ

*Helen Heliotrope: I am a fifty-year-old white working-class New Zealander. For most of his working life, my father literally pelted the skins off sheep at the local Freezing Works, and for many years my mother worked in the Freezing Works cafeteria. I was brought up a Presbyterian but was much more influenced by my mother's Irish-Catholic background. I have an M.A. in psychology and was married to an electrical engineer for fifteen years and have two children. I now think of myself as an upper-working-class lesbian-feminist pagan.*

*Noreen Penny: I am a third-generation New Zealander of British descent aged fifty-eight. I was married to a Methodist minister and have four adult daughters. In 1980 I found that my lesbian identification was of critical importance in my life, so I left the marriage and am now divorced. I have been a teacher, and I helped found the Kate Sheppard Women's Bookshop in 1982. Helen and I began living together in 1983 and now live out at my beach house, "Crone Cottage," which I had built in 1989.*

*Sharon M. Vardatira*

*&*     *Marian J. Wolfsun*

Sharon (left) & Marian (right)

*August 5, 1977*   ❧   *Massachusetts*

# A Nantucket Summer

Fairy tales are not politically correct. We have learned that over time. And we feel a little sheepish, on occasion, when friends are incredulous, fairly disbelieving. Maybe it would help if you imagine a movie set, complete with ocean spray and misty fog, windmills and heaths. That's how it was one summer.

We love to tell our story; in our private moments, we become mushy about it, pull out the pictures and reminisce. In public we are carefully autonomous, political dykes. And, still, when another lesbian asks how we met, we look at each other and smile because we get to tell our story. And then we tumble over each other, filling in different details, retelling this fairy tale of ours. We understand if you do not believe us; after all, happily ever after and princess charming are myths, things you do not believe after you've lived a quarter of a century, gone through a few relationships and gotten cynical. And maybe it is naive to think that two people could sweep each other off their feet and live happily ever after. But you have to remember that we met on Nantucket Island, and Nantucket is a magical place, cut off from the rest of the world, surrounded by ocean and inhabited by more ghosts than people.

*Marian:* I had never heard of a research program on Nantucket for women in science. I was the only woman majoring in physics in my entire university. One day, on my way to the planetarium where I worked, I saw a flyer advertising a conference for women in science. I found one other woman to travel with to Yale for the day of the conference, but despite our best plans, we arrived late, with only enough time to attend the last workshop of the day. I chose one workshop from the dozens available. I still clearly remember looking at all the faces and taking an empty seat next to an interesting older woman. Her face was lined, and her gray hair was piled in coils on top of her head. I later learned her name was Dr. Hoffleit. Early in the workshop, she mentioned that she directed a summer program for young women interested in science. I was terribly excited, and as soon as the workshop was over, I introduced myself to Dr. Hoffleit, described my planetarium work and asked about the program. At the time, it was unusually assertive behavior on my part, and I surprised myself. The planetarium work seemed to impress her, and she promised to send an application. Within a few months, I was accepted into the program.

*Sharon:* I had known about the Nantucket program for a year before I applied. I was going to Smith, a women's college, and majoring in astronomy and religion. It was expected that interested astronomy majors would spend a summer doing research at the Maria Mitchell Observatory on Nantucket. At the end of my sophomore year, I applied and was accepted. It was thrilling; I would be doing variable star research with Dr. Hoffleit, a renowned expert in the field. I was also engaged to work at the University of Bonn doing stellar spectroscopy for the month of May. I read passages from Newton's *Principia* and pondered the universe unfolding.

*Marian:* Dr. Hoffleit's letter listed the names and schools of the five women accepted into the program. I scanned the paper: Mount Holyoke, Smith, a Science Foundation Award recipient. No one else was from a state university.

My mother reminded me that my public school education—despite my high grades and scholarships—was no match for the likes of Smith and Holyoke. She advised me to work very hard and not expect to be easily accepted. I felt as if I were going to some weird, intense camp to see if I could prove myself.

To further complicate matters, I had just thrown out my knee in a parade kick line. After a few weeks, I was able to walk without crutches, and I tried to strengthen my knee by pacing the house and climbing stairs. I bought a yellow Nantucket slicker and enough shampoo for the summer—my mother was worried that I would run out. I sewed name tags into my clothes, all of which were freshly ironed.

On the first Sunday in June, I flew to Nantucket and then took a cab from the airport to the observatory on Vestal Street. Vestal Street was a narrow cobblestone road lined with grey shingled Quaker houses, weathered picket fences, vines and flowering gardens. As anxious as I was about this summer, I was also looking forward to retreating; it had been a hard year, and I was eager to get away from everything and be alone, introspective. The cottage where we would live for the summer was across the street from the observatory. Two bedrooms on the first floor slept one and four people, respectively. Amy Pierce—the gifted high school student and Science Foundation Award recipient—had settled in just before me. No one else had arrived yet.

Amy and I went to dinner at Dr. Hoffleit's house, and the two of them sat and talked about ambiplasma contraction and globular metagalaxies. I plastered a smile on my face, nodded at appropriate intervals and tried to appear intelligent. I had no idea what they were talking about. My mother's warnings plagued me. I considered my apparent inability to compete with these girls on their level. I believed they had all learned more than my classes could ever offer. And Smith and Holyoke had not even arrived. It promised to be a dismal summer.

I chose a bed in the corner, away from the others. Miss Junior Washington State showed up the next day, and Holyoke also came and claimed the single room. Miss Washington, recently crowned in her state contest, had long blond hair and a predictably sparkling, positive personality. She was also very intelligent—not exactly what I would have expected. Though globular metagalaxies were not her specialty, she could always turn the conversation to focus on other, equally complex astrophysical concepts. Holyoke, sporting a better-than-thou attitude, kept her distance from all of us. She was much what I had anticipated.

Sharon was the last person to arrive. I had already formed a sense about the other three, but Smith was still an unknown. The only bed left was in the middle of the room, and I was already feeling a little sorry for the latecomer. I imagined it would be hard to get the worst bed.

I distinctly remember that one of the first things she asked when she came in was if any of us knew a place nearby where she could do her laundry. She explained that she had just flown in from Germany and had not had a chance to wash her clothes. I was incredulous. There I sat with my name written into my clothes, a supply of shampoo to take me into next season and supplies for every conceivable emergency. And she had just flown in from Germany—with one suitcase of dirty clothes. I was intrigued by this mysterious woman. She seemed cool, cosmopolitan, adventurous.

*Sharon:* The flight from Bonn to Boston seemed long, and I was relieved to make my connection to Nantucket. I was suffering from jet lag, culture shock and the stress of leaving new friends; I felt acutely disoriented. I was particularly worried about arriving at the last minute without even one change of clean clothes. My anxiety increased when I arrived at the cottage on Vestal Street. I had, indeed, arrived last, and the only remaining bed sat naked in the middle of the large bedroom. Miss Washington, bent over in the doorway, was brushing her long blond hair. It was a disheartening sight: I was not expecting a cheerleader in the next bed.

The others watched me unpack. I dug a photo of the Orion Nebula out of my suitcase and passed around some prints of stellar spectra. My work in Germany involved photography and endless hours in the darkroom. I hoped the products of those weeks might break the ice.

Nantucket lies about twenty miles off the coast of Massachusetts. Fourteen miles long and three and a half miles wide at its broadest point, the island is a mix of low rolling moors, sandy beaches, cranberry bogs and a scattering of settlements. The main seaport town of Nantucket has cobblestone streets lined with rose-covered picket fences and hundreds of eighteenth- and nineteenth-century homes. European settlers arrived in the early 1600s and soon outnumbered the Algonquin natives who came before. On cool summer nights, fog rolls up the streets, and a golden mist hangs over the moors in the morning.

Maria Mitchell was born in 1818 in a modest saltbox cottage on Vestal Street. She received international acclaim when she discovered a comet in 1847, and she went on to chair Vassar's astronomy department for twenty-three years, until her death in 1889. The observatory and the program which sponsored our summer research had been founded in Maria Mitchell's honor. As "America's first woman astronomer," she had opened that previously male field to women. In time we would come to appreciate the significance of our falling in love in this setting.

Maria Mitchell had never married, and after her death, her body was returned to Nantucket and buried in a cemetery near Vestal Street. On walks to the newer Loines Observatory, Dr. Hoffleit would often lead our group past Maria's grave. Austere photographs of our sponsor's namesake hung over our desks; her presence was palpable, much more than a memory.

On that first evening, we all decided to walk the mile into town and dine at Captain Tobey's restaurant. I was eager to explore my new home; I was, after all, still searching for a laundromat.

*Marian:* I was not thrilled at the prospect of walking to Captain Tobey's. I detested clam chowder, and my knee was still weak. I wasn't prepared for a mile-long walk over cobblestones. At the same time, I wanted to keep up with everyone, and I worried that staying behind would further reinforce my sense of alienation. The mysterious dirty clothes woman noticed that I was falling behind, and she slowed down and started walking with me. I remember thinking how incredibly nice she was, and I enjoyed our conversation.

June had not quite faded into July when Sharon and I realized that something powerful and strong was growing between us. We had fallen in love. In the afternoons we took long walks down narrow, winding streets. On rare evenings when we were not scheduled to observe, we watched the sunset from the open gazebo by the harbor. We juggled the observatory schedule so we could spend more time together.

During the days, all five of us worked in one large room on the first floor of the observatory. Dr. Hoffleit's desk was in the middle of the room. When she was working, our group was sedate, quietly studious. When she left the room, Miss Washington would softly play the old office radio. Meanwhile, Sharon and I would discreetly drop love letters on each other's desks. We also got into little races as we moved through the collection of photographic glass plates.

*Sharon:* Of course, we didn't start out competing. Marian would take a stack of plates, and I would take some. Then Marian would take some more, and I would notice that she was moving precariously close to my section. I would put mine back and take a bigger stack. Then Marian would start worrying that I would slow her down by having the plates that she needed. So she would speed up. By then, it was a full-fledged glass plate competition. We would go through those collections in record time.

These are my memories of that summer: an isolated, fog-bound island; starry nights; a mix of salt air and blossoming flowers, and overpowering love. The future did not exist, and the summer stretched endlessly ahead of us. We barely noted the fact that we were both women; that this relationship meant we were lesbians. We had not previously identified as lesbians, we were not in contact with friends or family, not influenced by what was expected of lesbians and not swayed by the impressions of others. Our love felt right; it was at once ancient and timeless. And unexpected. We had been practical, sensible women. Marian had vowed to remain single well into her forties.

*Marian:* But there was no room for practicality. We were experiencing pure romance, and this was different from anything we had ever felt before. Sharon and I were private about our relationship, but not because of fear. For now, this was simply our private island paradise. Everything felt wonderful—the way love should always feel. It took two weeks for us to realize we were in love, and another two weeks for us to decide to spend our lives together. Two weeks after that we had a private ceremony; we called it a "wedding."

The only model we knew was traditional, and we adapted. We called each other wife. We believed we were the first two wives in history. Sharon, whose second aspiration was to be a minister, had found a small, simple chapel. It did not matter that Sharon was Christian and I was Jewish. I was overwhelmed by this new, magnificent love; it was more than I had ever imagined possible. Together, we picked out rings carved with a moon and star.

We didn't plan anything in detail; we only knew we wanted to get "married." The most substantial obstacle, our living arrangement, was easily resolved when the others decided to go away for the weekend to a telescope convention in Vermont. Sharon and I would be the only ones staying at the observatory. We decided to go to the chapel on Friday night and extend our honeymoon into the weekend.

*Sharon:* The others left, as planned. One major problem remained: we had been scheduled to observe on Friday night. We never considered asking Dr. Hoffleit to give us the night off. She was our mentor, and we wouldn't want to give the impression that we were less than serious about our vocation. On this night, like every night, we climbed onto the observatory's widow walk to survey the night sky. If Dr. Hoffleit decided that "seeing" was favorable, we would be observing until three or four in the morning. As the three of us gazed up into what was definitely a clear, starry night, Dr. Hoffleit pronounced it too overcast for observations. Elated, if not a little confused, we agreed and made our way back to the cottage to prepare for our wedding. Marian put on a long, cream-colored linen caftan, and I wore a white blouse and blue checkered skirt.

On our way to the chapel, we passed Dr. Hoffleit strolling through the observatory garden. When we mentioned that we were going to church, she beamed, hugged us and wished us well. Even though we knew the wish wasn't specifically directed at our wedding, we took it as a promising sign. We suffered a brief moment of panic when we realized we had forgotten "something borrowed and something blue," but the solution readily presented itself in the form of small blue roadside flowers (which we left at the church, since we had borrowed them). I don't remember passing another person, and the chapel, glowing with amber light, was empty. The magic of the evening and our sense of freedom was so complete that we never once considered that the chapel could have been locked, or occupied or unlit.

*Marian:* Accompanied only by the presence of island spirits, wind and the distant surf, we married ourselves in that little island chapel. We reconstructed the traditional vows to fit our needs. I cannot remember the words we used, but I remember thinking of forever, of marriage, of deep commitment.

That evening we made love in front of a crackling fire, and we pushed our beds together for the weekend. The whole cottage, Vestal Street and the island belonged to us.

That was 1977, almost thirteen years ago. A few weeks later, we would go back to our separate lives, the world. It seemed inconceivable that our summer in Nantucket would end, but we knew, despite all obstacles, that our relationship was just beginning. The commitment we made that summer carried us through two years of separation, while we finished college, and many hard times with family, friends and society.

I am still amazed by the fact that I met Sharon at all. On occasion, I consider what my life would be like if I had never seen that first conference flyer, or if I had missed the last workshop at the conference, or if I had not gotten a seat next to Dr. Hoffleit. I would not have discovered a variable star that summer, and I would not have met Sharon.

*Sharon:* Marian and I went back to Nantucket for our ten-year anniversary, and we go back in the fall from time to time to retreat from the world, go to the cranberry bogs and watch the fog roll up the beach. Neither of us are working in astronomy anymore, although it's in our hearts. We identify ourselves as radical lesbian-feminists, and we work in the women's movement. We have learned about oppression and political correctness. We are wiser about the implications of a state-sanctioned heterosexual union. Presented with the option today, we would have many conflicting feelings about committing ourselves to each other in such a semitraditional way.

And we wouldn't change a thing about our island wedding. We've seen more of the world than we had in 1977, and everything has changed.

*Marian:* Everything—except how we feel about each other.

*Sharon:* And that will never change.

—*Sharon M. Vardatira and Marian J. Wolfsun*

ข

*Sharon Vardatira: Sharon is a political activist, writer and feminist theologian. An organizer for over ten years in the movement to end violence against women, Sharon also works as a marine educator and assists with research on humpback whales. She is passionate about dolphins, the rain forest, breaching whales and sea turtles, and she still loves a dark, starry night.*

*Marian Wolfsun: Ever since she can remember, Marian has dreamed of voyaging to other planets, stars and galaxies. For now, she travels beyond our solar system through science fiction and an active fantasy life. A feminist activist, Marian has worked on such issues as pay equity, reproductive rights, lesbian and gay civil rights and anti-rape organizing. She is currently director of counseling and staff development at New England's largest abortion and women's health clinic.*

# Sheila Horowitz

## & Shelley Pearlman

Sheila (left) & Shelley (right)
photographer: Estelle Nichamin

*July 17, 1988* ⁊ *California*

# A Home Blessed by Shekina

My name is Sheila. I'm fifty years old. I was married for twenty-two years and have two daughters, ages twenty-eight and twenty-five. After my marriage ended, I lived with a woman for six years and then was on my own for about two years before I met Shelley. Shelley is forty-seven. She was married for twenty years and has two sons, ages twenty-eight and twenty-three. After her divorce, Shelley was in a relationship with a married woman for eight years. She had ended that relationship and had been on her own for about six months when we met.

Shelley and I met through our involvement in the gay and lesbian Jewish community. Neither of us are very religious, but we both feel a spiritual, traditional and historical connection to Judaism. The Jewish community offered something more than just a place to be sociable when we were single. We met through a minion, a women's group that was held at the home of a cantor named Debbie Friedman, a very special and talented woman.

After knowing each other casually for several months, Shelley and I started dating in February 1987. After about a year, we decided we were ready to make the commitment to share our lives. We wanted some kind of commitment ceremony that wasn't a "marriage" ceremony; we had both been married already, and we didn't want anything too much like a heterosexual marriage. We wanted to create our own kind of commitment and our own kind of ceremony.

At about this time, we also decided to buy a house together. We wanted a new space, someplace that we could each come to equally. We wanted to be in a house that wouldn't have a history of belonging to only one of us. So, in April 1988, we bought a wonderful house. The purchase of a home is an enormous commitment, and we decided then that our commitment ceremony would take the form of a house blessing. Having met in Debbie's home, we realized how special it would be to have her conduct the ceremony. We asked her if she would, and she agreed.

We invited friends and family members, asking them to make contributions to the homeless instead of giving housewarming gifts; our lives were quite full already, and there was really nothing we needed. It was a warm Sunday afternoon, and the ceremony was performed under our covered patio in the backyard. Both of my daughters were there, and the elder one, Lisa, videotaped it.

Debbie began by speaking of the tradition of putting up a mezuza to sanctify the home. A mezuza contains a small parchment scroll on which is written a quote from Deuteronomy about marking the gatepost of your home so you shall not forget to bless the Lord. The mezuza was put on our doorpost as a way of sanctifying our home and serving as a reminder of our commitment to Judaism.

Debbie then sang some songs of her own composition with lyrics from Biblical verse. She taught them to our guests, and everyone joined in. One of our favorite asks that "We be blessed beneath the wings of Shekina." The Shekina is the Divine Presence. We then did a Schehecheyanu, the blessing said for rare and joyous events:

> Today we stand before you
> To affirm our faith in the holy one,
> To God for giving us life, for sustaining us,
> And for enabling us to reach this season.

Then Shelley and I read a poem together from the Siddur of Shir Chadash, the New Reform Congregation:

> May the door of this home be wide enough
> to receive all who hunger for love,
> all who are lonely for friendship.
> May it welcome all who have cares to unburden,
> thanks to express, hopes to nurture.
> May the door of this house be narrow enough
> to shut out pettiness and pride, envy and enmity.
> May its threshold be no stumbling block
> to young or strained feet.
> May it be too high to admit complacency,
> selfishness and harshness.
> May this home be for all who enter,
> the doorway to riches and a more meaningful life.

At the end of the ceremony, my mother moved to Shelley's side, and Shelley's aunt came and stood next to me. Around our shoulders was the prayer shawl, or tallis, that my late father had worn at his Bar Mitzvah. Debbie and our guests sang; they wished us to be blessed as we went on our way, to be guided in health and joy, and to be sheltered by the wings of peace. My mother has since passed away, but I remember that day, and I can still hear her voice singing through the crowd.

It was really quite wonderful. We had a lot of straight friends there, and everyone was touched. Many of the guests didn't know each other, but they shared together in their happiness for us, creating a feeling of warmth and closeness. Shelley and I felt a sense of fullness. Although we didn't make any vows to each other, we committed our lives to filling our home with understanding, love and nurturance. We thought that was about as important a commitment as two people can make.

*—Sheila Horowitz*

ঽ঵

*Sheila Horowitz: I am a psychotherapist. I love my work, traveling, my daughters, movies, my friends, reading and my lifestyle. I am a committed social activist.*

*Shelley Pearlman: I am a realtor. I love the outdoors, fishing and camping. I'm a terrific cook and enjoy having intimate dinner parties. I love spending time with my granddaughter and being her "nana"!*

# Deborah L. Johnson

## & Zandra Z. Rolón

Zandra (left) & Deborah (right)

*August 7, 1983* ❧ *California*

# Mi Casa Es Tu Casa

*Deborah:* Zandra and I met almost ten years ago, in June 1980. We were both twenty-four. I was about to enter UCLA's M.B.A. program, and Zandra was working in women's health. Actually, we met while we were both involved in other relationships; my lover and I double-dated with Zandra and her lover. We didn't realize at first that we were double-dating with the wrong partners! That went on for about a year and a half before the two of us realized that we needed to get out of these other relationships and get with each other. It was all above board, but it was still an awkward situation. In a lot of ways, though, it was a good way to get to know each other; we had time to learn about each other as individuals and establish a friendship before becoming involved as lovers.

*Zandra:* When we first got together, we were these two mature women of the world who, of course, had decided that monogamy was absolutely out. We were going to have a very open relationship, and we were going to be very independent: Deborah was going to do her wash, I was going to do mine; she was going to have her checking account, I would have mine. Anything like a ceremony was completely out of the question. That lasted about two weeks. From then on, there was just no other choice but to commit to each other.

Deborah was actually the last person in the world I ever imagined wanting a ceremony. As far as she was concerned, it wasn't in line with her politics. But one night as we were eating spaghetti, she popped the question. I almost choked.

*Deborah:* We had probably been together about six months when I proposed to Zandy that we have a ceremony. In the past, the idea of a gay couple having a ceremony had seemed very politically incorrect. To me it symbolized all of our oppression in a heterosexual world; it seemed as though it was a way of trying to validate gay and lesbian relationships when they didn't need validation. I had been a pre-law student prior to going to business school, so I always saw marriage in a very legalistic way. Then I started living with Zandy, and all of a sudden I was with the woman I considered to be my soul mate. There was a new sense of a spiritual bond, a spiritual connection between the two of us. I remember telling her that for the first time in my life, I understood why people got married in churches. I finally understood that it was not just a civil proceeding, but that it was a very important spiritual union between two people: a union that you wanted to share and celebrate.

So it wasn't as though we were having a ceremony to become something that we were not already. It was more that this bond was sacred, and because it was sacred it should be recognized and celebrated. I also started thinking about it on a different level politically. I realized that in all cultures there are certain events that are always celebrated: birth, death, the beginning of adulthood and marriage. I felt it was important for us as a gay and lesbian community, in establishing a culture, to find a way to celebrate our own unions. I began to feel that I was being shortsighted in worrying about whether or not it was an imitation of heterosexual tradition. I realized that we had an opportunity to create our own tradition.

*Zandra:* I think the ceremony was an important symbol for our families and community, as well as for us. It showed people that we had more than a relationship; we had a union. It was also wonderful, as a lesbian couple, to be with so many people that were truly on our side and truly supportive. There were about seventy-five people there: all ages, all colors, men and women, gay and straight. And all of them were totally in our corner.

*Deborah:* There's another dimension that I think was also a factor that day. At that particular time, we had just initiated a major civil rights discrimination lawsuit in California. We were suing a restaurant that had refused to serve us in its section reserved for "romantic couples." As it turned out, we ended up winning the following year in the appellate court. At the time of our ceremony, we didn't know how far it was going to go, but it was obvious even at that point that it was really big. It was also extremely public: it was on the front page of the *Los Angeles Times* and was always on the news. We were really putting ourselves out on the line, and I think that at the ceremony there was a strong sense that people wanted to support us. We became symbols of being out there. This was not about something like housing or employment; it was really about our right to be a couple in public.

The suit also made us go even further out than we had already been. It took the glass door right off whatever residual closet might have been left.

*Zandra:* I had been working in the women's health field, so I had always been around gay women and being out had never been a problem. Deborah was working as a real estate investor at a major financial institution, though, and we were concerned about how corporate America would handle Deborah being out and also being in a very public lawsuit.

*Deborah:* The timing was the most critical element: I got my M.B.A. in

June 1982; Zandy and I started living together in July; I also started my new investment position in July; and within a year Zandy and I were in this major lawsuit. For a while I thought about how hard I had worked to get to that point in my career, and I wondered if I was shooting myself in the foot. But we decided it was worth the risk.

There was a time in my life when I was terribly, terribly closeted, and I understand the fears of all that. When it came to the bottom line, though, I felt like it was my mental health and well-being versus other people's discomfort. I felt that if I was going to be uncomfortable, they were going to have to deal with their discomfort, too. So I had entered the company not hiding anything. Zandy came with me on business trips, to conventions, to luncheons. I bought and sold large real estate projects, and I was also a commercial lender, so there was always a lot of wining and dining going on. I'd bring Zandy. She always got along well with everybody. It sent my company through some changes, but there was also a lot of support, and by the time the lawsuit came around, people were really rooting for us. And then came the ceremony, and a lot of my co-workers came and supported us there as well.

*Zandra:* For me, it's that I haven't been willing to entertain the alternatives to being out. What are my other choices? Denying Deborah, hiding Deborah, hiding my relationship, or calling our relationship something other than what it is? Those are just not options for me. I can see people tripping as I introduce Deborah as my spouse or as my lover. I can see them going through their changes as they're standing there realizing, "I know she said lover. I know that's what she said. Yes, she said lover." But I know that they're going to get over it. And what else can I call her? I can't call her my roommate. I can't refer to her as just my friend. I'm not willing to take those alternatives.

*Deborah:* I think that we have a high level of commitment both to ourselves and also to the integrity of the relationship. That's a lot of what was behind our ceremony. I knew in my heart that this relationship with Zandy was it, and the ceremony was a way of showing that we had made a one hundred percent commitment to each other. I had noticed in a lot of relationships that there was a certain lack of integrity, a lack of full commitment, and I wanted this ceremony as a way of showing that we were there for each other completely.

*Zandra:* It was also important to both of us that our families be invited to the ceremony. My family is from Texas originally, so they were unable to attend. But my uncle who lives in California was there, taking pictures for us. I think that if the rest of them lived in town, they would have been there. My mother would have had a hard time, but she would have been there because she loves me. My brother and sister would definitely have been there. And, of course, Deborah's father was the first to arrive. Her mother could not deal with being there at all, though she did send china.

*Deborah:* My mother is extremely religious, from a fundamentalist Christian tradition. The idea of two women having a ceremony together was more "blasphemy" than she could handle.

*Zandra:* We ended up creating the ceremony out of a number of different elements. I'm Latin, so the majority of it was in both Spanish and English. We also drew upon certain customs from Mexican tradition. One Mexican custom that we used was that the couple has godparents: a madrina and a padrino. We asked two friends of ours to be our godparents. In Mexican tradition, the godparents protect and shelter the couple. They're there for support and guidance. In the Hispanic community, you are absolutely protected by your godparents. It's as though you have God's eyes on you at all times. They support you financially, emotionally and spiritually.

We also did the dollar dance, which is another Hispanic tradition. People pay a dollar to dance with each member of the couple, and the money goes towards the honeymoon.

*Deborah:* One surprise was that forty-eight hours before the ceremony we ended up deciding to have a minister there. The Friday before the ceremony, the woman who had been like a second mother to me called me up and told me that I should have this event blessed. She had already talked to the minister who'd performed her daughter's wedding, and she told us to give this woman a call.

It turned out that the minister was a woman from a metaphysical tradition. I'm a practitioner in the religious science movement, and that had been her background as well. She said that she'd be delighted to perform a ceremony for us. We went over to her house, and she asked us a lot of questions, kind of like a premarital counseling session. It was great, because she ended up using a lot of that information in the ceremony itself. We felt like she really knew who we were and what we were doing together.

We had the ceremony itself in the backyard of a friend of ours. There was an altar at the front of the yard, and underneath a tree, a lunch buffet to be served afterward. A patio area had been set up for dancing—we wanted the celebration to be upbeat and festive, so we had hired a disk jockey.

After everyone had mingled for a while and then gotten seated, we started by playing "On the Wings of Love." Then one of our friends read a

welcoming statement that we had written. In it, we went through the ety-
mology of the word tryst. We talked about how it came from two words,
one of which meant a coming together, and the other of which meant
trust. So, in all, it signified for us a coming together in trust. We also
talked about commitment and the fact that all who were there were invited
to participate fully in this and to think about their own commitments.

Then we had two friends read the section on love from *The Prophet*
by Kahlil Gibran; one read it in Spanish and one in English. Then Zandy
and I and the minister came up to the front, and the minister made some
opening remarks. She started by saying that never before had she been so
grateful for the separation of church and state, which got everyone laughing and feeling more at ease about the fact that this was a lesbian ceremony.

Then she talked for a while about commitment and about some of
the things that Zandy and I loved in each other, which she drew from having talked to us for so long. I remember her telling the audience that I felt
like whenever Zandy spoke, I understood. I understood everything that
she said, and she understood me.

*Zandra:* That's true of our politics also. We understand each other's politics. My mother put it well once when I was trying to explain to her how I
felt about Deborah. She said, simply, that I had found my twin. And I
thought, yes, that's exactly it. We think alike.

The minister also talked that day about how much I love Deborah's
commitment to the relationship. The level of her commitment is just incredible; it's one of the traits that I'm really glad she got from her parents.

*Deborah:* The minister then did a candle ceremony, which is something
that we've since integrated into our relationship on an ongoing basis.
There were three candles, each in a separate holder, and Zandra and I were
each instructed to light one of the candles for ourselves, and then to jointly
light the middle candle, which was the family candle. Then the minister
challenged us to try to blow out all three candles simultaneously, which
couldn't be done because of the spacing and their size. She told us that that
was what our lives would be like; that it would be almost impossible to
blow all three lights out simultaneously, and that we could take solace and
comfort in whatever light was lit. So if my personal candle's out, and
Zandy's is burning, she can light mine. Or we can both go to the family
candle. Sometimes we're both jamming separately, but the family one's
out; we're not connecting. There are still times periodically when we feel
as though we need some centering, and we just go get the candles and de-
liberately light the one that we think is out. It's one of the things from the
ceremony that's been really helpful to us.

After the candle ceremony, we did our vow exchange. We had each written our own vows and hadn't shown them to each other until that moment. Since then, we've repeated them to each other on every anniversary. They still feel very appropriate:

*Deborah:* I consider it both an honor and a privilege to be the one standing here with you today in love, mutual respect and total honesty.

I believe our being here is but a small demonstration of our willingness to plan a life together in a style and fashion that is appropriate for the two of us. Let us continue to build a relationship that suits our needs and never try to force our needs to fit any preconceived concepts. We are forever evolving, and I want our relationship to always reflect our most current level of awareness.

I support you in your intellectual, emotional, spiritual and economic growth. No doubt we each will change as we grow. I want to know of your changes, and I promise to share mine with you. Never be afraid to tell me your thoughts. I believe it is the intensity of our intimacy that keeps us continually seeking the other for companionship. I love our spontaneity and our ability to laugh at ourselves and each other nonjudgmentally.

I will make myself a safe person for you to be around. I will provide a nurturing environment for your soul and care for the body in which it dwells. Tu eres mi familia y mi casa es tu casa. [You are my family, and my home is your home.]

My feelings for you were expressed so eloquently thousands of years ago when Ruth said to Naomi: "Entreat me not to leave thee, or to return from following after thee; for whither thou goest I will go. And where thou lodgest I will lodge. Thy people will be my people and thy God my God. And where thou diest, I will die, and there also will I be buried: All this the Lord do unto me and more, if aught but death part me and thee."

You are always welcome into my world. I place no limitations on the possibilities of our relationship. I hope we never truly discover just how high is high. As you go through life's ups and downs following your passions and your dreams, I want you always to remember that I believe in you and I'm rooting for you all the way. Te amo. [I love you.]

*Zandra:* Deborah, I am honored to stand here with you in front of God, our friends and family to declare the love, respect and trust I have for you and our relationship.

I declare that our relationship is a reflection of all that is good and arrived at through affirmation and belief.

Your mental and physical well-being is and will continue to be an important part of my life. May you always be well, baby!

May we continue to dream together and continue following our hearts.

May we continue to accomplish the goals we have set out for our lives, for I support your intelligence, your sincerity and your magnificence.

May we continue to communicate our concerns and our issues, and I promise to listen to your words and to your feelings.

I am certain that you and I have loved each other in another time and in another space, and once again we meet in trust to celebrate our joyous union.

Deborah, know that I am here for you, whenever you need me, want me, or desire me. For I love you! My heart, my mind and my soul loves you.

As in *The Prophet,* it states: "When love beckons you, follow her. . . ." I did! And it led me straight to you, and for this I am grateful.

Te amo, tambien! [I love you also!]

*Deborah:* After the vows, we exchanged rings. We had taken our own gold and diamonds and had them made into rings. For us, this was an important symbol. In part it represented our ability to take what we had and to reshape it into something that was significant for us. Everything that was in there was symbolic; we even had Zandy's mother's engagement ring. It was a collection of our mutual histories. We took all of that and turned it into something reflective of us. The other main point was that diamonds last forever, and gold is something that has had value all over the world and throughout history. The rings symbolized the value of our love.

*Zandra:* For me it was important that we were both contributing a lot of history. I felt that these rings were kind of like the family heirlooms that many people bring into heterosexual marriages. It was important to me that I was contributing to the relationship something symbolic of my heritage.

*Deborah:* After the exchange of rings, we kissed. Actually, what led up to the kissing part was very funny. When I was saying my vows, I was very nervous. I was trembling, and I had a frog in my throat. I do a lot of public speaking, but the honesty and vulnerability of what was going on was really hitting me. So there we were, facing each other, and Zandy just reached out and grabbed my hand to kind of steady me. And, as usually happens when we're in that position, she pulled me towards her to give me a little kiss. It's such a natural thing for us that I don't think we were even paying attention to it. But this was right in the middle of the vows, in front of seventy-five people, and the minister said, "Not yet." Then Zandy went to say her vows, and she reached out and kissed me again. And the minister said, again, "Not yet." And then it happened a third time, and that time everybody in the audience yelled, "NOT YET!"

*Zandra:* It was pretty funny. I still haven't been able to live it down. I think I was dealing with my nervousness that way. It was a way of saying, "Let's just go home, baby. Let's go home." It was a way of being together.

*Deborah:* And meanwhile there were seventy-five people calling, "NOT YET!"

Finally, though, we did the kiss. Then we poured champagne for everyone, and Zandy and I did six or seven toasts, in Spanish and in English. We turned around and faced everybody and acknowledged the people we wanted to say something special to. We acknowledged our families, our host, our godparents, our attorney and finally everyone who had come to support us.

Then we had a transitional song, and people started partying. The caterers had laid the food out like a formal picnic. The champagne was flowing. And then our madrina surprised us with a cake: a three-tier wedding cake.

I still remember that day as being one of the most moving experiences of my life. It was just very, very special in its depth, in its intensity. I was so glad that we had the consciousness to do it. I still consider it the happiest day of my life.

*Zandra:* And the next day we went on a honeymoon to Acapulco. It was a wonderful ceremony. We're thinking about having some kind of recommitment celebration again in a couple of years, when we have our tenth-year anniversary.

*Deborah:* We are such a unit together, and it all works so well. Even financially, we share everything; there are no hidden agendas. There are always people who say, "Well, maybe you should put a little aside," or, "Maybe you shouldn't share everything." And I look at them, and I say, "Show me a relationship that's better than this one that's gotten that way by all of that protective bullshit." Or sometimes somebody will say something like, "Don't you ever want something new?" I tell them, "Hell, this is new!" I have never done this before! I have started up relationships over and over again. There's nothing new about that! There's nothing new in the bars, in the clubs. I've done that; that's not new. This is new.

*Zandra:* When we passed the five- and six-year marks, everything after that was new. Neither one of us had had relationships that lasted longer than that. And certainly none that worked as well as ours works. We're committed to each other, and we're also committed to maintaining the relationship, the unity. So we spend a lot of time taking care of that and ironing out things that may be obstacles; we pay a lot of attention to the status of our relationship. I'm a chiropractor, and I see it as getting an adjustment. The relationship is constantly being adjusted, so that it stays centered. We go on vacations regularly, and we know what we need when we feel like we're off. We often need what I call a jammy night, where it's, "Get your jammies and we'll have dinner in bed and watch movies and go to sleep."

I think it also makes a big difference that my family loves her, and that her family loves me. I think my mother still hopes that maybe someday I'll come to my senses and realize I'm not lesbian, but she also thinks, "Well, if you're going to be gay, at least it's with her." And she loves me enough to support me. I think it's also that she sees that my life works. In some ways I've been a good role model for her to learn from. And my grandmother absolutely adores Deborah. When I speak to my grandmother, most of the conversation is about Deborah.

*Deborah:* Her mother and grandmother come out and stay with us; they sleep in our bed. Zandy's mother sends out Zandy's niece every year to spend the summer with us. And Zandy's brother has been living with us since November. My family is the same way. I think part of the trick has been that we have included our families in our lives, and we've actively participated in the family. I've also always been extremely respectful of her mother's position in the family.

*Zandra:* That just won my mother over. Deborah was in like Flynn after that.

*Deborah:* I treated her with the respect that I felt she would have wanted out of a son-in-law. When we first started living together, I told Zandy that we needed to go to Texas and meet her family. They needed to check me out. They needed to know what my intentions were, and the whole bit. So I've always been very reassuring. I made contact with her mother, and I let her know how much I loved her daughter. I told her I couldn't do anything about the fact that we were both women, but nobody (except for her) could possibly love her daughter more than I do. Her mother watched me financially support Zandy through her schooling, and she knows that our relationship is genuine.

I think our families got broken in on our earlier relationships. By the time this one started, we both had the attitude of "Don't give me any trouble. This is what I have been waiting for all my life. Be happy for me now or don't bother me, because I've got to go for what I know is right, and this is it." There's been a sort of finality about it all. Even with my father, who has never really embraced any friend or lover of mine before. Even before we were living together, I told him why I was splitting up with my ex. I told him that there was somebody else, and that this was it: this was the relationship I'd been waiting for. He met her, and he understood exactly what I meant. He has been like a prince ever since. He speaks very fluent Spanish, and so he always has these side conversations with Zandy in Spanish, "How's my daughter? She looks very happy." He introduces her as his daughter-in-law. He even told her that he thought she was the answer to his prayers for me. This is from the man who nearly threw me out of the house for being a lesbian years ago. But he realized that that was wrong, and I know that he really wants me to be happy. I believe that a lot of times what I thought was my parents' reaction to my gay relationships was really their reaction to the fact that those relationships weren't good for me. And sometimes it was hard for them to make the distinction between the two.

*Zandra:* I've been married to a man before, and this feels so different to me. In heterosexual relationships, it seems like a lot of times he has his friends and she has hers. She hangs out with the girls, and he's somehow not a part of it. Deborah's the first person that I call when I want to hang out with somebody. There are no topics that we can't bring up with each other; nothing we can't share. It's also different being with a woman, because we think so much alike. It's like being best friends and yet also being committed romantic lovers. That romance is a very important part of it for us. We're very romantic, and we go out of our way to keep that spark there: the flowers, the surprise parties, the dinners, the candlelight—the whole thing.

*Deborah:* There are some ways, though, that I think our relationship is similar to a heterosexual marriage. For all our New Age thinking, we're very traditional about family; we consider ourselves a nuclear family unit.

We have a spousal relationship with one another: I consider her brother my brother-in-law; her niece becomes my niece. All of that. Where it's different, though, is that we don't have those gender-based issues to deal with. In a heterosexual marriage, regardless of how open-minded people try to be, I think there's always an expectation, even subtle, for what a wife's role is and what a husband's role is. And even if the couple themselves don't subscribe to that, there's still a lot of societal pressure to conform to it all. Ultimately it seems that you find men having their allegiances to men, and women to women. There's a certain level of expecting not to understand the other party, because "after all, he's a man" or "after all, she's a woman." A certain amount of divisiveness is expected.

Our relationship is very different from that. I think we have a greater sense of possibility, because there are no rigid roles. There are no rules for this. We can do anything we want to do. There's a sense of freedom. It also means, though, that we have to assume a hell of a lot more responsibility, because it's no more than we make it. In that respect it's quite different from a heterosexual marriage. If you're heterosexually married, and you haven't lived, or even spoken, with your spouse for two or three years, you're still considered married. That person is still your spouse. With gay and lesbian relationships, there are no such definitions. Our relationships have only the significance that we give them. So it's a lot of freedom, but it's also a lot of responsibility.

*Zandra:* We've worked hard at our relationship, but at the same time it's been so easy. In April 1990, we will have been together eight years, and each year I feel more and more that I can't imagine living any other way. I love everything about being married to this woman. I love the comfies of it: the flannel pajamas, the chicken soup. I love being so familiar and so comfortable with somebody. I love having history with her and love having this unity. I feel as though we have a home with each other, no matter where we are. It's the feeling I used to get when I lived at home as a child, and I knew that once my Mom was home, and we were all home from school, that was it. It was six o'clock and we were having dinner, and I just knew that everything was secure because we were all home together. I feel that same way with Deborah. Once she gets home, that's it. We're together, and we're supporting each other. This is the world we've created together.

*Deborah:* I feel like our relationship is a total life partnership. I'm a builder. I like to initiate. I like to start things. I have a lot of tenacity. And to me, in addition to all the things that Zandy said, being married is an anchor in my life. I don't know what's going to happen to me in life; I don't know what kind of career changes I'll make, or where we'll move, or any of that kind of stuff. But the one thing that I know for sure is that no matter what happens, no matter what goes on, I will be with Zandy. Being married means knowing that I can count on her. That we can plan together. It just feels so good knowing I have a full-fledged partner. I look at the eight years that we've been together, and we've accomplished such an incredible amount together: we bought a house four years ago; we've already paid off one car; we're halfway through another car; we've got two dogs and a bird; Zandra's graduated from school; I've already had a corporate career; we have a business together; we won a major lawsuit. We've done it together. And we're going on together. We're both very strong and powerful women. I think that's part of our attraction to each other. We're finally at a place now of both being out of school, and we have big dreams of what we want for our lives. Nobody writes the manual for this. You don't learn it in school. You just work it through, together.

*This account is based on interviews with Deborah L. Johnson and Zandra Z. Rolón.*

ॐ

*Deborah L. Johnson: Deborah is a thirty-four-year-old Black woman who is a native of Los Angeles. Deborah and her life partner, Zandra Z. Rolón, are cofounders of The Motivational Institute, a consulting firm specializing in organizational development, interpersonal relationships and personal growth. Deborah is also executive director of the firm. She is a frequent group facilitator and public speaker who often addresses the issues of cultural diversity. Prior to her full-time consulting work, Deborah spent ten years in the real estate industry as an institutional investment manager. She has an M.B.A. in real estate finance from the University of California, Los Angeles.*

*Zandra Z. Rolón: Zandra is a thirty-four-year-old Hispanic woman who is originally from Texas. She is a doctor of chiropractic specializing in sports injuries. Prior to her chiropractic studies, Zandra was involved in the field of women's health, serving as a clinic administrator, counselor for battered women and advocate of reproductive rights. Zandra has also spent four summers studying at Palacios de Belles Artes (The Palace of Fine Arts) in Mexico City.*

*Both women are deeply committed to social change and to their own spiritual growth. In addition to being long-time activists in the civil rights, feminist and gay and lesbian liberation movements, both are also active members in the Agape Church of Religious Science.*

# Donale Chastain

## &  Laurel Holmström

Donale (left) & Laurel (right)

*November 1983    February 1985    June 1988*

*❧  California*

# Temple, Bathhouse and Grove

We decided to "marry" very early in our relationship. Realizing our deep resonance with each other, we felt compelled to formalize and celebrate our commitment. Being Pagans of the Wicca tradition, our "marriage" ceremony took the form of handfasting.* Wicca is the term used to designate those Pagans who follow religious traditions from pre-Christian Europe. Wicca practitioners usually call themselves witches, even though this word has collected powerful negative connotations in our culture. The reclaiming of the word *witch* is similar to lesbians' reclaiming of the word *dyke*. Both Wicca and witch come from the root "wic," which means a bend or shape, so our definition of witch is one who bends and shapes consciousness and therefore reality.

Handfasting is both a ritualization of commitment and a community celebration. Any number of people can handfast together, as the ritual does not assume sexual activity between participants. We suspect, however, that most handfasting rituals are between lovers. In Pagan thought, the handfasting ritual is literally a spell that two people cast on each other which binds them together for a year and a day. Because of this, the ritual can be repeated. This aspect of handfasting allows conscious evaluation of the relationship and provides room for growth and change. We have handfasted three times in five years.

Our first handfasting took place in November 1983 on the campus of San Jose State University in California. An old, lovely building that was due to be torn down was our "temple." We decorated the large room with flowers, gourds, images from Judy Chicago's "Dinner Party" and symbols of the season. We hung a picture of the Earth on the fireplace. The altar was placed in the center of the room and held symbols of the four elements—air, fire, water and earth. We used two purple candles to represent our lesbian selves and one red candle for the passion of our love. The Priestess who worked with us on the ritual told us that green and red are traditional colors for handfasting, so Donale wore a long green skirt with a plaid shirt, and Laurel wore a long red shirt with a black Chinese jacket. Laurel designed and made flower garlands of roses and carnations for our

---

*For more information on handfastings and Pagan ritual see Zsuzsanna Budapest's *Holy Book of Women's Mysteries* (1980; reprint, Berkeley: Wingbow Press, 1989) and Starhawk's *The Spiral Dance* (San Francisco: Harper and Row, 1979).

126

hair. Donale strung together Indian corn for beautiful necklaces.

We had invited almost everyone we knew, parents and relatives included. Laurel's mother, father and stepfather attended, and Donale's niece and nephew were there for her. Donale's parents are deceased, but were there in spirit. Laurel was so nervous she had diarrhea all morning. While it was scary to be with all those people, it was also empowering. They all loved us. Everyone joined hands in a circle, and the Priestess and her Consort led the ritual. It began, as almost all Pagan circles do, with meditation for grounding, casting the circle to create sacred space, calling in the four directions and invoking the Goddess and the God. After that ritual we stopped invoking the God at our circles and handfastings; we are Dianic and feel that the God gets his due from others. Dianic is a word coined by Zsuzsanna Budapest and refers to a particular form of Wicca that is completely womon-centered. Only the Goddess is invoked in the circle, and the circle is always made up of only wimmin.

Once the sacred space was created, we were led to the center of the circle. The Priestess anointed us with oil and blessed us fivefold: "Blessed are your eyes to see Her ways. Blessed is your mouth to speak Her many names. Blessed are your breasts, formed in strength and beauty. Blessed is your cunt, which gives life and pleasure. Blessed are your feet to walk Her path."

She then took gold and silver cords, representing the sun and moon energies, and tied our right hands together. (This is the literal handfasting.) Facing each other, we placed our left hands on each other's heart chakra and spoke our "vows." Our vows were not pre-written or memorized. We spoke directly from our hearts, to each other's. Our exact words did not stay in our memory, but people present remarked that it was very moving. That moment of speaking, of looking into each other's eyes and feeling the immensity of the love generated between us, was one of the most powerful and profound moments in all our handfastings.

Once the "vows" were spoken, our hands were untied, and we were each given one of the cords. This part of the ritual represents the fact that we are individuals as well as a couple. We took the chalice full of cherry juice from the altar and gave each other a drink saying, "May you never thirst." We then took the chalice around the circle, addressing each person by name and asking each for a blessing. They held the chalice as they spoke and then drank. We received many, many wonderful blessings, including happiness, creativity, peace and truth. After our blessings we jumped the broom, a symbol of jumping into our new life together. As soon as we landed, Bach's Brandenburg Concerto began, and we encouraged everyone to dance and make merry. Unfortunately, practically no one else at the circle was Pagan, so they didn't know quite what to do. But we danced and hugged and kissed anyway. People brought lots of glorious food and presents. We feasted and talked and took pictures. All in all it was a very exhilarating experience.

Our next two handfastings followed a similar ritual pattern but had very different energy. Our second was at a wimmin's bathhouse in San Francisco. Everyone wore togas, which to our delight kept falling off! Our togas were blue satin, marvelously loose and slinky. A dear Crone friend of ours was Priestess for us. (A Crone is usually an older womon and is considered wise in our tradition.) She was so pleased to perform the ceremony and radiated such love and power that we felt wonderfully blessed. Afterwards we all hot-tubbed together and gave our Priestess a massage.

One friend showed up late, but certainly added a lot to the feeling of celebration. She had brought us a gift, but mysteriously told us that we would have to go into the bathroom before she would give it to us. Knowing that she worked in a sex shop, we wondered what outrageous thing she was going to do. Once in the bathroom, with great mischief in her eyes, she presented us with a lavender silicone dildo. We laughed and blushed as she instructed us, in her practical style, in how to take care of it. As we were about to leave the bathroom, she dared us to wear it out in front of the rest of the wimmin. We didn't do that, but we did put it on the altar. When one of our straight friends came out of the hot-tub room, she walked over to the altar saying, "Oh, what's this?" Suddenly, she realized it was a dildo and was very befuddled for a moment. Then we all laughed together. It was a very sexy, sensual and lively handfasting.

Our third was held in a small redwood grove with three close friends. It was a very hot day. Donale wore a white pants outfit with big iris flowers on it, and Laurel wore a sleeveless pink jumpsuit. Previously, we had gone to the woods and found a perfect circle of trees a little way off the main path. On the day of the handfasting, there were people sunbathing not too far away. Undaunted, Laurel approached them and said that we had planned to do a ceremony there and hoped we wouldn't bother them. They were very respectful and quiet. By the time the ritual was over, they had left without us even hearing them.

We were supremely honored by our circle sisters at that handfasting. They did most of the ritual for us, and it turned into a deep sharing between all of us. Not only did they give us a blessing as we passed the chalice around, but we gave them a blessing as well. One of the greatest moments of our third handfasting occurred as we were leaving the park. We were wearing baby's breath wreaths with long ribbons flowing down the back, and all of us looked festive and happy. We asked some people walking by if they would take a picture of us. They agreed, and as the man looked through the lens he remarked, "Looks like someone's getting married." The look on his face when he realized there were no men in our group was priceless.

In a world where lesbian relationships are rarely honored outside of the lesbian community, handfastings have strengthened our belief in ourselves and helped validate our lesbian experience. If we do not honor ourselves, we cannot expect the world to honor us.

—*Donale Chastain and Laurel Holmström*

ॐ

*Donale Chastain: Donale is funny and bizarre. Working full-time in an academic library, she lives for vacations. She made her acting debut this year in a street theatre production of* The Lorax. *She loves sex and dogs (not necessarily together), is an Eco-feminist witch, and is a great masseuse.*

*Laurel Holmström: Laurel is an Eco-feminist witch trying to keep her sanity while finishing a B.A. in anthropology and teaching a course in women's spirituality and feminist theology in the Women's Studies Department at a nearby university. When not studying or teaching, she does a unique form of massage therapy with Donale, performs guerilla theatre and constantly endeavors to create her own lesbian-feminist utopia in the present moment.*

# Anna
## &
### Deborah

Deborah (left) & Anna (right)
photographer: Richard Krause

*June 20, 1987*  🕊  *Michigan*

# Born to Be a Bride

*Anna:* I was born in the Netherlands and first came to the United States eight years ago when I was twenty-four. I was working on my master's degree in the Netherlands and would come here every summer and go to the Womyn's Music Festival in Michigan. The summer before I finished my degree, I was working at the festival with a good friend of mine. Deborah was with a guy at the time. I don't know if they would have gotten married, but it was pretty serious. Some of the women she worked with were also friends of mine, and these women didn't think much of Deborah's relationship. They didn't believe she was that straight. Anyway, in those days, I was the kind of person that liked to seduce straight women. So our friends set us up. The first afternoon, Deborah was pretty nasty to me, trying to put me off, but I just kept my natural charm and by night we were together. Deborah ran off to her boyfriend the next morning, but she called me four days later, having broken up with him, and then we got together for good.

In the beginning we wanted to get married right away, but we decided that we should try to be rational and reasonable and live together for a year first. Neither Deborah nor I had ever been monogamous; we had never felt like that was something in our lifestyles. Then, when we met, we both knew we wanted to be monogamous with each other. I was so in love with her that I couldn't be with anybody else, even physically. That was something that had never happened to me before. We both felt like this was a different kind of relationship, a different kind of commitment. And we wanted to get married as an expression of that commitment.

We knew we didn't really need to do it in a traditional way, because obviously the government wouldn't accept it anyway. But we weren't happy about feeling that we weren't *allowed* to do it in the traditional way. If Deborah had married a man, she probably would not have chosen a traditional wedding because she doesn't agree with a lot of the roles that are expressed in that kind of ceremony. But for us, we felt that this was something we supposedly couldn't have because of being gay, and I think it was the opposition that made us want such a traditional ceremony. It was also very important to Deborah to make a real commitment in a real church.

So we ended up having a very traditional church wedding at a Metropolitan Community Church. We did the whole bit: Deborah had on a bride's gown, I had on a tuxedo, and we had women and gay male friends standing up with us. The women that stood up for Deborah were wearing coordinating dresses, and the women and guys that stood up for me were wearing tuxedos. We changed the vows a little and put in nonsexist language, but for the most part it was a traditional church wedding.

I don't know how to explain it, but there's a certain emotional bonding that goes along with having a wedding. I'm not very Christian or anything; I'm not even sure if I believe in God, but after the wedding I felt I had made a commitment that related to my spirit. There's just something spiritual that gets involved with it.

The whole process ended up having a big effect on our relationship. I feel much more deeply committed now. Every relationship runs into trouble, and if you're gay it's relatively easy just to walk out on it, because usually you don't have social or family support for your relationship. But I take it more seriously now. I'm not going to go out and look for somebody else if we don't get along for a week. I would fight much harder for this relationship because I know I made a commitment; I actually went to church and made this commitment in a wedding. I'm not a very traditional person, nor a conservative person, and from a radical view, I wouldn't argue that I "believe" in weddings, but we grew up in a society where we acquired certain emotions and associations, and there's a part of me that acquired the association of making a commitment with a wedding.

Even though we did it very traditionally, I'm also clear that we approached our wedding totally differently than heterosexual couples approach theirs. We did it so traditionally partly because we were *not* supposed to have it that way. We kept the words about traditional roles out of the ceremony, and of course, no one was giving anybody away; we just walked into the church as individuals. Being two women we are not bound to the traditional roles of society. We chose the traditional ceremony because we wanted to do it that way. It was a choice. And neither of us is a man, so neither has the role of traditionally being more powerful than the other. That in itself changes the whole meaning of a wedding for lesbians.

*Deborah:* I never thought I would get married. I always had a hard time sustaining one-on-one relationships, regardless of whether with men or women, so I had just assumed that marriage was something that wasn't in the cards for me. Until my mid-twenties I had tons and tons of relationships with men, and even though I lived with a number of them, none of the relationships were monogamous. None of the men were really very interesting to me, certainly not interesting enough to inspire any sort of emotional commitment. Then at about twenty-four I had my first long-term relationship with a woman. I didn't even consider a gay wedding though; at that point I thought that gay weddings were just kind of weird. They seemed pathetic to me, as if people were trying to break into the heterosexual mode. So neither form of marriage seemed very likely, or even desirable, to me.

When I turned thirty I went through a real life change. I finally started to feel established in my work. I had been practicing law for about five or six years, and I was starting to realize that no one was going to take the degree away from me. I felt like I could start to put energy into other aspects of my life; and one thing I started thinking about was that maybe I didn't really want to end up bouncing from person to person for the rest of my life. I think that the last guy I was with was kind of my last-ditch attempt to settle down and be "normal," so to speak. So even though he wasn't the right person for me, the process got me thinking that maybe there wasn't anything wrong with commitment, per se. It wasn't like I was going to marry the next person that came along, but at least I had started to feel that commitment in itself wasn't an impossible idea.

That was about the time Anna and I got together. So much was going on for me emotionally. I was so in love with her, and I wanted very much for the relationship to work. I found myself wanting to make a commitment, but not really knowing how to do that. I had told other people, "I'll love you 'til the day I die," and that, to me, didn't seem sufficient. I felt differently about Anna than I had about anyone else. My past relationships hadn't been bad relationships, but this one was so much deeper. For the first time, I really wanted a commitment. And I think that on some level the commitment wouldn't have been meaningful if it hadn't been something like a marriage.

There are two parts to me, parts that I think a lot of other people have but just don't want to deal with. One part is what I consider my post-eighteen-year-old, or my post-feminist-awakening, self. That part consists of things that I believe intellectually: things that fit my values, make a lot of sense to me and are politically correct. The other part of me consists of the first eighteen years, during which I grew up as a traditional little girl. I could probably think away all of those early values if I wanted to spend the next ten years in psychotherapy, but in reality those values still exist inside of me. I think that it's important to acknowledge and support those feelings to some extent, because I don't think that they just go away if you ignore them. And so in addition to wanting a commitment, there was also something important to me about getting married and being a bride, even though intellectually I thought there was a lot of garbage that went along with that. If I had gone with just my intellectual side, I don't think that my whole being would have been involved in the commitment. I wanted to make sure that I didn't ignore an important part of myself. I also felt very strongly that we shouldn't be denied anything because we are gay. So, given all those factors, we decided to have a traditional wedding.

Part of wanting a real church wedding was also because I wanted the ceremony to have a spiritual component. For me, getting married includes a spiritual commitment, and I wouldn't have felt the same if we had had our wedding out in a field with everything but a minister. The presence of that religious aspect denotes a certain seriousness to me. My philosophy about religion is that all religions are valid, and that the important thing is not what religion you are, but how you treat people and what sort of values you integrate into your life. I knew I wanted my wedding to include an expression of spirituality, and although other people might express it differently, the most familiar expression for me was in a church with a minister.

Both of our families knew about the wedding. Anna's mother ignored it completely. She didn't want any part of it. I only have a mother and a sister, but both of them were around. My mother came to the wedding, to the rehearsal dinner and to the showers. I don't think she was particularly happy about it, but she had just gotten divorced and frankly I'm not sure what could have made her happy, although I do think it would have been different if I had been marrying a man.

My sister was very supportive, but I'm not sure that she accepted it as much as she said she did. She called me two days before the wedding, just as I was dressing for the rehearsal. It was fifteen minutes before she was supposed to be there, and she said, oh, by the way, Glen (her husband) wouldn't be coming to the wedding. We had already bought him this special boutonniere, trying to help him feel comfortable. At that point I just lost it. I said, "This is my wedding, Cheryl. How can you tell me that your husband is not going to come to my wedding?" And she said, "Well, he's busy." I said, "This is bullshit. This is discrimination." I asked her how she would feel if it were reversed. She said, "Well, I'm sorry, but he just has something else going on." I said, "Then don't come. If your husband can't come to my wedding, then I don't want you there either." Frankly, at that point I didn't care if she had to force him to come. You just don't miss your family members' weddings that lightly. She called me back five minutes later saying they would both be there.

One thing that emerged as a real issue for us in planning the wedding was that we look so traditionally butch and femme: Anna is a big six-foot-tall woman, and I am five-foot-two and very straight-looking. We're often mistaken for a straight couple; we've even been stopped going into gay bars by people saying, "Excuse me, but this is a lesbian bar." Because we do appear so traditionally butch and femme, it was hard to convey to people that the wedding was an outgrowth of our relationship, not just us

trying to fit into some straight mold. We had to justify that almost immediately, because traditional butch/femme-looking people can get extremely
hassled by other lesbians. People assume that they look that way because
they're trying to fit into some straight ideal; but in reality, it's sometimes
just the opposite. When I first came out, I tried to be butch. I tried to be as
butch as I could: I grew out the hair on my legs, didn't wear any make-up
and didn't curl my hair, which was then my idea of what butch was. It just
looked horrible; I couldn't do it. I felt awful, so I went back to being myself. And since Anna looks fairly masculine, together we look like a real
butch-femme couple.

It's pretty much just appearances. There are a few divisions: Anna
does the yard work. I don't like doing it, but I wouldn't like doing it no
matter whom I was with. We share cooking. We share cleaning. I do more
of the sewing and do things like cook Anna brownies, but that's just the
way we are naturally. It doesn't come into play at all in our decision-
making; we're very equal about that. So really it's just appearances, but the
appearance issue can be pretty intense.

There were a couple of times when I was trying on wedding dresses
and the store employees wouldn't let Anna into the room at first because
they thought she was a man. When I first met Anna, I would be outraged
when something like that happened. I would think, "You narrow-minded
person, how dare you accuse her of being a man?" From my perspective, it
would be awful if someone thought I was a man. But with Anna. . . well,
you have to know Anna. She really doesn't care. She thinks it's funny. We
have these little neighbor boys, and they'll come up and ask her, "Are you
a man or a woman?" And she will just laugh and say, "Why is that important?" When older people have asked her, she's said, "Whatever you want
me to be."

After the wedding, we ended up spending two nights in a bridal suite
just to recuperate before we went to the Virgin Islands for our honeymoon. The second night, we went out to a really nice dinner in the hotel,
and we told them we were a honeymoon couple. We were all dressed up,
and during the dinner it became clear that the waiter, who was gay, assumed that Anna was a man. He kept calling her "the bridegroom," which
Anna thought was really neat.

I think this aspect of our relationship contributed to the problems
some of our friends had with our wedding plans. I do civil rights law for
persons with disabilities, and some of what we do is pretty radical stuff. A
lot of the women that I work with, and am friends with, are very open and
political lesbians. Anna and I have always been the couple that they got a
kick out of but never really understood. When we asked them to be in the
wedding, they were very skeptical. They thought that it would look like a

circus, and they couldn't figure out why we were intentionally putting ourselves in those "traditional" roles. They kept saying that women had been stuck with this stuff for centuries, and why were we perpetuating it? And we kept saying, "But there's no man here." We had changed the wording so there wouldn't be any repressive language, but they still initially couldn't understand. They thought it would look ridiculous.

Anna just refused to answer such questions, but I felt that I had to keep justifying what we were doing. And, at the same time, I was going through my own inner questioning: "If she's kind of masculine, and I'm attracted to her, then why aren't I with a man?" I couldn't answer that. I still can't really answer, except to say that I love Anna, and I don't want to be with a man. I was also thinking, "Well, maybe I'm narrowly identifying women. Who says men are the only ones that can look this way?" I went through a lot intellectually, trying to figure out why we are who we are. It was hard to be going through all of this internally and at the same time trying to justify it to friends.

We had a celebration party, early on, after we chose the attendants. The women and the men who stood up for Anna didn't have any problem with doing it so traditionally. They said, " Well, if this is what you want, this is what you want." The women who were standing up with me, however, got me in a room and said, "Why are you doing this?" and "We don't want to wear matching dresses. We don't even want to wear dresses." They just drilled me on it. I didn't really know how to explain our relationship or how right it felt to be doing this way. I just knew deep down inside that I wanted it, and I knew that if I didn't have it this way, I would feel, on some level, that this wasn't really a wedding, and that as a lesbian I was cut out of something else. I said, "Damn it, if this is what we want, why can't you just support it? It's hard enough anyway. I don't expect you to get married using this form. You can get married out on a rock over an ocean. I don't care." I would have supported them, and I wanted them to support my form of commitment. That was about nine months before the wedding, and after that they stopped being so vocal about their objections. Plus, I stopped explaining it. Then about two months before the wedding, I started thinking to myself, "My God, why am I doing this? Maybe this *is* really sick. Maybe this *is* going to look ridiculous. Maybe I'm just trying to lay some straight mold on top of our relationship." I went through those fears for about five weeks, and then about a week before the wedding they went away. Suddenly I was absolutely sure that it was the right thing to do, and since then I have never regretted a single second of it.

When it all came together, our friends felt that the wedding didn't look ridiculous at all. Now they sing higher praises of the whole ceremony than we do. We had so many comments afterwards about how affirming it was for gays and lesbians, and how it was wonderful that we had had the strength to go through with it. One guest came out as a lesbian after the wedding. She came up to me at the reception and said, "You don't know what you've done for me today."

What I really appreciate is that if Anna had been a man, I would never have done this whole bride business. I couldn't have ignored the inequalities that go along with traditional heterosexual marriages and weddings. It would have seemed too much like a chaining. But because we are two women, no one was chaining the other. We could have fun with it, and preparing for it became a wonderful process. There's a side of me that really loved to sit in the bathtub and read the five bride books I had bought. I'm glad I could indulge that. I said at the time to my friends that I was born to be a bride. I loved buying the invitations. I'd read what one book would say about the invitations' wording, and then I'd read another book. Actually I thought briefly about going into a consulting business for lesbian weddings! There really is a lot in the process that you don't know how to do until you're in the middle of it.

The process of preparing for the wedding was a very powerful period of bonding for us. There were a lot of stresses, but for me it was also nine months spent anticipating the commitment of my lifetime. I thought it was a very healthy process to go through, because you have to think about what you're doing every step of the way. It gave us a lot of opportunity to let the idea of the commitment sink in at a very deep level.

The process ended up also being just really wonderful and fun. Before going through with the wedding, I had always wondered why people spent so much time and energy on them. For us it was really a nine-month project. It ended up being very lavish: we had seventy-five guests, a sit-down dinner, an open bar, and then we took a honeymoon trip to a little gay resort in the Virgin Islands. We spent $8,000, including the honeymoon. We took out a loan for part of it and were lucky to have enough money to pay for the rest of it.

I'm still glad we went "all the way." Sometime before our own ceremony, the MCC minister invited us to sit in on a lesbian wedding. It was a traditional wedding, but not in the same way that we were doing it. It was two women in tuxedos, which was fine for them, but their reception was in the church basement, and someone brought a cake, which had cracked on the way over. It just seemed kind of sad, and for us it reinforced what we were doing. It's not that you have to spend a lot money on it, but for such an important ceremony we really felt that we wanted to make it exactly the way we wanted.

I felt very differently about the wedding at the beginning of those nine months than I did at the end. At the beginning, I was afraid that what I wanted were things I couldn't really have. I just couldn't believe that the option of a traditional wedding was open to me. It started when we went to a bridal shop to look at dresses. I had decided to get a bridesmaid's dress; I didn't want a suit because I wear suits every day. I would just get a nice dressy outfit. So I started looking at the bridesmaid's dresses, but over on the other side of the store were these beautiful white wedding dresses. I started to feel like a second-class citizen. There I was looking at these bridesmaid dresses, but I kept looking at the other side of the store thinking, "I don't want this bridesmaid's dress. I'm the bride. I want a wedding dress." And finally I said to Anna, "I think I would prefer a wedding dress." (But, of course, at that point I was thinking I could never wear a wedding dress.) And Anna said, "You're the bride, get a bride's dress." And I said, "No, I don't think I could do that." And she said, "Of course you can." And so I started thinking, "Yeah, I'm the bride. I can get a bride's dress." And I went over there, and we started looking at wedding dresses. The wedding dress was the big symbol for me. Once you buy a white wedding dress, everything else seems to follow.

I kept waiting for someone to say, "You can't do this." I don't know whom I expected to say that, but I sure expected somebody to say it. We used as many gay services as we could, but there were a lot of straight services we used, too. For instance we bought our cake from a regular German bakery. They knew that we were the bride and groom and didn't bat an eye. We also got the tuxedos from a regular tux rental place. The so-called best man went with us. We had been talking to the salesman about whether if we rented six tuxes we would get the groom's tux free. He said that yes, that was the arrangement, and then he said, "Now, who's going to be the groom?" We kind of looked at each other, and Anna said, "Well, I'm the groom." The man replied, "Oh, of course. I'm sorry," and he wrote the order up. I don't know what I expected to happen, but I guess I expected somebody to refuse us. We also went to Hudson's, a local department store, to register for the bridal registry. There were four couples, including us, and they just stuck Anna with the men and me with the women, and we registered. Again, nobody batted an eye.

The same thing happened with the reception hall. When we were first thinking about where we could have the reception, I was thinking about the basement of the lesbian bar, but realized we'd have to have the reception on a Sunday because they wouldn't close the bar on a Saturday night. It seemed like we didn't really have many choices. On the other hand there was this country club that I had wanted to get married at since I was a little girl. I just figured it was out of the question. Then Anna said, "Let's call up the country club and see if they'll accept it." She called and said she wanted to make an appointment to look at the facilities for a wedding reception, adding, "There will be a lot of gay people in the wedding party. Is that a problem?" The person got off the phone for a minute and then came back on and said, "No, that's not a problem." After we hung up, I said, "Maybe they think that we've got some gay friends, but that it's a man and a woman getting married." So Anna called them right back and said that the so-called bride and groom were two women and asked if that was a problem. "No, that's not a problem." It's a very lavish place, and we went out there thinking, "Well, they're going to say that the dates aren't available." But they said the dates were fine, and they even tried to convince us to have the actual wedding there in the garden. We just couldn't believe it. If gays and lesbians would just try things, there are a lot more options open than one might think.

I got more and more confident as the process went on. Different companies would send you promotional items if you wrote and told them that you were going to be a new bride. Generally what they asked for was a copy of your invitation, which of course had our two names on it. I sent one to Lipton, and they sent us all of this food with a little cover letter, "To the new bride . . . "

Once things really started coming together, it couldn't have been any better, especially the day itself. It was literally the best day of my life. The actual ceremony was a nondenominational Christian ceremony in the Metropolitan Community Church. Anna walked in first with the minister. They were followed by the wedding party, all very traditional. My sister came down right before me, and then I did the traditional walk. I didn't want to be given away by anyone, so I walked down alone. We didn't have the traditional wedding music, but we picked out some music with the organist. I even wore a blusher, or veil, which I wasn't going to wear until they put one on me at the bridal store. To be honest, I can't stand the concept of it, but it looked so cute, and I thought, "What the hell, I've gone this far."

The ceremony was based on a standard wedding ceremony, except our vows were identical to each other's. We had also picked out our scripture. I picked out something that said not to be judgmental: Don't take the splinter out of someone else's eye until you get the log out of your own. We took communion and offered communion to everybody there. I felt that that was a nice way to include all of the guests and the wedding party. About half of the people took it, and at least three or four people who were Catholic told me that that had been the first time they had taken communion in at least ten years. It was really very powerful.

Of course there were the rings, too. We had bought the wedding rings in Germany. Anna had wanted to get me a diamond, but in Germany most of the rings just have tiny diamond chips in them, and many people don't get diamonds at all because they're considered to be American and gaudy. So we got standard matching wedding bands. Unbeknownst to me, however, Anna had gone out with my mother and bought a very nice diamond. Before we exchanged the rings, they had us hold the rings up while they blessed them, and there was Anna with this beautiful diamond ring that I hadn't known anything about.

We ended up having a wonderful time at the reception, too. Usually after weddings, everybody leaves pretty early. Well, our reception lasted until they kicked us out at two in the morning. It was just a wonderful experience. We had probably forty lesbians, twenty-five gay men, and the rest were a smattering of straight people. We had the disc jockey from the lesbian bar in Detroit doing the music, and it was great. Everybody danced with everybody; it was incredibly high-spirited. The people at the country club also turned out to be wonderful, especially the waitresses. We asked some of them if they had known this was going to be a gay wedding, and they said that they had been told just before we arrived. A couple of them said that they had been scared and hadn't really known what to expect, but then as soon as we got there everything was fine. In fact the country club manager came and offered a toast to us.

The wedding ended up having a profound effect on our relationship. Among other things, it had a big effect on our sexual relationship. That was something that neither of us had anticipated at all. Sex was immediately better for me. From that day onward, it's been so much deeper and closer and spontaneous. It was like I woke up in a different body.

I think the wedding changed the relationship much more than either of us anticipated. It definitely made us more committed. Even up until the day of the wedding, I sometimes thought, "Well, I could walk out of here, and yes, it would be tough, but I wouldn't be breaking a commitment." I now feel that I've made a promise, and when I promise to do something, I do it. I had nine months to think every day about that promise, and I still decided to make it. I'm going to put every effort that I can into making this relationship work. I will be honest, I will be open, and if we need to, we will go into intensive psychotherapy in order to save the relationship. Anna is the most important part of my life, period. I don't think, "We'll try, and if it doesn't work, it doesn't work." I think, "We'll try, and somehow we'll find a way to make it work."

*This account is based on interviews with Anna and Deborah.*

ð

*Anna:* I have a Ph.D. in linguistics, and I teach at a nearby university. Presently thirty-two years old, I have been a lesbian since birth and am very pro-woman. I am into all sports, especially weights, and am very comfortable with myself. I feel that I am just now coming into my own professionally.

*Deborah:* I am thirty-five years old and a civil rights attorney. I am very happy being with Anna and am currently learning how to relax and feel centered. Anna and I are both strongly feminist, much more so than we may appear in the story of our ceremony.

*Linda*

*&*

*Susan*

*January 4, 1989* ❧ *Rural South*

# The Commitment Trail

*Linda:* It all began twelve years ago. My brother was getting married, and my sister and I were arranging the reception for him. She and I were checking one of the tables to make sure everything was all right, and I looked up and saw Susan walk through the door. I fell in love with her right then and there, the first moment I saw her. I knew she was the love of my life. I was too shy to say anything, though, so I didn't even ask her name. After the reception was over and things kind of settled down, I described Susan to my sister-in-law, Jackie, and I asked her who she was. Jackie said her name was Susan, but she didn't tell me her last name, and of course I was too embarrassed to ask.

During the next couple of years, every time I saw Jackie, I would ask "How is Susan?" She'd say she was fine, but she also told me that Susan was in a committed relationship with another woman. I didn't want to step into that, but yet I was still in love with her. I knew I just had to wait. At that point I was married and had three kids, but I knew that someday Susan would come to me, and I knew that when she did I would leave my husband and be with her. I still don't know how I knew she would come to me, but I knew. There was no doubt in my mind. But meanwhile she was living a couple of hundred miles away, and I didn't even know her last name.

Then, about two years after the wedding, my brother had to have open-heart surgery, and I went to wait at the hospital with Jackie. Who else should arrive but Susan and her lover, who had also come to keep Jackie company. I was still too shy to say anything. They asked me to play a game of backgammon. I knew how to play, but I said I didn't because I was afraid I'd do something stupid during the game and Susan would think I was dumb. So I just sat there and looked at her the whole time and didn't say anything.

*Susan:* I think Linda was so shy because she was afraid that I'd think she was just some country bumpkin, and I wouldn't be attracted to her. A lot of that's because Linda didn't finish high school, and I have a college education and have traveled more than she has. So she perceived me as this really intellectual worldly being, which is kind of a joke. At the same time, she didn't perceive herself as a well-educated person, which is as far from the truth as you can get, because Linda is an extraordinarily bright and extremely talented individual. I never cease to be amazed at the things that she can do, and has done, in her life. She was a nurse for fifteen years, is a very skilled carpenter, has built her own house, and now she's a well-known artist. She's very, very talented, and I'm very, very fortunate to be with her. But at the time she was too shy even to play backgammon with me.

*Linda:* Well, anyway, about ten more years passed, and every time I saw Jackie I would ask how Susan was. Jackie would always say she was fine, but what she never told me was that Susan wasn't with that other woman anymore. Then my brother had to have open-heart surgery again, and when I went to the hospital to be with Jackie, there was Susan. I was still really shy, and the waiting room was really big, so I sat in one part of the waiting room behind a potted palm, so I could look at Susan without her knowing that I was staring at her. Two or three days after that I asked Jackie, "Would you tell Susan that I would like to be her friend?" She said she would. Then two or three months later I mentioned it again. Jackie said, "Well, I'm sure she'd like to be friends with you, and I'll let you tell her yourself, because she's going to move up here." I was just astounded. Jackie told me that Susan had taken a job twenty minutes from where I lived.

*Susan:* You can imagine Linda trying to act real calm, cool and collected with her sister-in-law and brother while her little heart was beating ninety miles an hour.

*Linda:* It really was beating that fast. I loved her the first time I ever saw her, and here she was getting ready to move practically up the road from me.

*Susan:* I went ahead and took this new job, and before I moved up here, I called Linda to ask her if she'd take me around and introduce me to some people in the area. She, of course, was delighted to do that. I knew that Linda was an artist, so I guess I was expecting to travel around and meet some of the other local artists, but when I pulled up to her house, Linda came out all dressed up and took me to a really nice place for lunch. She did introduce me to one person, but she really wasn't much interested in introducing me to other people.

At some point during that first day, Linda shared with me that even though she was still married, she was a lesbian. Of course, when I moved up to the mountains, the last thing I expected to do was to find Ms. Right. And when I first met Linda, I certainly didn't think she was Ms. Right; she was on the tail end of a relationship with a woman, she was still married to her husband and she had three kids. I had been in relationships before with married or otherwise committed women, and I had said I would never do that again. I told Linda that; I told myself that; I told all my friends that. I was bound and determined not to put myself in that position again. But, of course, during that summer, I did put myself in that position again. During the two months before I moved up here, I came up every chance I got. I sent Linda little presents via her brother, and we had long telephone conversations.

I could tell that Linda wanted to be with me, and I felt like I wanted to be with her, but I didn't want all that excess baggage she was carrying. And, of course, she wasn't prepared to give it up until I was ready to make a commitment, which I was afraid of doing. Getting out of my last relationship was one of the most painful things I had ever experienced, and I knew that when I made a commitment again, that was going to be it. I never wanted to go through such a separation again.

So Linda and I started out by making commitments for four days at a time. Then we got up to a week, and then two weeks. And then one night, when we were watching a movie on TV, I just knew all of a sudden that this was the woman I wanted to be with. In the midst of munching popcorn, I turned to this woman who had been chasing me, blatantly chasing me, for four or five months, and I said, "Will you marry me?"

Well, after all of this chasing, she couldn't answer me! I understand now that she couldn't just say "yes." She was still married, and saying yes to me would mean changing a lot of things in her life. But, of course, a little later she did say yes.

A couple of weeks after that, we were walking out on the property where I work. There's a beautiful trail there that's all grown over with mountain laurel and rhododendron, with a tiny little stream that runs beside it. It's a very serene, peaceful, beautiful place. We had been talking for several days about making a long-term commitment, and while we were walking along the trail, we just spontaneously decided to stop then and there and actually make the commitment. So we call that trail our Commitment Trail, because it was there that we stopped and shared with each other what our commitment meant for us, what we wanted to do for each other and what we wanted from each other.

For me, making the commitment meant that I had found my lifetime mate and that there weren't any back doors. It was a relationship in which we would work through whatever came up. There would be no giving up and walking away. We also talked about what things were essential to us in a relationship: things like honesty, a sense of nurturing, fun and caring.

*Linda:* We wanted to be forthright with each other and tell each other our feelings directly and honestly, without being pouty with each other. That was one of the things that we decided right away: that we wouldn't make each other play guessing games about our feelings. I think that was the most important part for me. It meant a total sharing. It meant that if I had a bad feeling, or if something didn't go right, then right then and there, or as quick as I could, I would let Susan know that something was bothering me. No secrets. No hiding of feelings. I had never been totally honest with a lover before; there had always been feelings that I just kept inside of myself. In this relationship, we would take care of things right away instead of having to deal with them later on.

*Susan:* And we promised each other we would never go to bed angry without dealing with it and that we would be faithful to each other. Both of us knew that we couldn't live in a relationship in which we weren't physically faithful to each other, as well as emotionally and spiritually faithful. The spiritual component of our relationship is very important to both of us.

So we made our real commitment in the fall, towards the end of September. Linda began proceedings for her divorce, and I finally got to move into our home in December. After we were living together, we decided we wanted to formalize our relationship. We had been told by a friend that January 4 was the New Year for the New Age, kind of a spiritual new year. So we picked January 4 to be our wedding day, and on that day we again shared our vows with each other. It was just the two of us, and we did much the same thing as we had done on the Commitment Trail: made vows of honesty, trust, nurturing and fidelity. We did it all again because when we'd been on the Commitment Trail, Linda had still been with her husband, and we wanted to say our vows again once we were actually living together, with the slate cleared. So we recommitted to each other, and we chose January 4 as our anniversary date.

*Linda:* I was worried for a while about how people around here would react to Susan and me getting together. We live in the same town that I grew up in, and it's a very small town up in the mountains. I think I'm the only woman from here that has ever openly come out and said, "I'm gay." It's not like I ever walked outside and yelled it up the street, though my husband did. But when Susan and I moved in together, I didn't try to hide what was going on. I didn't know what to expect from the community; it's hard to know how people will react when you're one of their own. As it turned out, everybody was really accepting. Several of my straight friends called up and said, "I very much admire what you're doing. I don't know if I would have the courage that you have." My kids have been great about it, too. They had just thought that I had been acting weird, so I think it was kind of a relief to them when I said I was a lesbian. It got everything out in the open. I think it gives you a lot of strength when you tell the truth, and I think my kids know that.

Things have just worked out really well. I used to spend so much time thinking about Susan, and hoping, and I used to envision her here in this house. I used to envision us both here together, and sometimes I notice that something will happen just exactly like I had envisioned it; exactly, with each of us doing what I had seen us doing in those fantasies.

*Susan:* I guess the bottom line of the story is that Linda saw me "across a crowded room," and waited twelve years for us to get together. And now our love just seems to get stronger and stronger. We believe we have a very long future together, and we're looking forward to it. We'll be sitting on that front porch in those rocking chairs many, many years from now.

*This account is based on interviews with Linda and Susan.*

ᕽᕽ

*Linda: Linda is a woman in her forties who has spent her entire life in Appalachia. She is an artist and a woodcarver.*

*Susan: Susan is forty-plus, was raised on the coast, loves the sea and is greatly affected by the tides. She is most happy in the out of doors and loves animals, skiing and scuba diving.*

# Marion Hansell

## & Barbara Hicks

Marion (left) & Barbara (right)
photographer: Photo-Decor

## June 4, 1988 ❧ Australia

# A Gift of Love

When Barbara and I first met, I had no idea that my life would be dramatically changed. I was working as a nursing unit manager in a palliative care unit. Barbara was hired as the social worker. On Barb's first day, we eyed each other up and down, and as the days and weeks passed, we developed a great professional respect for one another. I wanted to get to know this lady better.

Barb was living on her own and had not had a relationship for some months prior to our meeting. I was living with two other women, one of whom I had shared a home with for nearly ten years. The three of us were close friends and were deeply involved with the Evangelical Church.

I had known I was "different" by the time I was in high school, but it wasn't until my twenty-first year that I realized I was a lesbian. The Church's teachings were very strongly against homosexuality, and I denied my sexuality, locking it away in a cupboard. Barb had had a similar background, but had moved beyond this point. She had come to feel loved before God, accepted as a woman loving a woman.

It was with this background that Barb invited me to dinner. Barb had prepared enough food to feed an army, and I ate only one potato! We talked. We shared our lives. I was amazed at how easily we opened up to each other. I didn't consciously know that Barbara was a lesbian, and it was both a shock and a great relief when she told me.

That was the beginning of our life together, and it was twelve months (to the day) from that first evening that we made our public commitment to one another. I wanted a public commitment because I wished to live our lives to the fullest, openly and honestly. I wanted to stand beside Barb as her partner, and I wanted to do this in the presence of friends and relatives. In making such a declaration, I lost old friends but gained new ones.

My commitment with Barbara is a commitment for life. It is something we work at daily, just as daily I give thanks for our love and our life together.

—*Marion Hansell*

ès

Marion and I decided to have a ceremony for a number of reasons. For Marion, it was because she had hidden away, denied even, her sexuality for over twenty years. After much soul-searching, she had reached a point of being able to rest in the knowledge that she was still worthy, lovable and precious in the eyes of God. Having come out, she felt good and whole about being who she was, and she wanted to make a public declaration of this fact. Second, we both wanted to share our deep joy and happiness with others. We also wanted to ask our friends to be willing to help us should we ever get into strife and need counseling or deep caring and understanding.

I felt an inner certainty that this relationship would be long-term; hopefully, "'til death do us part." By making a public statement of my love and commitment to Marion, I was saying to others, and, perhaps more important, to myself, that this was no flash in the pan, short-term affair: Marion would not be dumped by me when things became difficult. I had had several relationships of short standing over the past ten years, but I had never lived in a relationship with another person, never shared my life with another. In joining my life with Marion's, I was sure I was doing something I needed to do in order to develop further as a person, and I thought that Marion probably also needed me in order to develop untapped potential in herself. The ceremony, and the commitment that came with it, was not a step we took lightly: we only did it once we were quite sure we had the basis for a long-term, loving relationship. We courted for twelve months and had the ceremony on the anniversary of our coming together as lovers.

The ceremony itself was intimate, sincere, friendly, warm, affirming, informal and, apparently for those watching, very moving. We were living in a small flat, and over thirty people crowded in to share the half-hour ceremony with us. They came early for drinks and nibbles and then came as our guests to a Vietnamese banquet afterwards. Marion and I left during the evening to catch a ferry across Sydney harbor to a beach-side suburb called Manly where we had a late supper in a big international, beach-front hotel.

Gathered for the ceremony and banquet were work colleagues, friends and a member of Marion's family. None of our parents were present. Marion's were not there because they could not emotionally handle our relationship; mine were unable to make the journey but sent a card that they asked to be read during the ceremony. There were heterosexual couples, gay female couples, divorcées, lovers, three children and one single gay male. The youngest there was ten, and the eldest was a woman in her seventies.

The ceremony was a combination of Anglican church service and New Age philosophy. We wanted an ordained minister to bless us and our relationship, and we wanted friends to be present and to later share what we called a Love Feast. We exchanged vows and rings using words that we scripted ourselves. The essence of what we said was that we believed we needed each other in order to grow and develop. We said that we expected to stay together for as long as it was fruitful to do so. When it ceases to be fruitful, and efforts to make it fruitful have failed, then we expect to separate; we hope, amicably. We did not want to make vows or oaths of allegiance to each other that would tie us into a situation that could become detrimental to our growth, either as individuals or as a couple. We plan to celebrate our anniversary each year and to make that a time to review our relationship, its goals and the manner and means by which we are achieving those goals.

I was raised in the Anglican faith and, after several years in charismatic communities, left the Church when I was thirty. Marion converted to Christianity as an adult, and it was Christian attitudes, in part, that prevented her from acknowledging her sexuality until recently. Both Marion and I have strong, if somewhat different, spiritual beliefs. A recognition of our spirituality and of the existence of spiritual forces working in our lives and in our relationship was an important component of our ceremony.

In much of this, our ceremony and celebration might not differ from heterosexual marriage ceremonies today, at least from those that are modern and based on equal relationships. There were, however, some major areas of difference. One was that we were selective about whom we invited; we knew that some people would not cope well with such an event. For most heterosexual couples, it would be expected that all friends and relatives would be invited and would come joyfully and expectantly. This is often not the case for lesbian couples. I have experienced persecution and discrimination from my employer because of my sexuality, and Marion has met rejection and ostracism from the Church that previously called her a friend.

It will remain a grief to me that none of my family was present at our ceremony. My parents have been marvelous in accepting my sexuality, despite my fears that they would not be able to cope with it. One sister, here in Australia, had known of our relationship only for a short while when we had our ceremony. Against all my expectations, she coped very well with learning about the relationship. However, when I invited her to the ceremony, she declined for reasons I felt would not have been given had I been getting married in a conventional way to a man.

Another difference from a heterosexual marriage was that we did it all ourselves. There was no doting mother to help with the outfits or make a wedding cake; no bridesmaids; no gifts from family, and no honeymoon. We had one friend who helped in any way we asked, and she and her two sons took part in the ceremony, reading selected verses and holding the rings. She also acted as hostess at the banquet and arranged the bill after we left.

Friends expected us to go away for the night to a hotel or motel. We felt we could not justify the expense. Our relationship is wonderful, and we try to make our leisure time quality time, so every day is something like a honeymoon. We give thanks daily for each other, for the gift of love and for the relationship.

*—Barbara Hicks*

## The Ceremony

*Reading*: I Corinthians 13:1–13

*Marion:* Barbara, it is without fear or shame that I stand with you before our friends, declaring my love for you and my need of you.

Barb, I open my hands to you as a symbol of what I offer you:
Freedom, not possession;
Openness, not restriction;
Honesty, fidelity, warmth and gentleness; acceptance and respect.

Friends, by your presence with us this evening, you show love and acceptance of us and good wishes for us. I am delighted to share this momentous occasion with you and ask: will you rejoice with us in the good times and assist us in the rough times?

Barbara, I have chosen to love you and give myself to you. In this love I desire to serve you and to encourage you in your spiritual growth and devotion. I will contribute to the atmosphere of our relationship that allows you freedom and room for personal growth.

I desire that we maintain the quality of relationship that we now enjoy, and if that quality should begin to deteriorate, that I should seek assistance to resolve the cause of that deterioration.

*Reading*: From *A Sleep of Prisoners* by Christopher Fry

*Barbara:* Thank you all for coming to share this occasion with us.

I want to share with you that I love Marion and have great respect for her. I am blessed with the gift of our relationship and feel a responsibility to nurture and foster its development. We have come together to fulfill a task in the world that could not be achieved if we remained separate. We have joint and separate tasks needing others' support and encouragement; others as in you.

To love Marion and to be loved by her is essential to my present and future development.

I say *Yes* to the opportunity to make my life into the future with Marion. I hope we will work side by side for many years to come; living and loving the questions; knowing that the exploration is into God.

I intend to love, cherish and nurture Marion; to encourage, foster and support her free development—the development of her inner potential: intellectual, emotional and spiritual.

Marion, I have no claims on your love. You are a free spirit to be and do what you are destined for.

I intend in times of conflict to communicate the difficulties to you and to own my part in them so that together we may problem-solve and resolve any conflicts. If necessary I will seek the help of friends or counselors.

I am committed to our development—individually and together.

*Reading by Marion and Barbara in unison*: From *Making Contact* by Virginia Satir

*Exchange of Rings*
*Marion:* Barbara, I give you this ring so that you may choose to wear it and in so doing be reminded and re-experience my deep love and regard for you.

*Barbara:* Marion, I give you this ring: a dolphin ring—a symbol of health and right relationships between people as well as between humans and the creatures and all creation. A ring, I hope, of healing and joy.

I give it to you so that you may choose to wear it and in so doing be reminded and know my deep love and regard for you and my wish that you may have a long life and a beautifully rich and creative one.

*Marion:* I will wear this love gift with honor and joy as a sign to others that I am committed to our union.

At this point guests were invited to speak. About eight spoke of their regard for us, of their understanding and appreciation of our relationship, and of their wish that we have a long and happy relationship.

This was followed by an address by the Anglican minister we had invited to help us with our ceremony. Gay himself, he spoke of the way in which any relationship of love is one that is inherently of God as well.

*A Jewish Blessing*—given by Father John
    The Mother's Sabbath Prayer (adapted slightly)

    May the Lord protect and defend you.
    May he always shield you from shame.
    May you come to be in paradise a shining name.
    May you be like Ruth and like Esther.
    May you be deserving of praise.
    Strengthen them, O Lord, and keep them from all dangerous ways.
    May God bless you and grant you long life.
    May God make you good partners for life.
    May the Lord protect and defend you.
    May the Lord preserve you from pain.
    Favor them, O Lord, with happiness and peace.
    Oh hear our Sabbath prayer. Amen.

*Reading by Marion and Barbara*
"Song of Songs" from the Song of Solomon 4: 1 through 5: 1

*Marion:* Behold you are beautiful, my love, behold you are beautiful!
    Your eyes are doves behind your veil.
    Your hair is like a flock of goats, moving down the slopes of Gilead.
    Your teeth are like a flock of shorn ewes that have come up from the
        washing, all of which bear twins, and not one among them is
        bereaved.
    Your lips are like a scarlet thread, and your mouth is lovely.

*Barbara:* Your cheeks are like halves of a pomegranate behind your veil.
    Your neck is like the tower of David, built for an arsenal, whereon
        hang a thousand bucklers, all of them shields of warriors.
    Your two breasts are like two fawns, twins of a gazelle, that feed
        among the lilies.

*Marion:* Until the day breathes and the shadows flee, I will hie me to the mountain of myrrh and the hill of frankincense.

You are all fair, my love; there is no flaw in you.

*Barbara:* Come with me from Lebanon, my bride; come with me from Lebanon.

Depart from the peak of Amana, from the peak of Senir and Hermon, from the dens of lions, from the mountains of leopards.

You have ravished my heart, my sister, my bride; you have ravished my heart with a glance of your eyes, with one jewel of your necklace.

*Marion:* How sweet is your love, my sister, my bride! How much better is your love than wine, and the fragrance of your oils than any spice!

Your lips distill nectar, my bride; honey and milk are under your tongue; the scent of your garments is like the scent of Lebanon.

*Barbara:* A garden locked is my sister, my bride; a garden locked, a fountain sealed.

Your shoots are an orchard of pomegranates with all choicest fruits, henna with nard, nard and saffron, calamus and cinnamon, with all trees of frankincense, myrrh and aloes, with all chief spices—a garden fountain, a well of living water, and flowing streams from Lebanon.

*Together:* Awake, O north wind, and come, O south wind! Blow upon my garden.

Let its fragrance be wafted abroad. Let my beloved come to her garden and eat its choicest fruits. I come to my garden, my sister, my bride, I gather my myrrh with my spice, I eat my honeycomb with honey, I drink my wine with milk.

*All:* Eat, O friends, and drink; drink deeply, O lovers!

≥●

*Marion Hansell: I come from a large family. I am the last of five children and am the fourth daughter. I was educated to the age of seventeen and then started nursing, which I have done for twenty years. I was thirty-five when Barb and I met and I declared my sexuality. Since then, I have found a church that loves and accepts me as I am. The response from my family has been mixed: my mother finds it very hard to accept that I am committed to another woman. We don't see much of each other. Barb's parents, though, have been very accepting and loving.*

*Barbara Hicks: The middle child of seven, I was born in the United Kingdom and immigrated to Australia in 1972. Of my siblings, I am the only one in a same-sex marriage and the only one without children. I was trained as a social worker and feel as though I'm also a frustrated, or perhaps unadventurous, Greenie politician. I feel strongly about injustice, corruption and pollution. I am an enthusiastic social developer who also loves gardening, bushwalking and camping. Because I am scared of people, my work is painful for me, but essential if I am not to become a recluse or hermit.*

# Eleanor Soto

## & Yvonne Yarbro-Bejarano

Yvonne (left) & Eleanor (right)

*March 17, 1990* ❧ *California*

# An Affirmation of Community

*Eleanor:* Yvonne and I met in September 1987 at a slide show about Asian lesbians. I had gone with a friend of mine who is a straight Asian woman. At the time, I was dealing with the death of my mother, and I was also trying to resolve and let go of past relationships. I was single and was feeling very protective towards myself. I had a lot of distrust at the time.

*Yvonne:* I had gone to the slide show with a Japanese-Hawaiian friend. I was also going through a hard time. My lover and I had gone down to the Bay Area from Seattle for a year's sabbatical to write a book together and then had broken up a week after we got there. That was about a month before the slide show, and it was still very present for me.

That night, the woman I was with introduced me to Eleanor. I remember feeling very attracted to her and thinking that she was really cute, but I thought she was coupled with the friend she was with.

*Eleanor:* And I thought that Yvonne was dating my friend and that I shouldn't interfere. But I remember checking her out and feeling that there was some attraction or interest in her eyes.

At the time we met, we didn't realize that we were both planning to go to the Encuentro of Latina lesbians that was going to take place in Cuernavaca, Mexico, in October. I had gotten together with a group of friends and was going to go to the Encuentro and then go to the Yucatan; my friends had already rented a house on the beach near Cancun.

*Yvonne:* For me, going to the Encuentro was part of putting myself back together after the break-up. I had been brought out by my ex-lover, so I was working on creating a lesbian identity on my own. I was also trying to make more connections with my Latina lesbian self and make connections with other Chicanas and Latinas. My ex-lover was white, and when I was with her, it had never occurred to me to go to this conference. The decision to go was part of healing myself and affirming myself as a Chicana lesbian.

*Eleanor:* In Mexico, my friends and I had waited for several hours for the bus from Mexico City to Cuernavaca, and had then traveled several more hours. The bus driver had gotten lost and made several phone calls at gas stations. We were a little dubious about this guy's ability, but we finally arrived. We were hungry and tired and weren't really sure where we were

160

going to sleep that night. The first person I ran into as I was heading out into the kitchen was my ex-lover, whom I wasn't very happy to see. Then, as I backed out of the kitchen, I nearly ran into Yvonne. I remembered her as a woman I had been attracted to, but I couldn't remember where or how we had connected.

*Yvonne:* I immediately recognized Eleanor. Right from the start, I was pleased by the way we communicated. It just seemed like we cut through a lot of crap real fast. We had very meaningful conversations and were very open with each other.

At the time, I was sort of a baby dyke; I didn't really know what moves to make or how things were being interpreted. I was trying to flirt and trying to make my intentions known, but I was having trouble reading Eleanor's signals. We managed to clear things up fairly well, though, because we got together at the end of that week.

*Eleanor:* We got together on the last night of the last day. It had been kind of a wild week; hardly any of the women at the conference had ever been around so many other Latinas, much less around so many other Latina lesbians. There was a heck of a lot of flirting, and a lot of people were totally high from the experience. We had to cut through a lot of that to determine that our intentions were longer-lasting than just flirting at the Encuentro.

I mentioned to Yvonne that my friends were going to take a trip afterwards, but she kept saying that she was going to stay in Mexico City and go to this feminist Latina conference. I was kind of bummed that she wasn't considering traveling with us.

*Yvonne:* Of course, I had asked her if she'd like to travel around with me after the conference, and she had said that she was going to the Yucatan to spend a week in this house they had rented. So I said, "Well, I guess I'll have to go to this feminist conference," hint, hint. I was waiting for an invitation, which finally came at the end of the week.

*Eleanor:* We did go to the Yucatan together. There were times when I felt very open and really felt that I was falling in love with Yvonne. Then every critical part of me would come out and I would step back again. I just couldn't completely trust that this wasn't some deep plot to hurt me. I ended up doing some really important work around trusting and letting go.

*Yvonne:* We kept seeing each other after we got back to the Bay Area. We spent quite a lot of time together during the rest of October, November and December. In February, we broke up for two days, mostly because we had come into the relationship with different expectations. I felt that I still needed more time to heal after the separation from my ex-lover, so I wanted the relationship to be open-ended. Eleanor, however, wanted to know where things stood and wanted to know if we had a commitment.

*Eleanor:* I had come out of a relationship in which things had been open-ended for two years, so I wanted to have this one clearly defined. One of my "nevers" was that I was never going to be involved with someone who couldn't make a commitment to me. During the short break-up with Yvonne, we talked several times on the phone and came to an agreement about commitment and also about needing to explore our relationship more slowly.

*Yvonne:* I've had a pattern of burying my own needs in relationships, so it was really important for me to express to Eleanor what I needed, even if it meant hurting or angering her. It was interesting to me that once I was able to express that I needed more space, I realized that I did feel really strongly about our relationship. I considered us partners, and I missed her in my life.

*Eleanor:* The other thing that was happening at the time was that Yvonne was going to leave for two months at the beginning of May, so I felt a pressure to know what was going on with us.

*Yvonne:* I had made plans to go to Berlin for two months, which I went ahead with. Eleanor came to see me for two weeks while I was there, and we also ran up a huge phone bill. It was around then that we started talking about whether she should move up to Seattle when I returned to my job in the fall. That was a real struggle. We went back and forth about it quite a bit. First, I wrestled with whether I was ready. One day after I had returned from Berlin, I called Eleanor and said that I did want her to move up here to be with me. She freaked out and started backing off, but we continued to work that through over the summer, and in October she moved to Seattle. I think that was a major testing ground for our relationship; I think any time one partner moves for the other, all kinds of issues come up.

*Eleanor:* I didn't want to be "the replacement." Yvonne had left with one lover and was coming back with another. I didn't want just to fill in the blanks of her life.

*Yvonne:* We had lots of discussions during which we gradually worked through some of our issues. That's when the consideration of getting married came up. The actual proposal came from me, which I think was important. Eleanor had already manifested her commitment to the relationship by leaving her life in San Francisco. It was important that I showed my commitment by proposing, which I did on the freeway. We were coming back from a trip, and Eleanor's mouth was open for about fifteen miles. She made me repeat the proposal at home, in a proper setting, so she could say yes.

*Eleanor:* After Yvonne asked me, I spent several months backing off. A lot of times, when I'm trying to convince her of something, I'm not really aware of my own fears and anxieties. Then, when she accepts, I suddenly have to work through all of my own issues. We spent quite a while talking about it, screaming about it, having serious discussions and joking discussions, and thinking about what it would mean to us and how we actually wanted to do it.

*Yvonne:* I think one of the anchors dragging on me during this process was stuff around my mother. I had come out to her in the fall of 1986, when I was in the relationship with this other woman. It was a struggle and very traumatic. Right before I had gone down to the Bay Area for the sabbatical, she had finally accepted my partner and me as a couple. I had made a point of keeping her informed while I was on sabbatical and told her about meeting Eleanor. I told her that we were consolidating our relationship and that Eleanor was going to move to Seattle, but my mother was still in denial about it. Part of this was because she had gotten married in the interim, and she was very much in the closet about me to her new husband.

When I realized that having to deal with my mother was making me reluctant to have a ceremony, I came to the decision that she didn't have to be involved. At first, this was a great relief. Then, as we got within a couple of months of the date we'd set, I started to feel very uncomfortable about not telling her; it felt like I was in the closet again. Why had I bothered coming out to her in the first place if I wasn't going to share this with her? Finally, I did tell her, and it wasn't pretty. She didn't understand why we had to do this public thing. I told her that I was upset about how she felt and that I didn't want to talk with her or see her until after the wedding. It has been a long slow process since then, but we have recently begun talking very openly, which is new for us. During our last conversation, she made it very clear that she has accepted me and accepted Eleanor in my life, and that she understands what we mean to each other. She is seventy-five years old and traditionally Mexican, and I think she just couldn't deal with this unconventional gesture.

My younger sister and I also had quite a heavy time for a while and had to deal with some of our old sibling stuff. It was remarkable for me to see that when you make the decision to have a same-sex wedding, it brings up all kinds of things, especially for yourself and for your family. Your life changes and the world changes.

*Eleanor:* For me, the process of getting married made me realize that even though I had been out in my jobs, there's a big difference between people knowing that I'm a lesbian and involved with Yvonne and people really acknowledging it. Having a same-sex wedding is a political move; people can somehow ignore your relationship with another woman, but when you really say that you want to make this commitment, it zings a lot of peoples' reality recorders. They just can't deal with it. And that's what happened with many people I knew; they just had to deal with their own stuff around it. And I had to deal with *my* own stuff around it. It was another level of coming out for me.

In terms of my own family, I had come out to my two sisters at different times. I have a pretty close relationship with my younger sister, and I told her immediately and invited her to come to the wedding. My father and I don't have a very good relationship. It's cordial at this point, but I wouldn't say that it's open. My strongest connection was with my mother. I never really said, "Mom, I'm a lesbian," but I think she understood. She was very open and loving. I'm still sorry that Yvonne never met her and vice versa. It would have been a nice connection.

*Yvonne:* Neither of our mothers were at the ceremony. My sister and Eleanor's sisters came, and as part of the ceremony, we mentioned the absences: the absences because of death and because of other barriers.

We decided to hold the ceremony in the Bay Area, and our friends, Trinity and Des, offered their house. We had also decided that we wanted Cherríe, a Chicana friend of ours, to officiate. It was sort of astonishing when we sat down with Cherríe and started putting it together, because we realized just how special it was going to be. Cherríe came up with some very beautiful ritual elements. She commented that as Chicanas, we live in the borders of so many racial and cultural identities. Ceremonies and rituals become a mix of different things; sometimes we ground ourselves in Indian cultures and rituals, sometimes in Catholicism and sometimes in Anglo-American culture.

From Mexican tradition, we had a home altar for the ceremony, covered with cloth and candles and flowers. The ceremony began with us entering to music played on pre-Columbian instruments. Then we burned incense and had the invocation of the ancestors, especially the mothers. After the invocation, we took turns speaking about ourselves and about what we brought to the relationship.

*Eleanor:* I said that I was a mixture of everything that had come into me, including the influence of my mother, the influence of my culture, the work that I do, the corny jokes that I crack and my old dog who has been with me for twelve years. I talked about choosing to work in the community as someone who supports and heals and empowers people to make changes in their lives.

I tried to say all that in a very condensed form. I was scared and anxious, and I was amazed that everything felt so special and sacred. There were fifteen of our friends sitting around us, all looking very bright and loving, and there was this beautiful altar, and there was this beautiful woman standing there, waiting for me to make a commitment to her. I just kind of swallowed a lot of my thoughts. I was just in love at that moment.

*Yvonne:* I, of course, had written everything out and memorized it compulsively. I talked about loving women, about being a mixed-race woman, about being a sister and an aunt, about my professional commitment to being a teacher and a writer, and about my feminism and my commitment to making changes in the world for women of color. Then I said that what I brought to Eleanor was my love, which was very strong and very loyal, and I also brought a desire to respect Eleanor as an individual human being with her own feelings and problems and joys. I didn't want a merger. Then I cracked a joke or two about the professorial air I have that Eleanor finds erotic.

At the end, I said that I also brought to the relationship a commitment to take care of myself; if I'm not true to myself, I can't be a good partner to Eleanor. If I am not supportive of myself and love myself, I can't really support her and love her the way she deserves to be loved.

There were three candles on the altar: one for each of us and one representing the relationship. While we talked about ourselves, we each lit our individual candle. Then our sisters gave us our rings, and as Eleanor and I gave them to each other, we talked about why we were getting married.

*Eleanor:* I was still enraptured and kept it pretty short:

> For me, the ring represents mi amor y mi carino, my love and care, that I have for you, and my respect and dedication que tengo para ti. I want to make these feelings, the love and commitment, public. I want to celebrate the discovery of this joy in my relationship with you with the group of people here. I want to honor us and declare us a union, to declare us just us—who we are as a couple.

*Yvonne:* Then she almost broke my finger.

*Eleanor:* I was trying to put the ring on.

*Yvonne:* Then I talked about what having a ceremony meant to us and what commitment meant. There is a perception in the lesbian community that long-term relationships are very difficult, and I said that one thing we wanted to do was create and make public a perception of lasting commitment among lesbians. In that way, getting married is an important part of building lesbian community. I felt that there was a very strong political aspect to what we were doing. We weren't imitating an oppressive and sexist heterosexual institution; we were demanding the same rights and privileges of heterosexual couples. Our goal is not to imitate it but to transform it in progressive ways. If people continue to do this, maybe one day we'll also have the legal and economic privileges that go along with heterosexual marriage. I see getting married as part of the gay and lesbian movement. It really does make a difference. That difference was brought home to me very personally and powerfully as I saw how it brought things up for my family, sometimes in a very painful way. It has been, and continues to be, very important in clarifying who I am in my family and in the world. More personally, the bottom line of why I was getting married was the knowledge that Eleanor was the person I wanted to make a life with. To her, I said:

> I love you for who you are, not some ideal person I think you could be. I love your values, your passion, your feminism, your caring and commitment to the disenfranchised people in the world, your clarity, your sense of humor, your smarts and, of course, your smile and eyebrows.

(It was the eyebrows that I first noticed when I met her at that slide show.) Then I talked about the way we are together in bed, and kayaking, traveling, hanging out.

> I love it that we can speak Spanish together and share our individual experience of being Chicanas, even though they are very, very different, and I love the way that we talk about things and have talked about things from the beginning. And I think with you I am learning more than with anyone to talk about what is going on with me. Te quiero mi amor. This ring is a way of making my love and commitment to you concrete and public.

*Eleanor:* Then we kissed.

*Yvonne:* Cherríe had brought some clay from Chimayo, which is a shrine in New Mexico with healing powers. This clay is especially healing for women and women's ailments. She put a little of the clay in a goblet of water, so that all four elements were involved in the ceremony. She then asked people to take a sip and one by one say something about Eleanor and me—about our relationship and their commitment to supporting us in our marriage.

People said some really wonderful things. Several wrote wonderful poetry for us. Others talked about our relationship and how they perceived us. What was interesting was that three people said that they had been skeptical about a lesbian marriage, and that they'd had questions about why we were doing this. All three said that by being there and experiencing the ceremony, they really understood why we were doing it. They said that it meant a lot to them.

There was a very strong feeling of community at that point. It was as if we had created a real joining—a community event that was beyond just our relationship. There was a recognition of our relationships with each other, and of the importance of those relationships.

*Eleanor:* At the end of the comments from our friends, we lit the third candle. I said, "When we light this candle of our relationship, we light the room with our love y cariño and happiness."

*Yvonne:* The third candle was the "we" of the relationship, but the "we" did not subsume the "I." It was a statement that we needed to respect each other as individuals and not merge into one.

*Eleanor:* We both struck matches and lit the candle together, then we kissed. There was a huge sigh from the crowd, and our family and friends came up to congratulate us and to give us wonderful hugs. Trinity had prepared her sister's convertible with all the traditional banners and balloons and tin cans, and we drove around the Castro, honking horns. There was something wonderfully releasing in doing it publicly. It was both a personal and a public act of acknowledging our relationship and our commitment.

*Yvonne:* In all, the ceremony combined a lot of elements from different cultures. Going around in a circle and having everyone say something is Quaker. We used elements of Indian culture, and we had some the traditional things that are part of both Anglo-American culture and also Chicano culture: we had a traditional wedding cake with two love birds; we smashed the cake into each other's faces; we had a champagne toast with the ribbons on the glasses; and we danced together to the first song.

*Eleanor:* I think our friends were strongly affected by it. Most of them now feel a commitment to help us get through our hard times together and to help us remain together as a couple. Lesbians often don't get family support, and I think a commitment from friends to help keep you together is really important.

*Yvonne:* One of the most meaningful parts of the ceremony for me was listening to what our friends said as they each spoke. I'll never forget it. It wasn't just an affirmation of our relationship but also an affirmation of our friendships. I felt so blessed to have those friends. Since the ceremony, I've felt a real deepening of my bond with Eleanor, but what's surprised me is that I have also felt a deepening of the bonds with my friends. The whole event felt like building community.

*This account is based on audio recordings made by Eleanor Soto and Yvonne Yarbro-Bejarano.*

୬

*Eleanor Soto: I'm originally from Los Angeles. My mother is from Monterrey, Mexico. My dad is a Chicano who grew up in Chicago. On a visit to Mexico, he met my Mom. They were married in 1946 and came to the U.S. at that time. When I was growing up, we spent several summers in Mexico and once spent a year there as well. My early life was one of confusion about where I belonged: when I was in Mexico, I was a pocha for half the summer, then I was a regular norteña for the rest, and then when I came back to the U.S., I was always just a Mexican. I don't think I have ever been thoroughly accepted as, or ever completely felt like, a North American. I'm a social worker. I've worked in the fields of drug abuse, violence against women and children, and sexual/physical abuse recovery for about sixteen years. I have also been doing private practice part-time, working primarily with women. I work at a community public agency and do community education around racism and homophobia. I was involved with the National Coalition Against Domestic Violence for three years and was also involved with California Women of Color Against Domestic Violence. I'm thirty-nine years old and freaking out about forty.*

*Yvonne Yarbro-Bejarano: I was born October 10, 1947, in Oklahoma City. I am the daughter of a southern white man and a Mexican mother. My mother was born in Mexico and crossed the border into El Paso, Texas, with her family. When I was about eight months old, my mother and father moved to Seattle, where I grew up. I became Chicana-identified in the early seventies and began working in the field of Chicano literature, especially theatre and writing by Chicanas. For me, there is a political dimension to teaching and writing about the works of Chicanas and other women of color. I have taught Spanish language and literature, and comparative literature, at the University of Washington since 1974.*

*Sussi Gustafsson*

*&   Lena Isberg*

Lena (left) & Sussi (right)
photographer: Elisabet Hemgren

*September 1, 1985*  ❧  *Stockholm, Sweden*

# Head Over Heels

Sussi and I have been married since September 1985. We decided to get married very suddenly soon after we met. We both entered the relation ship with a desire for it to last a lifetime, and we wanted to have a ceremony to show that—in short, a wedding.

We had heard about people, that is, homosexuals, going to Denmark and Holland to get married, so we were thinking about hitchhiking to Denmark to try to find a church there, but neither of us was sure quite how to go about it. Then we went to EKHO here in Stockholm, a church organization for homosexuals. We asked somebody there what to do to get married. "Ask the lady over there," was the answer. We asked "the lady over there," who told us that there is no country in the whole world that allows marriage between two people of the same sex. Legally, that is.* The ceremonies we had heard of were not legally binding. That's when we decided that we might as well get married in Sweden, but we had to find somebody who would be willing to perform the ceremony for us. "I can do that," said "the lady over there." It turned out she was a priest. To get our "marriage" legally equivalent to those of heterosexuals, we made up a will, with each other as beneficiaries.

A few weeks later we were standing in front of the priest in a church and promising to love each other for better or worse and to be faithful, till death do us part. We had invited about a hundred guests and a flutist who played the hymn we had chosen, "In This Beautiful Summertime." We exchanged rings, and people threw rice (and alfalfa seeds) on us as we left. Camera flashes were blinding us; unfortunately there was no film in the camera. Sussi's whole family was present, as well as our friends from work and a whole bunch of lesbians. Several of those invited from the last category did not show up. They were mainly women I had had relationships with before I met Sussi. After I married they disappeared from my life, for some reason or other.

Of course, we were terribly nervous before the ceremony. I had never been that nervous in my whole life. We rode the subway to church together with the flutist. I had brought a bouquet of red roses, and one

---

*Editor's Note: Since this account was written, Denmark has legally recognized same-sex unions.

170

flower fell. "What the hell are you doing? Are you going to ruin them?" Sussi yelled. She was so nervous she didn't know what she was saying. We giggled. We did not wear wedding dresses because Sussi hates wearing dresses. We had run around town for a whole day before we eventually found her a pair of pointed pink shoes. For myself I bought a pair of Chinese moccasins that hurt the back of my foot. I wore Sussi's old tuxedo shirt, which I had colored purple, and a pair of new pink pants (on sale). Now I think the clothes we were wearing were awful.

In the morning we had showered, applied facials from the supermarket, blown up purple and pink balloons and made a cake that was constantly on the verge of collapsing (wedding cakes are not easy to make). I'd gotten so furious at the cake that I started throwing cake pieces on the floor, but Sussi saved it. We used a knitting needle to keep it together. We decorated the top with two brides made of construction paper. We had tried to find brides in plastic, but for some reason we did not manage to.

Sussi was very beautiful all day long, radiant. . . with her curly hair and blue eyes.

We didn't choose a church ceremony for religious reasons. Sussi is an atheist, and I am not a member of any church, though I have my own "homemade" religion. But I think that there is a certain special atmosphere in churches. It also felt important somehow to have a ceremony where several people were present: "In front of God and the community," so to speak. It was also the only ceremony we could think of that heterosexuals could understand. Married, we have received more understanding from heterosexuals than from lesbians. Somewhat surprising, but then life is surprising.

Our relationship is very comfortable and feels right. It was definitely a big step to get married. I think I had looked for a lifetime companion for many years but had not found the right one because I was not mature enough.

Of course, we don't know what it would be like if we were not married. But somehow our relationship feels special because of it. We have made a pact. We have been blessed. A hundred people wished us well. Those things are important.

One thing is for sure—if we had not married during our early passion, we would not have done it. We would simply not have dared. To stand up in front of a lot of people, to go and ask a priest, those are things you do when you are head over heels in love and capable of anything. At least if you are a lesbian.

—*Lena Isberg*
(*translated from Swedish by Rene Searles*)

ᷰ

*Sussi Gustafsson: I was born in 1960 under the sign of Scorpio and am currently working as a saleswoman in the building industry. My interests include my beloved wife, Lena, our dogs, our home, carpentry and sports.*

*Lena Isberg: I was born in 1955 under the sign of Capricorn and grew up in a working-class family. I have two occupations: I write (for the soul), and I work delivering mail (for the money). My favorite pastimes include being with Sussi and our dogs; spending time in nature; keeping our home pretty; looking after our hamster, aquarium and potted plants; reading; and living a healthy life. My goals in life are to get a house with a beautiful garden and to live on what I earn from writing.*

# Kilby Clark

## & Janet Osimo

Kilby (left) & Janet (right)

## May 19, 1984 ❧ California

# An Almost Traditional Catholic Wedding

*Janet:* Kilby and I got together in 1983, when I was twenty-four and Kilby was twenty. We had actually met in June 1980 and had been friends for three years before getting involved with each other. At that time we weren't out, either to the world or to ourselves.

*Kilby:* Both Janet and I had had similar previous relationships, relationships which we had considered "special friendships." Neither of us had really acknowledged that we were gay: we knew that we were in love with these other women, but we each thought we were just going through a phase.

*Janet:* I had always assumed that someday, after my relationship with that woman was over, I would end up marrying a man and living happily ever after, and I would look back on this "special friendship" as a strange and intense time in my life. It was completely different when Kilby and I fell in love, though. We fell madly in love, and I knew that this was no "special friendship." I knew that this was the woman I loved, and that I wanted to spend the rest of my life with her. It was impossible to think that it was anything other than love. I couldn't call her just a friend.

Our love affair moved along quickly, maybe because we had been friends already. I knew within two weeks that I wanted to marry her. I had never even thought about marrying a woman before, but the desire felt very natural to me. We wanted to somehow express our desire for a lifetime together publicly to our friends and to each other. So it was really only three weeks after we got together that we started to talk about getting married.

*Kilby:* It seemed like the natural next step for the relationship. I knew that Janet was the person I wanted to spend my life with, so the logical thing to do was to marry her.

*Janet:* I think that for me it was also a way to validate that my feelings were real: to make very clear what this relationship was. Since we were relatively closeted at the time, we became distinctly aware of how many lies are involved to stay in the closet. That had seemed all right in our previous relationships since they had only been "special friendships," but once you actually name something, then I don't think you can really lie about it anymore. Words are very powerful to our subconscious selves. When you

174

constantly hear yourself answering questions by saying, "No, I'm not married," or "Yes, I'm single," somewhere in your subconscious, you believe you're really not married—that if this relationship doesn't work out, you'll just go on to the next one.

*Kilby:* I wanted to make a statement that we were a couple and that we were committed to staying together forever. It was a way of saying, "Together, we are one."

*Janet:* It was also a statement that "Yes, I am a woman, and I am marrying another woman." It was a way of saying to everyone out there that this was the person I was choosing to be the focus of my life. I wanted others to share that with us.

Since neither one of us was involved in the gay community (we were barely out to ourselves), we didn't know if such a ceremony even existed. When I started asking around, I expected people to say, "I've never heard of a gay wedding. I don't think anyone's ever done that." I was absolutely astonished to find that not only were there lesbian and gay weddings, but that there was a church, the Metropolitan Community Church, that performed them.

Deciding what kind of ceremony to have was easy for us. Since we both had Catholic backgrounds, we had a similar vision of what we wanted, which basically was a Catholic wedding ceremony.

*Kilby:* It was important to me that we have a somewhat traditional wedding. We talked about having it outside or at home, but I think that it might not have felt as real or traditional to me outside of a church.

*Janet:* There were a lot of people that we told we were getting married that just immediately hugged us and were happy for us. A lot of my friends were Catholic nuns, and they were all very supportive. We were always really elated when friends shared in the spirit of celebration, and we'd think, "Wow, we are normal, and this isn't so odd." Then there were a lot of other people, even in the gay community, that just looked at us with confusion and said, "Can you do that?" It was rather deflating. It felt as though the whole message of two people being in love was overlooked. One of our friends, a lesbian, was totally blown away by it. She kept talking about how much courage it took. It's funny too, because it didn't feel like it took courage. It just came naturally. It wasn't a matter of pushing myself up the aisle. It felt like the most natural thing in the world.

*Kilby:* The ceremony itself was at the Metropolitan Community Church. We met with the minister a few times, first to talk about why we wanted a ceremony and then to talk about the details of the ceremony. The MCC has a prepared ceremony, and we just went through it and changed some of the language. It ended up being a fairly traditional Catholic wedding service. If you can call a lesbian wedding traditional at all!

*Janet:* We were both wearing silk dresses, and we walked in together holding hands. It was wonderful to walk into a church full of friends. We started with two Catholic songs. Then the minister spoke. When she read us the words, "Will you have this woman to be your wedded spouse. . . . " I could feel Kilby shaking. I myself was cultivating a nice red rash up my neck! This was definitely the biggest moment in our lives. We exchanged gold bands. Then, after more songs, we shared communion, giving each other bread and wine. After communion, we both approached the altar, each holding a lit candle, and together we lit a third candle. As we came back before the minister, her final words were, "I do publicly declare and state that you are one. What has been joined by God, let none of us disband." Then we did the traditional kiss, a friend sang a final song, and we left the church.

*Kilby:* What was really amazing was that when we were outside after the ceremony, we saw that almost everyone had been crying. One gay man who had been there came up to us and said that he had been to lots of straight weddings, but this was the first time that he had really understood why people cry at weddings. I think he finally could relate to what was going on. I think that there were a lot of people who were touched that way. The feeling of community was exhilarating.

*Janet:* It was pretty wild to start hugging people and to find that person after person had tears in their eyes. We felt like, "We really did something here." What we had started out to do for ourselves had also touched others. The whole thing has really made a big difference, both for us and for the people who were there.

*Kilby:* Janet and I had been living together for a year before we got married, and we had really already made a commitment to each other. But I was still so nervous before the ceremony: I was hyperventilating the night before. I knew that the next day was going to be the most important day of my life.

I think to this day our friends see how important our ceremony was to us, and therefore it's become important to them.

*Janet:* It's inspiring and strengthening to hear friends refer to us as being married, or talking about our wedding day. It's made a difference in our relationship to have more social reinforcement. To be able to look at our wedding pictures, or to read over our vows; it's just a constant reinforcement of our commitment to each other. I think that's really important in a world where you're so often writing "single" on tax forms and insurance policies. A wedding is something that helps to remind you of your commitment. The support, the reminders, the encouragement, the anniversaries—they all continue to strengthen our relationship.

*Kilby:* I feel like we're also accepted as married by both of our families. Actually, when we had the ceremony, the only member of my family I told was my sister, so my mother and brother didn't know about it. My sister was incredibly supportive. She just thought it was great that I was getting married. Since then, though, I've come out to my whole family.

*Janet:* I also only told my sister at the time. She's a Catholic nun, and she was terrific. I think she was really proud of us for doing it, and both she and Kilby's sister came to the ceremony. Since then I've told my mom and my dad. My dad has been very supportive. Although he's not very verbal, I know he's glad I'm happy, and I know he cares about both of us, individually and as a couple. My mom is incredibly supportive and curious. It's amazing to me. She was the last person in the family I told, and the one I was most worried about. She had an extremely strict Catholic upbringing. She's the kind of person who could barely even say the word sex, let alone entertain the thought that I had it, and with a woman! Then, when I told her about our relationship and the ceremony, she was completely accepting, embracing us both with open arms. I was overwhelmed.

Since then she's asked a million questions about it. She and my dad once sat down with us, and we showed them our wedding slides. I've also shown her the invitation, and she wants me to take her to the church where we had the ceremony. I think she feels like not being there was a real loss. That was a big point in my life, and I feel like she's trying to put the pieces together to make it real for her. I think she really feels like she missed something very important.

*Kilby:* I'm six years older now than when we were married, but the one thing that I would do differently is that I would be a lot braver about inviting people to the ceremony. As the years go by and I come out to more people, including my family, and I see that it's okay, I start to feel that same loss that Janet's mother feels. I wish that those people had been at the ceremony to share it. I wish that I had been brave enough to reach out and invite them. A lot of people have said, "Why didn't you tell me? I would have loved to have been there!" I think that if I had been able to do that I wouldn't feel that sense of loss. But we were younger and more scared then. We were doing the best we could.

*This is based on an account written by Janet Osimo and on interviews with Janet and with Kilby Clark.*

ஐ

*Kilby Clark: Kilby is a fourth-generation Californian, and it is from this that she draws most of her sense of roots and history. She has a great creative family and believes that she is the most conservative of the group. She loves her current job as a technical support specialist for a software company and can't wait to live out her future with Janet.*

*Janet Osimo: A native of California, Janet was raised in an Irish-Italian Catholic family. She is currently pursuing a career in international business. Her lifetime goal is to see all seven continents, and her most exciting adventure was when she and Kilby quit their jobs, packed up their belongings and toured the United States and Canada for four months.*

*Dusty Blue*

*&   Ali Marrero*

*October 21, 1984   ❧   California*

# Festival Days

*Dusty:* Ali and I met in May of 1984 at the first Southern Womyn's Music Festival. I was living in Charleston, South Carolina, at the time. Coming out in the South had been hard. It's really closeted, and it was hard to identify as a lesbian without feeling even more isolated than I'd felt already. I'd been looking for a person who could take me seriously and who could help me take myself seriously, because I wasn't really getting much support.

The Southern Festival was so beautiful: so many southern womyn who had never been to a festival and so many womyn from the West Coast who had never been to the South. We all worked together and had such a great time. Ali and I worked in the kitchen together. There were a lot of sweet and beautiful womyn there, but something about Ali really attracted me. She had a real essential side that was no bullshit.

*Ali:* When I first saw Dusty, I was attracted to her red hair.

*Dusty:* I had gotten into being a hairstylist and was trying all sorts of different things. I'm a natural blond, and I had short hair with a perm on top with some red dye in it. When I heard that womyn from the West Coast were tired of blondes, I asked my friends to get another bottle of red dye when they went into town. I wanted to have an in with those West Coast girls.

*Ali:* When she said she was a hairstylist, we all lined up for hair cuts. That was the first time Dusty touched my head. I was falling asleep and drooling at the same time. There is something in your hands that brings out the love that you have for your work.

*Dusty:* That was the first time I had cut hair in the nude. It was such a free feeling; I felt no sense of self-consciousness.

Actually, we made our first real connection to each other on the pre-festival kitchen crew. You were coordinating the breakfast crew: coordinating everything and everybody, everywhere. Your knees were hurting from standing on your feet too long. The girls were so sweet; they brought you a chair, and they wanted you to take care of yourself. You are such a doer of everything. That's when I put my hands up and cupped your face and made you look in my eyes. I said, "When are you going to sit down?" Your face just kind of melted. You were so sweet. There was a

180

heart connection, but you were also kind of embarrassed that somebody had pinned you down. That was an interesting dynamic that started there. The next night, we had sex up in the bumper pool room. It was weird. To me, it wasn't satifying.

*Ali:* It wasn't satisfying to me either. I don't even know why that happened.

*Dusty:* I think it was a miscommunication of expectation. That heart connection just stayed there, though, and for the next week we were together in the kitchen.

*Ali:* The most exciting night was the night the festival ended, and a few of the performers stayed behind to give the workers a show. There was this place called The Motel where the performers stayed, and that was the first place we actually made love. It was the greatest sex. We went all night long.

*Dusty:* I felt so deeply touched. I had never been made love to like that. I had never received so much love in such a short amount of time. My fear was that it was going be another sex scene, and I was really looking for something more than that. I didn't have an orgasm, but I felt this love inside of me. I started crying. You were holding me close, so close. Oh, that was beautiful. It sealed it for me.

*Ali:* We started this relationship, but it was really crazy. I was involved with two other womyn and was dealing with incest and sobriety issues at the same time. I didn't know what was going on. I was so afraid. Dusty is white, and I let that be a barrier for me because of my own concepts of what that might mean. I was having all these feelings that were tearing me apart. I talked to some friends about it, and they said, "You have to follow your heart." My heart was going in all these different directions, but mostly in Dusty's direction.

*Dusty:* After the festival, we had from May until the end of July before the Michigan Womyn's Music Festival. I went back to South Carolina, and Ali went home to California. We had phone sex almost every night. That was so hot, not to be touching each other but to be imagining what we were doing. We also sent letters. I had a photo booth fetish. I went down to the Woolworth's black and white photo booth, tried on different hats and clothes, and did different poses. I cut the pictures up, xeroxed them, made letters out of them, and sent them to Ali. She thought I was pretty wild. We started this summer-long affair. It was the most exciting time of my life.

*Ali:* Then there was Michigan. I did overnight security at the front gate because I knew Dusty was coming in the morning. I thought maybe she would get there early. One of Dusty's friends and I spent the night out at the gate. Then, in the morning, I wanted to go to this little store that was ten or fifteen miles down the road. We were heading towards the store when I spotted you way on top of the hill. All I could see was this little tiny yellow dot; I couldn't even make out if it was a car or a motorcycle, it was so far away. But I said, "Ah. I'll bet you anything that's her."

*Dusty:* Something in your heart was calling. I had driven with a group of girls from the Southern Festival in this VW van. We had driven overnight, and I had been telling everybody about Ali. They were really excited for me, because it was the hot romance of the summer. When I saw you, we started yelling. We were driving down the road hanging out the windows, yelling. We passed by each other and did U-turns three times.

*Ali:* We looked like a Keystone Cops movie the way we kept turning around each other.

*Dusty:* We were together all the time there, working in the canteen. The womyn that we worked with became a very sweet family. It was great for me, because I had never been comfortable making new friends. There it just came so naturally and so easily. There was such a high about that un-conditional love. It was the greatest part of the summer.

It felt real, too; it wasn't just a fling. We got so much closer. We also began our bonding around incest issues. You shared with me that you had started writing in your journal about your incest. It started churning some place deep inside me and started getting me in touch with my own incest issues. It was such an opening. It was such a vulnerable place to share. I felt so protective of you and so loving.

*Ali:* I felt such an emptiness when I got home after the festival. I missed you so much. And then when you first called, you said you had decided not to come to the West Coast. You didn't want to lose your job. It was just horrible. I was devastated.

*Dusty:* What kept happening was that every time I tried to take time for myself, I'd get fired from my job. It was so frustrating; as a hairstylist you can't just go from job to job. But after Michigan, I lost my job anyway. I was kind of freaked out; I have big issues around money and independence. Then I decided to just throw it to the wind. I decided to go to the West Coast Festival and not deny my heart's longing.

*Ali:* You called me, and you said, "I'm coming. I'm coming to the West

Coast Festival. We should be there in about four or five days." I started counting the days.

*Dusty:* The way you greeted me—I felt like we were the oldest friends and the best buddies. You always make me feel like you have always known me. There's this warmth, this glow, that just brings me right back to myself.

We went over to your apartment. It was the first time we'd made love on a bed. That was so beautiful. I remember the feeling. It had an environmentally-specific feeling: the smell and flavor of being on that king-size bed. I felt so held, so safe with you.

*Ali:* You had an orgasm that time.

*Dusty:* That's right. I had my first orgasm with a womon. That's something I'd always reserved for myself. I'm sure that's totally incest-related; I wouldn't give that control or power over to anybody. But you felt so right, so safe.

That was a beautiful time, the West Coast Festival. We got a chance to just play around. We played down in the dried-up river rocks. We drove through the Santa Barbara Mountains on your motorcycle; hung out at the guard post late at night, talking; and did overnight security on the stages together. I'm sure we didn't sleep that night. And the leather pants on the motorcycle—that was very hot.

*Ali:* You look hot in leather. That was one hot moment. I think we freaked out our next-door neighbors.

*Dusty:* I started getting a hold on who you were and who people *thought* you were. I remember the first time you wrote me. You said that you were into being butch and into dildos. You knew I wasn't, but you wanted to know if that meant I wouldn't try them. I wrote back to you saying, "I'm willing to explore this with you. I also know that is who you *think* you are, and I know that you are more than that. I see you as Ali, a very, very sweet womon."

*Ali:* That's when I started asking you to marry me. You said you were not the marrying kind. I said, "Neither am I, but I'm willing to give it a try." I was tired of the game playing. I was tired of going to bars even though I wasn't drinking. And I couldn't see having an open relationship anymore. I had to come to grips with the fact that I was basically monogamous. It's like the song says, "I may look over my shoulder, but I will never leave your side." You said that to me once, and I didn't understand it until I heard the song. I needed that kind of commitment. That's what marriage meant to me: making a commitment to work it out no matter what.

*Dusty:* That's what felt so great about being with you. You kept reminding me of that. My first reaction in an argument has always been to turn around and leave: to say, "Fine. Forget it. I'll do fine by myself." You kept saying, "Dusty, come on. Don't walk away from this. We can work this out." It's been almost six years now, and I am finally getting that it's not the end of our relationship when old buttons get pushed, or when something is frustrating because I haven't developed the tools to deal with it yet. So I made my decision to stay on the West Coast. I went back to South Carolina, sold everything, and hitched back across country. I got back just in time for Ali's birthday; I wanted to be there when her family of friends were celebrating her. It was wonderful. It was a homecoming.

When I woke up that first morning in California, I felt so freed. I was lying in bed, and the thought just hit me: if I am here, and I am making a commitment to this relationship, then go all the way. So rather than saying, "When do you want to get married?" I rolled over to Ali and said, "So where do you want to get married?" Her eyes popped opened. That was Friday. She wanted to hold the ceremony on Sunday.

*Ali:* October 21. I wanted it to be at sunset, and I wanted to do it at the beach. The weather had been so beautiful. I was amazed that the weather was so bad on Sunday.

*Dusty:* Sunday was grey, grey, grey.

*Ali:* The place that I picked was San Gregorio beach. It's a small area that has a little lagoon as well as a beach. I wanted the beach because I wanted to be close to the ocean. I wanted the power of Yemaya, the Yoruba Goddess of Life who rules over the salty oceans.

*Dusty:* I had never been to any gay marriages or bonding ceremonies, so we made up what we wanted to do. We pulled from the Yoruba faith, from matriarchal faith, and a little bit from Sufism; the spiritual was very important. The people that came with us were Ali's roommate, who later became a really good friend of mine, and her girlfriend, who later lived in the same household with all of us. There was also another womon friend there that Ali had come out to about her incest issues. The womon's kids and current lover were there, too. We were a pretty tight little group. We all thought it was funny that Ali and I were wearing the only white clothes we had between us: Ali's cook pants and shirts.

Driving down to the beach, we wrote our vows. We set up this little wooden box as an altar, and we offered the day and the ceremony to the four directions. We lit a candle, and one womon made a circle around all of us with sage for protection. We had brought some circular Tarot cards that were special to us, some womyn's poetry, and little gifts to give to each other and to the other people there.

The moment that I saw the altar, and Ali kneeling down in front of it, this real Catholic thing of church and altar hit me. I suddenly freaked out. Ali said, "No, you can't back out now. We're here. Let's do it."

*Ali:* We'd gotten there about five o'clock. The whole day was so cloudy and overcast; I was afraid that we wouldn't have a sunset. Then, just as we started the ceremony, the clouds broke, and the sun was setting into the ocean an orange-fiery-red. It was awesome. It was a beautiful, beautiful sunset. I felt like the Goddess was just smiling and giving her blessing to what was about to occur. We both got on our knees and put a hand over each other's heart. Then I read my vows to Dusty. This is what I said:

> Dusty Blue, I give to you my love, my trust, my openness, my honesty, my strength. With you, I will confront and walk through my fears and pain. With you, I will grow, learn and change, for I truly love you. I will stand with you for as long as there is ocean to cleanse, air to breath, earth to ground and the fire of our passion. You have touched so deep inside my being that I no longer feel alone. With you I will heal. Our love, truth and strength will be our magic. May all the forces with us today bless this bond.

*Dusty:* I read mine:

> Dearest Alida, my sweet, sweet love. Yesterday I realized I am in love with you, open to the heart of my soul to you. Today I will marry you in a ritual of bonding. The two of us, bonded to the love in each other. Ali, love between two womyn is such a precious thing. It is not a possession. I no longer need to possess to complete myself. True love becomes my freedom. I am so happy to be with you. Your love in me is like the ocean, wide and deep and blessed, and lived in with Yemaya. You wash over me and heal me. I want to hold each moment as the only one in time. I will live for each one with you as I am now, in celebration of living a life of love. Ali, you know there were deep secrets hidden in my heart, never said to any womon for fear they would turn away. With you, at last, I can reveal my sufferings, my needs, my deepest desires. For the strength I once felt in silence has lost all its power. Knowing, my love, is the key to speaking, which is the key to my power. With you, I shall hold safe the trust of this moment. I thank you now for being the space, the one in which

I could find myself and let the truth out, the one I can open myself to and let my love flow to. Come, nena, let us grow together as we have, and teach others this healing love. Te amo [I love you].

It was so exciting. I still shake reading it, even now. When something comes so deeply from the heart, it's not like you're sharing: it's like you're witnessing to a really deep, deep love.

After our vows, we asked our friends to choose something to read, then we gave gifts. I gave Ali a necklace I had made from a sand dollar from South Carolina. She gave me a charm of bells and beads. Then we had everyone stand in a circle around us as we sang a Sufi song: "All I want from you is forever to remember me as loving you. All I want from you is forever to remember me as loving you." We just sang it and sang it until it faded of its own accord. Then we went down to the ocean, Yemaya, and washed our hands and our faces and each other's faces in the ocean. It was a cleansing and a bathing in that power of strength. The sun just fell out of the clouds and hung there forever. We had the longest sunset. Deep, deep orange. It was so beautiful.

*Ali:* There was nothing hard about it. There was no doubt in my being that this was the right thing to do. There was so much trust. It was so new for me to feel that much trust: to become part of a commitment, a relationship; to really work out issues; to put ourselves in a place of not running away from anything; to give ourselves the permission to confront and to talk about anything; and to explore the depth of our love. It was amazing.

The other thing that was really significant for me was how mixed a group we were. One friend who was there is Italian, and her lover is Filipina-African-American. Another is Native American and Jewish, and her lover is Asian. Then Dusty and I, American-Anglo and Latina. There was a lot of representation and affirmation. There wasn't any negativity around being one race or another. There was so much respect and so much love in that circle; there was no place for any negativity.

We had children there, also. It felt important to have children at something as significant as a bonding. To give children that feeling that this is something that's really good. That it can happen. It can happen between two human beings, whether they are two womyn or two men. That was really special and significant.

*Dusty:* After the ritual, we went back to the city to plan our honeymoon. Ali wanted to take me up to see the Russian River. We stayed at a little place up there, and then the next day we went to the redwood forest, Armstrong Woods. It was so beauitful. It was kind of misty, so all the wood was a deep red, and all the leaves were deep green. We drove up to the very top, above the trees, and we could see all the mist on the mountains. It felt so real and so right. We saw deer and stood out there in the silence together. Every year we go back to the redwoods.

We also went to Jenner Beach, where the river meets the ocean. We've made that trip many times since, too. That in itself is kind of a ritual of renewing who we are together: that empowerment, that peace, that openness. At Jenner Beach, we found this huge stretch of empty beach where someone had built a big driftwood windblock. We sat there and watched the sunset that afternoon. It was so sweet. We were married. And we still are.

*Ali:* My parents were freaked, of course. They are so loving, though, and we've been so consistent with each other, that they have pretty much adopted Dusty as another daughter. I have my uptightness sometimes. I don't show the affection and the love that I have for Dusty when I'm around my straight family. That's probably something that I'll outgrow. I'm learning to let go of that a little more, but I think it's a cultural thing.

*Dusty:* About a year after our ceremony, Ali's family asked us to come and stay with them, because we had given up our apartment and had been living in a van for about six months. It was a little uncomfortable at first, because her cousin's wife was also staying there, waiting for her husband to come back from the Air Force. She didn't speak any English, and I didn't speak any Spanish. But Ali's parents were very sweet; they really worked on loving everyone the way God would want them to. I had never seen that put into action before.

That was a very important time for Ali and her parents; they got to know each other again. Ali had been clean and sober for four years, and her parents were trying to let go of old expectations. They didn't want her to work in a cafe. They didn't want me to cut her hair short. They didn't want her living in a van. They wanted her to be this responsible, femmy, professional girl that she wasn't. And straight, too; I'm sure they would have loved that.

One night, her mother got very emotional and very lovingly just kind of cried to me: "Well what do you expect? How am I supposed to feel? If somebody looks at my girl in a negative way, that's my insides they're looking at." I really understood how protective she felt about her daughter. I had to say very lovingly to her, "I don't expect you to like it; it's not something that you were brought up to understand. However, the womon is forty years old. I don't think she's going to change anytime soon. And if you want to have a loving relationship, it might be better if you accept that this is how she is, and this is who's in her life. Find the most love that you can." Her face just relaxed. I'll never forget it. It was a wonderful, loving moment. And it was the truth. Being with Ali has helped me tell the truth.

*Ali:* My family is very, very important to me. First is my path, which is Siddha Yoga, then there's Dusty, then there's my family. I have a lot of components: I am a spiritual person; I am a dyke; and I am a Puerto Rican. I have very deep roots in my island. It's an important part of who I am: that Indian/African/Canary Islands/ Spanish/Italian blood. And when I am affected by something, all those parts of me are affected. As a lesbian, as a womon of color, a lot of buttons can get pushed. Dusty has pushed some of those buttons sometimes, just as I push some of hers. But we have a commitment to talk about it honestly, not to run away. To confront the fears and work through them.

*Dusty:* It's real important for me to be in a relationship with a womon of color. I'm sure I have had previous incarnations that have made it easy for me to affirm womyn of color and womyn of different backgrounds. I also grew up in the air force, where you have everyone mixed together all over the world. I think that made me a culturally sensitive person. I feel so much more comfortable in a mixed marriage, in mixed groups, and in mixed neighborhoods. It's the way the world is, and it's the way I am. I have also never really felt rooted in a white identity, and I wanted some connection to a strength of culture that I had never felt. Being with Ali, that strength of culture has affirmed me as a human, as a womon, as deserving of self-love and respect.

While my family hasn't let go of their dualism or of their fear of difference, I feel fine telling my mother, my sister and three of my brothers that I am very happily married in a lesbian relationship, and that my spirituality is based in Yoga, or unity consciousness. I've never had any doubts that being with a womon, and being with Ali, is the right choice. I was at a "Healing the Heart" seminar with Stephen Levine, and he talked about how when you have two people moving down the same path, supporting one another, you get there much faster. My sadhana, the way that I'm going, is speeded up by being with Ali.

Our meditation master, Gurumayi Chidvilasananda, a womon, stresses that your higher Self is inside yourself and inside everyone else. That heart connection, I believe, is what Ali and I have always had. We are always uplifting one another to that space. It's joyful, it's wonderful, and it's spreading to both of our families and to all of our friends. We're constant and consistent in love. I think we're keeping our vows.

*Ali:* I really think that we were destined to be together, and I think our love is much stronger than any hardship that we've faced in the past or any that we may face in the future. I think we bring self-love out in each other in a way that I've never experienced before; it makes me feel solid, and it makes me feel that we will continue to grow. And nobody outside of our relationship can affect that. We've learned that it doesn't matter what anybody else says or does; we know what we feel for each other, and we know that what we have with each other is lasting and strong. The commitment is so strong, the bond is so strong, the grace in this relationship is so immense, that it can't be touched.

Jai Gurumayi!

*This account is based on audio recordings made by Dusty Blue and Ali Marrero.*

ð

*Dusty Blue: I'm a white southern girl, thirty-three years old. I've known since I was four years old that I preferred bonding with female energy. I've been living in California for six years with Ali. Previous to that, I was living in South Carolina for ten years. I have a strong spiritual base; it is a gift that Ali and I share. I coordinate a pre-teen program at a Siddha Yoga meditation ashram and am currently a hairstylist in San Francisco. I'm thinking about having a child. I know I would make a great mother, and Ali would make an absolutely wonderful mother. I know that a child in our lives would only add to our joy and would give love back to the world. I'm into finding out what's inside of me; I want to find out why I am here. I think the answer is just to love unconditionally. My mother taught me that, through the way she served with love. My goal is to unite my true Self to the love in all people through equality consciousness.*

*Ali Marrero: I was born in Puerto Rico. I left the island when I was five. I am an army brat. I spent some of my formative years in the South, where I learned a lot about who I was and who I wasn't. I am a recovering drug and alcohol addict. I am butch. I came out when I was around eight years old in Alabama, brought out by my babysitter who was thirteen years old. I've got very strong roots with my Latina community and with my family, now that I am in recovery. Currently, I am working at the Shanti Project in San Francisco: a nonprofit AIDS direct service organization. I recruit volunteers for our programs. I am forty-two years old this October.*

# Terry Kime

## &   Sally Meiser

Sally (left) & Terry (right)
photographer: Stelmach/A. Jacko, Jr.

## August 8, 1987   California

# A Unity of Hearts

*You share in our lives*
*with friendship and love*

*Please join us in celebration*
*as we proclaim*
*the unity of our hearts*
*and our lives together*

We got married August 8, 1987, in San Francisco. We had lived together for more than two years in a deeply committed relationship and decided it was time to claim our right of celebration as life partners. We wanted the blessings of our community, its formal recognition, love and support. And we wanted the special blessings of a religious ceremony.

Both of us are members of the Unitarian Universalist denomination, which has a long-standing commitment to lesbians and gays; in fact, it is one of the few denominations which performs "Services of Union" for same-sex partners. There were several Unitarian Universalist ministers and a good number of ministerial students (including Terry) present at our wedding. While a number of them offered to lead the service, we decided on a friend of ours, Linda Hansen, who is a professor of philosophy. We rented the perfect space, both spiritually and physically, from a lesbian and gay synagogue in our neighborhood.

The content of the ceremony itself was very important to us. We spent hours and hours looking through materials we gathered from a wide variety of sources. Brainstorming, we would write and rewrite, and write some more.

We also took great care with the visual, symbolic aspect. We hung the gay, rainbow flag from the podium. The altar table was covered by a white linen cloth with needlework done by Terry's great-grandmother, Kate Kirkpatrick. At one end of the table was a large, clear glass bowl containing symbols of the four natural elements: rocks and fossil sand dollars; spring water; a floating, rose-shaped candle; and, of course, the air inside the bowl. In the middle of the table was the book *Women-Church* by Rosemary Ruether, tied with ribbons at the place describing a lesbian wedding ceremony. At the other end of the table were three candles: two tapers (one purple and one blue) in small, brass holders and a bright rainbow pillar candle between.

Preparations involved a million details. Decorations, music, rentals, food and drink, cleanup, photography, guest book, audio recording of the event—all required the help of so many friends, who needed to be organized. We were overwhelmed with concern and excitement right up until the ceremony began.

Taped music played as people gathered. The presider entered and lit the candle in the bowl and the processional music began: Alix Dobkin's "Over the Banks," a special love song. Carrying leis, we entered from separate doors at either side of the front. We walked slowly around the sides to the back of the sanctuary and walked together up the center aisle to the front. There we met our matron of honor, Jen Kitselman, and patron of honor, Jeff Stelmach (who coined his title); they were also holding leis. We put the leis we were carrying on each other, and so did they. (Following our color scheme, Terry's purple dress was complemented with white flowers and Sally's white dress with purple flowers.) We joined the presider up front, and all stood in a semicircle facing the people gathered.

After welcoming words and prayer by the presider, a friend of ours, Ann Jordan, did a reading by Walt Whitman. Then we had a time for introductions during which people could talk to those they didn't know by sharing how they knew us. We were pleased with how this broke any tension from the formality of the occasion and created a good means for the eighty-five people to feel present and connected. In fact, the presider joked about how hard it was to interrupt the buzzing conversations! We then affirmed our intention to be married (the "Will you. . . ," "I will" part).

One of our favorite parts of the ceremony was next. A minister, Tom Anastasi, a gay man who had been a classmate of Terry's at divinity school, gave a rousing, enthusiastic and moving sermon on lesbian and gay love, while people in the pews vocalized their agreement. "Soaring," our very favorite love song by Cris Williamson, provided a musical interlude before the exchange of vows. Following this, our matron and patron of honor each lighted a match from the rose candle in the bowl and then lit the tapers, which represented our individuality.

Our presider then announced a time for blessing of the rings. Jen and Jeff tied the rings onto the open book and with the presider stepped down to the pews. Everyone joined hands, making a physical connection to our wedding rings, in order to send their silent blessings to us. (We believe their blessings are always present with us in the rings.)

We exchanged the rings with vows and, with our individual tapers, together lit the rainbow candle, which represented our lesbian partnership.

Repeating after the presider, our community proclaimed us married:

> In the presence of this good company
> By the power of your love
> Because you have exchanged vows of commitment
> We recognize you as married.

A spontaneous cheer arose, with loud and long applause. The enthusiasm and sense of celebration was incredible.

The presider gave a benediction, and we closed with the song, "Give Yourself to Love," by Kate Wolf, with all of us joining in.

Our reception was held in the same building, with champagne, coffee or mineral water, and wedding pie, instead of cake. The centerpiece on the pie we cut together was homemade, and besides the traditional two doves, included two black cats (representing our B.B. Louise and Little Bit) and two kewpie dolls with wedding rings around their waists, standing on a purple stage with lavender flowers. As memorabilia we offered engraved wedding matchbooks and baskets of chocolate kisses wrapped in purple netting.

We were inundated with bird seed as we ran to the car: a red Mustang convertible decorated with "Just Married" signs and the obligatory string of cans. Several carloads of friends, madly beeping their horns, followed us on a drive through our neighborhood (the Castro in San Francisco), where we were greeted with cheers and waves while traditional wedding music blared from our tape deck.

—*Terry Kime and Sally Meiser*

## The Ceremony

*Opening Words*

Dear Friends,

Out of affection for Sally and Terry we have gathered together to witness and bless their mutual vows which will unite them in marriage. To this moment they bring the fullness of their hearts to share with one another. They bring the dreams which inspire their lives together. They bring two unique personalities and spirits out of which grows the reality of their relationship. We have been asked as a community of loving friends to share their joy with them and to pledge ourselves to support and honor their love. No matter how strong their love for each other, they will need our support. I ask each of you present today to do all in your power to aid, sustain and encourage Terry and Sally in their commitment to one an-

other. We rejoice with them as the outward symbol of an inward union of
hearts, a union created by friendship, respect and love.

Please join me now in prayer.

*Invocation*

Holy and Creative Spirit, known in the deepest hearts of people everywhere and called by many names, whose essence is revealed to us in the
elements of nature—water, air, fire and earth, we come this day feeling joy
and warmth and affirmation to be companions to Sally and Terry as they
join their lives together in marriage. Bless this place in which we gather.
We declare it to be a Holy Place. And bless this occasion that brings us all
together, that what we do and say here reflect our deepest selves and our
sense of the sacredness of life.

Blessed Be.

*Reading*

> Stop this day and night with me and you
>     shall possess the origin of all poems,
> You shall possess the good of the earth
>     and sun, (there are millions of suns left,)
> You shall no longer take things at second
>     or third hand, nor look through the eyes
>     of the dead, nor feed on the spectres
>     in books,
> You shall not look through my eyes either,
>     nor take things from me,
> You shall listen to all sides and filter
>     them from your self.
>
>                 . . .
>
> All seems beautiful to me,
> I can repeat over to men and women You have
>     done such good to me I would do the same to you,
> I will recruit for myself and you as I go,
> I will scatter myself among men and women
>     as I go,
> I will toss a new gladness and roughness
>     among them,
> Whoever denies me it shall not trouble me,
> Whoever accepts me he or she shall be blessed
>     and shall bless me. . . .

Allons! to that which is endless as it
    was beginningless. . . .
To know the Universe itself as a road,
    as many roads, as roads for traveling souls. . . .

Camerado, I give you my hand!
I give you my love more precious than money,
I give you myself before preaching or law;
Will you give me yourself? will you come
    travel with me?
Shall we stick by each other as long as we live?

Selections from *Leaves of Grass*
by Walt Whitman

### Introductions

We are a community who share the bond of loving Sally and Terry. We are here to witness publicly to our love for them as well as theirs for one another, and to pledge our support for the commitment they are making. Terry and Sally have an advantage on us. They know all of us, but since we have been drawn from different parts of Sally's life and Terry's life, we don't all know one another. Terry and Sally want us to have a chance to come to know one another a little better in light of the bonds we have to them. Let me start by telling you who I am and how I know them.

Now I ask you to turn to someone near whom you don't know, and introduce yourselves by saying how you know Sally and Terry.

We hope that was a good start and that your conversations can continue at the reception.

### Questions

Will you, Sally, unite your life with Terry's life? Will you honor her, support her, cherish her and stand with her all your days? (I will.)

Will you, Terry, unite your life with Sally's life? Will you honor her, support her, cherish her and stand with her all your days? (I will.)

Trials will come, and tests, for there is much in this world of ours that would long to pull you apart. Do you bring strength and vision to your relationship, courage and understanding? (I do—unison)

Joys will come, graces and blessings will warm your souls and give you wonder. Do you bring thanksgiving and rejoicing to this relationship, laughter and abandon? (I do—unison)

*Vows*

Repeat after me:

I, Terry, take you, Sally, to be my beloved partner
To love and to cherish all my days.

I, Sally, take you, Terry, to be my beloved partner
To love and to cherish all my days.

### Blessing of the Rings

At this time, we ask that everyone join hands and share in the blessing
of the rings.

One of my favorite theologians and philosophers (as Terry and Sally
have had to hear many times) is a man named Bernard Loomer. And one
of my favorite lines of his, paraphrased slightly, is, "What we make out of
what we have received is who we are." That seems a very appropriate way
to think about the meaning of the blessing of these rings. All of you who
are here have been significant parts of the web of relationship out of which
Sally's and Terry's lives flow. You are what they have received, and out of
your gift of yourselves to them, Terry and Sally make themselves who they
are. It is to acknowledge that web of relationship and the flow of that gift
and your continued presence in their lives that we have asked you to join
your hands and form a web and let the energy of your love flow into the
rings.

All of us are now connected. Let us have a moment of silence as we
send our blessings for the union of Sally and Terry through the symbol of
these rings.

Out of your gift to them, Terry and Sally make themselves gift to one
another and gift back to you.

Sally and Terry, these rings will from this time forward be a symbol
of the love here declared and the vows exchanged. Let these rings say that
your commitment, which flows from our commitment to you and back
again, is deep.

### Ring Vows

Repeat after me:

With this ring I join my life with yours.
May it be a symbol of my enduring love
and the blessings of our community.

### Pronouncement

Sally and Terry, you have proclaimed your commitment in this holy place before your community of friends. I now invite everyone to join me in the confirmation of this marriage.

(To congregation) Please repeat after me:
In the presence of this good company
By the power of your love
Because you have exchanged vows of commitment
We recognize you as married.

### Benediction

May your lives together be joyful and content,
And may your love be as bright as the stars,
warm as the sun, accepting as the ocean
and enduring as the mountains.

### Singing

"Give Yourself to Love" by Kate Wolf

❧

*Terry Kime: Growing up in Nebraska farm country, Terry developed an appreciation for nature early. She lived for many years in San Francisco, where she delighted in the cosmopolitan atmosphere and fell in love with Indian food and cafe lattes. Studying for the ministry at Starr King School in Berkeley deepened, affirmed and changed her life. Currently Terry is the parish minister of a Unitarian Universalist congregation in Pennsylvania.*

*Sally Meiser: Sally is a green-eyed, enthusiastic, warm-hearted woman with a generous sense of humour, integrity and a lifelong quest for personal truth. She loves cats, hawks, communing with nature, energetic dancing and singing, Indian food, reading mysteries and getting massages.*

*Frieda Feen*

*&    Naja Sorella*

Frieda (left) & Naja (right)
photographer: Patti Smith

*August 2, 1987   🐚   California*

# Working Towards Access

Of the twenty-eight womyn that Frieda and I invited to our celebration, about two-thirds were disabled. Most of the preparation for the celebration went into making the event safe and accessible for those of us with disabilities. Much of this involved making it environmentally safe for the seven or eight of us who have severe Environmental Illness.* Where to have it was the first major problem. We decided to have the celebration outdoors, since we couldn't think of an indoor place that suited our size requirements as well as our need for environmental safety. We decided on Frieda's backyard, as it was spacious, had many trees to give us privacy and was wheelchair accessible. Frieda canvassed the neighborhood the week prior to the ceremony and asked her neighbors not to barbecue on the day of the celebration. She also arranged with her two housemates for the use of the kitchen and bathrooms by us and our friends. We chose a Sunday, because Frieda's home is in an industrial area and the fumes would have been unbearable any other day of the week. Also, the Senior Citizens' Recreation Center next to Frieda's house was usually closed on Sundays, which meant there would be plenty of close parking spaces. This was important since many of us have mobility impairments. Since the center was sometimes used for weddings on Sundays, Frieda called ahead to find out which Sundays it would be closed. If the center had been open, not only would there have been no nearby parking spaces, but cooking smells, smoke and perfume would have drifted over and made some of us ill.

We chose August, so it would be warm enough to have it outside, and we chose mid-afternoon, so that womyn whose illnesses kept them from functioning either early in the day or later in the evening would be able to attend. We checked to make sure there would be some shade in the backyard for womyn who were sun- and/or heat-sensitive. Since some of the womyn had limited stamina, we planned to have the bonding portion

---

*Environmental Illness, or E.I. (also known by many other names, such as chemical hypersensitivity, complex allergy syndrome, and so on), is an immune system illness. Environmental Illness literally makes people allergic to the world, because damaged immune systems can't deal with the chemicals in everyday products. Car fumes, smoke of any kind, carpets, synthetic clothes, petroleum products, most foods and all personal care products, cleansers and laundry products that contain chemicals and/or scent are just some of the items that make E.I. people ill. [Naja Sorella, "A/part of the Community," *Sinister Wisdom* 39 (1989/90): 104]

of the ceremony first, then the meal, say goodbye to those who needed to leave, and then have the part of the celebration where the remaining womyn could share poems, stories or songs about loving relationships between womyn. I called able-bodied womyn ahead of time and asked if they'd be able to stay afterwards and help clean up.

I sent out a two-page access information sheet well in advance of the celebration. In addition, I called individual womyn about their specific needs. In the access sheet, I listed specific personal care products womyn needed to use in order for those of us with Environmental Illness to be safe, as well as those products they needed to avoid. All the womyn coming had some contact with E.I. womyn, so I didn't need to go into a discussion of what E.I. was and why it was important for them to use the specific products requested. Since we had the advantage of being outdoors, womyn needed to use these products only a week in advance, as opposed to two or three weeks for indoor contact. I knew there was a better chance of womyn using the products for one week versus two or three. I gave names and addresses of stores where the products could be purchased and offered to send them to anyone who was unable to get them herself. Frieda picked up clothing from womyn unable to wash their clothes themselves, and she hand-washed the clothes several times in safe laundry products, returning them in time for the celebration. My mother came from out of state, and as her clothes weren't quite safe enough, she wore some of mine. I requested that womyn bathe with safe products before arriving; wear specially laundered clothes that they'd kept tightly wrapped in plastic so as not to pick up laundry scents from other clothes; and refrain from smoking, burning incense, chewing gum or using hand lotion. Womyn were asked not to smoke at all during the celebration or during breaks; even if they went a block or two away, smoke would cling to their hair and clothes and make many of us ill. Frieda bought several tubes of sun screen that we knew none of us would react negatively to, and before the celebration started we announced that these were available. For womyn who wanted to bring flowers, I recommended ones that weren't scented.

Organizing the potluck took the most work. In the access information sheets, I listed certain foods that many of us were allergic to and asked that no one bring them. I also informed womyn that I'd be calling them personally to discuss what they should bring. First I contacted those who had food allergies, and I made a list of what each person could and couldn't eat. Many of us had only fifteen or twenty foods we could eat. I also listed those who were vegetarians and those who were meat eaters. My goal was to eliminate all the major allergic foods, such as wheat, cow dairy products, sugar and fruit, because they tend to be addictive, and I didn't want anyone, including myself, going into a binge cycle from food she was allergic/addicted to.

My second goal for the potluck was to provide each food-allergic womon with at least three different dishes she could safely eat individually and in combination with the other two dishes. I had almost thirty womyn to call. I talked to each one, figuring out what she could bring that she herself could eat, that the food-allergic womyn could eat, and that she could afford. I asked each womon to write the ingredients of her dish on a card (including condiment items such as lemon, salt, spices, and so on) and to note if the ingredients were organic, nonorganic or unsprayed. I told womyn that organic ingredients were preferable, but not to go broke getting them. I made sure that those who could bring organic food made the dishes that womyn with food allergies could eat. I knew that out of roughly thirty womyn invited, probably twenty would come. When talking to womyn about food, I asked how likely they were to show up. If womyn were absolutely sure they'd be there (except for unforeseen disability reasons), I asked them to bring the dishes I was counting on. If womyn weren't really sure, I asked them to bring food we could do without if they didn't show. If a womon wasn't sure she was coming, I didn't assign her a dish that was needed as one of the three dishes for a food-allergic person.

It took several weeks of nonstop calling to pull this all together. Not everyone remembered every food they were allergic to the first time around. Sometimes I'd have dishes set up, and someone would remember she was allergic to an ingredient in one of them. Some womyn had limited energy and had to figure out if they could realistically make a particular dish. Other womyn wanted to make a specific dish but were missing a key ingredient, and their attendant was gone for two weeks. And on, and on, and on. The work was immense, but worth it. The result was an incredible potluck that was awe-inspiring to look at, delicious and satisfying to eat, and safe for those of us with complicated food allergies. Womyn with no food allergies commented that the food was amazingly varied and scrumptious, and that, to their surprise, they didn't feel deprived at all. They'd expected a very limited menu, considering the extent of some of our food allergies. Those of us with food allergies were delighted to share food with other womyn and to not get sick from, or be tempted by, food that we couldn't safely eat. For many of us, it was the first time in years that we'd eaten in any type of social setting.

Frieda and I decided that we wanted matching paper tablecloths, napkins and plates, all in Lesbian colors. We bought them about a month in advance, and as they were quite stinky from the dye, we opened everything up and let them air out in one of Frieda's rooms. We also set up regular plates, cups, silverware and white napkins for womyn who were sensitive to the dyed paper products. We provided spring water and herbal teas that everyone could drink. Since it was a hot day and womyn with certain disabilities need frequent access to water, we made sure we had more than enough water and tea. We put the water and tea in a variety of different-sized containers, so as many womyn as possible could serve themselves.

Many of the womyn invited used wheelchairs. Some were full-time wheelchair users, others weren't. In the access sheets, I informed womyn that there were stairs leading up to the closest bathroom. I described the number of steps, the shape they were in, how secure the railing was, and how wide the door to the bathroom was (in case some wanted their wheelchairs carried up the stairs). I also called each wheelchair user and discussed her needs with her. I offered to have someone available to help womyn up the stairs or to help empty urinals. This turned out to be unnecessary. One womon said she felt fine scooting up the stairs on her butt. Another womon was fine with using her urinal in the bushes. Several womyn said they would be able to make it up the stairs with the help of the railing or their canes. The important thing was to inform womyn of the situation and make plans ahead of time so no one would be left unprepared. Frieda made sure the bathrooms weren't cleaned with any unsafe products, and she took out all the shampoos, soaps and other unsafe items.

I also called each womon about her seating needs. Many of the womyn were fat womyn and needed comfortably wide chairs. Some womyn needed to lie down. Others had back problems and needed straight-backed chairs. Some had bone problems and wanted cushy chairs. In talking to each womon, I made sure either she, myself or someone we knew could provide the seating she needed. I made calls to find the chairs needed, and if womyn couldn't bring their chairs themselves, Frieda picked them up. We ended up borrowing a few of the metal folding type from the Senior Center next door, just in case, but ended up not needing them. We tried to have as many chairs as possible ready ahead of time, since Frieda and one of her housemates had all the setting up to do the morning of the celebration. Some chairs were put in the shade for sun-sensitive womyn, and enough room was left around all the tables and chairs for wheelchair access.

In terms of access, the celebration was mostly a success. Towards the end, a neighbor Frieda had been unable to reach started a barbecue. Frieda requested they keep the lid on it for another hour while we finished, and they agreed. Unfortunately, by then several of us were already ill from the smoke.

If I were to do this again, I'd check with diabetic womyn about their meal schedule needs. We ate when people decided they were hungry, not according to any specific time frame. As a hypoglycemic person, this works well for me. I know now, though, that diabetic womyn need to eat on schedule. I'd check that out next time.

## The Celebration

Frieda and I created our own ceremony. It never occurred to us to have someone else perform it, not even another Lesbian. In both our minds, we were the only ones who could bond us, not some outside power or authority. Neither of us had any attraction to the structure of "straight" marriages (church, white dresses, exchanging vows, wedding music, and so forth). We acted as though we'd never known of these customs and, instead, invented our own.

First of all, we only invited the womyn we were closest to. To us the number of guests wasn't a measure of the success of our celebration. We invited about twenty-eight womyn, including my mother, and about twenty showed up. The celebration was to share our bonding with our friends, not to impress anyone with extravagance, so we planned a down-home party.

We decided to have three parts to the event: Frieda and I sharing our bonding statements; the potluck; and womyn sharing their poems, stories and songs about loving relationships between womyn. For our bonding statements, Frieda and I chose to write on the following: why it was important to have a Lesbian Relationship Celebration; how we met; our first date; major components of our relationship; what we love/like/admire about each other; what we love about the relationship; and what we want for our relationship in the future. We worked together on the statements about how we met, our first date, and why we thought it was important to have a celebration, but we didn't show each other our writings about what we liked in each other, our relationship or our hopes for the future. We'd each hear what the other had to say at the ceremony itself. We wanted our statements to be a true sharing with each other, as well as with our friends, and we didn't want them to be rehearsed.

Since we're Lesbians and greeting cards for our bonding celebrations don't exist, we let our imaginations run wild. Thinking up different designs and making them was pure fun. Armed with a borrowed Polaroid camera, we took shots of each other in goofy positions (for example, looking like we were about to take off flying). At the photomat, we made many copies of each picture and cut the little Friedas and Najas out of them. We'd brought along different background designs, including the front of a traditional wedding invitation. We arranged the cutouts in different positions on top of the background, taped them down, and photocopied it all onto the heavy paper we'd chosen for the invitations. On the other side of the heavy paper, we photocopied all the information about the party. This was time-consuming but lots of fun. We spent the next couple of weeks hand-coloring each invitation with watercolor pens. Each card was very different, quite wild, and looked more like a notice to an art exhibit than a wedding invitation. Some of our friends told us it was the best art they'd seen in years. We had a good time doing them, that's for sure.

On the big day itself, Frieda set up a table with our personal items: crystals, Goddess figures, pictures of the two of us, the tiger lily plants my mother had given us and a few other significant objects. Frieda set up some shelving on the table, making it multilayered. It looked quite beautiful and made a wonderful background for our ceremony. Frieda's backyard was the perfect place, as it had plenty of trees for privacy. After everyone arrived, put their food on the table and visited for a few minutes, we started the celebration.

ఎ

*Frieda:* For me, creating a time and space to share my feelings of deep love and to make public my bonding and commitment with Naja feels very important and special, because this kind of sharing is something we as a couple seldom get to do. As Lesbians in this society, the restrictions are already far too limiting. Naja and I are also forced to have an isolated relationship due to her Environmental Illness and the world's unwillingness to change.

*Naja:* Today, I celebrate the love of my life partner, Frieda. I celebrate the years we've had and the ones to come. I wanted this celebration to make our love visible to the world. Straight people have engagement parties, weddings and anniversaries with family, friends, neighbors, strangers, the courts, the churches and even Hallmark Cards behind them. Since Christianity started 2,000 years ago, society has condemned womyn loving womyn. When Hallmark comes out with dyke anniversary cards, we'll know they're taking a step in the right direction. Meanwhile, I can't wait for Hallmark, T.V. commercials or Hollywood to validate womyn together. Our culture actively seeks to destroy us and our relationships. T.V. evangelists now reach forty percent of America every single day of the week, and a lot of their messages are queer-hating. This puts us in an especially dangerous time. Unfortunately more and more of us are creeping back into the closet out of fear. Every group of people since the beginning of time has celebrated certain events and used the celebrations to both validate the event itself and to bond the community. Forced to keep our relationships hidden, Lesbians don't receive the same societal support hetero couples do. Within our own community, there are few celebrations to validate our loving each other and to bond as a community. We need group events to publicly acknowledge our bonds as lovers and as a community. Today is about that. Today is having you, our friends, our family, our community, here to celebrate our relationship: the one we've had and the one we continue to have. I'm really glad you're all here.

*Frieda:* I first noticed Naja at the flea market from a distance, and I thought "Mmmm, she's beautiful." A voice came from deep in me that said, "Be patient." Who knew what that meant then, but I listened and went on my way.

A few months later, on a Sunday morning in May three years ago, I woke up with this very strange and powerful knowing that I had to go to the flea market *that morning* to meet the womon who was going to become my lover. My mantra in those days had been, "I'm ready now," and I was. I was ready to open myself up to a positive, supportive relationship.

I walked out of the BART [Bay Area Rapid Transit] station, and the first person I had contact with, besides some children giving away puppies, was Naja. I turned towards Naja's beautiful beaming face and felt these tingles deep in my belly. We probably stood talking and smiling at each other for no longer than five minutes. But I felt like I had been charged up, and a smile found a home on my face for the rest of the day.

*Naja:* Instant overwhelming attraction describes my first meeting Frieda at the flea market. I kept saying to myself, "She is sooo cute. Too bad she has a lover." This incredibly strong urge to ask her to go somewhere for a cup of coffee kept pounding at me. My certainty that she had a lover prevented me from asking.

*Frieda:* A week later Naja and I met again at a singles' party in Rockridge. I remember feeling deeply comfortable with her immediately, like we had known each other forever. I remember following Naja into the bathroom and standing there talking to her while she peed, then suddenly feeling like perhaps this was a little too familiar for our second meeting. It was okay, though, we both were so comfortable. We closed down the party that night with a watermelon seed spitting contest. It was then I realized that mouth was something special.

*Naja:* Out of 150 Lesbians at the singles' party, the very first person I saw was Frieda. She was in another room, about forty feet away. Rushing over to her, I blurted out, "If I'd known you were single, I would've said something to you at the flea market." Then I died of embarrassment as Frieda and the womyn around her stared silently at me. "What a fool," I said to myself. I just wanted to die and fall through the floor, disappear through the woodwork or something.

*Frieda:* After the party, we walked out to our cars together. When we got to our cars, Naja and I hugged, and I kissed her on the neck. That kiss came so naturally, but I was sure I had gone too far.

*Naja:* Leaving the party, Frieda kissed me on the neck as we gave each other a good-night hug. The other womyn disappeared, the trees disappeared, the houses, the streets, the cars disappeared. I was only aware of Frieda's warm lips, her very soft body and my total desire to go home with this womon.

*Frieda:* We did exchange phone numbers at the party. We talked every night during the week after the party, and we made a date. I came to find out that Naja was living right across the street from me. On our first date we went down to the Berkeley Marina for the sunset, an event that shortly after became known as "Our Sunset." Naja told me she was attracted to me... I got shy... We both got silent... We held hands... I told Naja I was attracted to her, too. That night we stayed together and held each other and talked. In the morning we made love.

*Naja:* My incredible attraction to Frieda kept me nervous. After a freezing walk at the Marina, we sat in the car. Somehow I managed to tell her I was attracted to her. She reached over and held my hand. Silence prevailed for a few minutes. Then we discussed what I found to be a mutual attraction. I remember a calm feeling that anything that developed between us was fine. I had no attachments to whether we had an affair or a major relationship. It was the first time I felt no desperateness with a new lover. I was aware of a tremendous relief at this lack of desperateness. It allowed me to trust that everything would work out the way it was supposed to.

*Frieda:* We began to spend a lot of time together, becoming very close, very fast. Over the past three years we have gone through a lot of struggles, along with our gentle loving times, and we have always had the immense support we give each other to make it through. We decided to live together due to the lack of resources. During that time we lived through Naja's being hit by a car—the surgery, the hospitalization; Naja's dad's death; my family's issues and their lack of support and lack of acceptance of my Lesbianism. During this time, I was very busy and gone quite a lot on tour with a band. All of these challenges and hard times seemed to bond us deeper and deeper.

Some of our stuff takes dealing with in an ongoing way and on ever-changing levels. The level on which Naja's illness affects my life is quite profound. I am sometimes so very afraid of losing her. The threat of losing your life partner definitely makes living for the moment take on new meaning. Naja's illness is almost like having a third person, with her own individual needs, involved in our relationship.

During this past year I have stopped getting high, which for me has been a daily occurrence for over twenty years. Now I am face to face with my moods and feelings: I no longer can round off those raw edges that seemed to make my world easier to deal with. I am trying to discover new ways.

*Naja:* A major component of our relationship is my illness. There is Frieda, me, and the illness, a third individual. Much of our early relationship was spent learning to deal with the illness in relation to each other. Frie learned she couldn't fix me when I was in crisis and learned to detach enough to leave me alone at those times. I learned to be patient with her concern for me, rather than viewing her concern and suffering as clinging and a pull on my energy. Also, from seeing her sick a few times, I learned how painful it is to watch someone you love be very ill and that the helpless feelings that arise create the overattentiveness. I discovered how difficult it is to detach and gained more understanding of why she gets pulled into my suffering.

Out of necessity, Frie and I moved in together after being lovers for three months. One musician and one severely ill womon together in a small one-bedroom apartment does not make for a good situation, let me tell you! We both tried to stay aware that our stress was due to external pressures and didn't stem from our relationship itself. Nonetheless, after one and a half years of this, we were both tremendously relieved when we had separate living spaces. Our relationship has blossomed in ways that were impossible in cramped living situations. Another positive effect on our relationship was Frieda quitting pot and starting the NA [Narcotics Anonymous] program. This allowed us to grow further in our communication. And when my father died and I was more withdrawn, this required patience and understanding on Frieda's part.

Our third year has been a settling in. Even though my illness has been progressive and we still deal with crises, we weather them better. This third year was the year the shoes finally felt comfortable, with no tight rubbing spots. For me, there is a definite feeling of having completed the prerequisites, and I now feel ready to begin the actual course. We've established a deep bond, and with it has come a trust that we can deal with whatever we need to and the relationship won't break up. Now, at the end of our third year, Frieda is starting music school. It's an exciting time for both of us, and there's a willingness from both of us to make school and the relationship interface smoothly.

*Frieda:* I found Naja to be beautiful. There is a way her beauty finds its way into my belly like a seed and then radiates out. What gets me every time is those eyes, those deep, warm brown eyes that melt into me. She smiles, and her crows' feet deepen, and her whole face is soft and loving and accepting. I truly love that face.

Naja is an old, old soul whose wisdom goes way beyond this life. I love her consideration for the Mother and all of life, and the respect with which she approaches her life's choices. I love her sense of wonder, curiosity and amazement. Her child within is still so alive in her involvement with nature. She is fun to play with.

Naja has this wonderful ability to see the larger picture. I can go talk out a problem or situation with her and get such centered, grounded advice. I love Naja's gentle, soothing voice that reassures me when I am filled with self-doubt.

I love the feel of Naja's body. My hand in hers as we walk. Or leaning my shoulder against her knee as we watch a movie. Or laying full body to body, feeling belly to belly, breast against breast, sometimes soft and restful, other times soft and full of passion. But always soft. I love burrowing into one another the moment before falling into sleep. Safe and feeling so at home.

*Naja:* Frie, there is so much I love, respect and admire about you. Before I even saw you the first time, I heard your marvelous laugh. Your laugh is like no other. It comes from your deep love of life, wonderful sense of fun and joyful spirit. Your gift of laughter has been healing for me. I love your ability to be happy and excited by the little things in life: a delicious meal, crawling under your covers, singing, flowers, sleeping in late. Immediately after hearing your wondrous laugh, your magnificent smile caught my heart. Girl, after three years, you can still melt me with your Frieda Feen smile. I love your Jewishness, how it is the very core of you. I love your fatness, how voluptuous it makes you; how round and full and soft and cuddly it makes you. Being enveloped by your sensuous body is to be embraced by the Goddess herself. Your beautiful blue-green eyes reveal every nuance. Whether you're excited, impatient, happy, angry, mischievous, worried, horny or tired, I know it all from those sensitive eyes.

You approach life with a flair of creativity, whether it's arranging food on a plate, picking a bouquet of flowers or singing. Womon, you have an incredibly beautiful voice. Besides your natural singing ability, your theatrical instinct makes you a wonderful performer. I love that you've made your dream of music school come true. I admire the perseverance you've had in making this dream come true. One of the qualities that attracted me to you, Frieda, was your love and respect for yourself. You take your own needs into consideration before extending yourself. You state your needs and limits to me. It is such a relief to me not to have to figure out what you can and can't do. You're a very good role model for me in this.

Frie, one of the first qualities I noticed about you was your deep respect for all life. You have a very keen sense of how to treat any person with fairness and consideration. I love these qualities about you. I like that you're a womon who questions all the suppositions in life. I love the rebel in you. You've been my best support around my illness. Your complete willingness to be totally environmentally safe for me all the time means the world to me. Thank you for never challenging me around what I say my disabilities are about or what I say I need for my disabilities. When I'm in pain, your hands always have a way of massaging the points that hurt the most. Honey, one of the qualities I cherish most about you is that your words and actions towards me always match. I've never felt any discrepancy between your saying "I love you" and your behavior towards me. Every interaction you have with me is an expression of your immense love. You are a wonderful supportive friend with a gift for listening. Besides being a thoughtful, sensitive lover, you are my best friend.

*Frieda:* In my three years with Naja, we've grown into best friends, playmates, confidants, teachers, problem solvers. We are life partners in so many ways.

I like that Naja and I are both working-class girls. There is a way that this similarity means we speak the same language. For me, there is also a mutual respect and support and understanding that comes with this similar life experience.

I love our day-to-day comfort. It feels so good to check in and know that there's a genuine caring about how each other's day has been going. The mutual support I feel and the special attention we pay to celebrating each other's individual growth are so rewarding. We're great food partners; it is so wonderful as a fat womon to feel so absolutely comfortable in my obvious enjoyment of food. I love that both of us are very satisfied and pleased by each other's body type, and that there is no pressure to change into someone else.

Most of all—I'm so happy that this isn't a drama-identified relationship. (Naja interjected here, unplanned, "We get a video if we want to see drama.") Although it isn't crisis free, the crises feel so much more sane; we deal—we go on. Naja honey, I feel so mated and bonded with you. I am comfortable, satisfied and very excited about our relationship.

*Naja:* Despite the external pressures on us, this relationship is the most loving, supportive and stress-free one I've had with a lover. Our relationship is a safe place for each of us to communicate what is happening on our most vulnerable levels. I desperately need this with a lover, and I love that we have this together. I also cherish our treating each other gently, even when we disagree or are upset. We're both aware of our personal issues and how they can get in the way of our relationship. I treasure the support we give each other to be who each of us is individually. We have a lot of fun together, just hanging out, even though most of the time we lie in bed due to my illness. Frie, you are my best friend. I know I'm yours. I cherish the deep respect we have for each other. I also love that violence in any form, whether emotional, physical or psychic, has never been a part of our relationship. The element of high drama is very low, and this is an incredible relief. I treasure the basic calmness of our relationship and the lack of bickering and nagging. We support each other through crises, as well as in personal achievements, and this is important to me. Being with you, honey, is pure joy. There's a calmness and trust with you that I've never had with a lover before. We have a healthy, relaxed, nurturing relationship, and I love it. On a very deep level, you are family.

*Frieda:* I want to continue growing as individuals and as a couple. I want our willingness to work on our baggage from the past to continue and to help free each of us to be present in the present. I also want us to be wise enough to know that this work will fill our lifetimes.

I want to find a home that cares for each of our needs. With air you and I can breathe, water that is safe and beauty that invites us in and cradles us. A home with a community that continues to inspire and support us like the community we've found. And music enough to quench the thirst.

I want us to remember the depth of our caring for one another when our times are less smooth. I want to be your partner for as long as is healthy for both of us. I'm hoping that is for a very, very long time. Naja— I love you very, very deeply, sweet womon.

*Naja:* Frie, I love what we have together, who we are as lovers. My hope is that our intimacy will continue flowering through the years. My wish for us is that we will always learn and grow from being together. I want to be an old womon with you, Frie. I'll try to keep my heart open to you, to us. I'm willing to take pleasure and joy in the good times. When hard times overwhelm and scare me, I tend to panic and run away. I'm willing to recognize this as my own fear and not make decisions based on my panic. I can't promise I'll never do anything that hurts or pains you. I can promise to listen to what you say is hurting you as well as to what you say you need from me. Always, I'll treat you with gentleness and respect. I'm committed to this relationship taking care of both of us. As well, I want our relationship to be a safe haven, a place for us to be nurtured and revitalized. Honey, rather than give you a ring as a symbol of my love, I give you my love itself, to wrap around you, soft as a cloud and warm as the sun.

ঌ

This was the end of our statements. Frie and I were hugging and kissing, and womyn were saying "ahhh." I said, "This is kiss-the-brides time." When we finished with the hugs and kisses, I made this announcement: "We wanted to have something that each of you could take home that would be a memory of our relationship and the loving community that's here today, so we have in this appropriately shaped box some little stones. There are enough here for everyone, so you can take your favorite." We had planned to take a little break then for snacking, but instead we ended up making it the main eating time. Most womyn were able to stay after the meal for the sharing time, though some womyn left due to exhaustion or other disability reasons. The sharing time was wonderful. There was a large variety of poems, songs and stories that womyn shared. Each womon seemed to have put a lot of thought into selecting something that would be special for me and Frie and for the occasion. Frieda and I took some time during the sharing to open presents womyn had brought. Most womyn left after the sharing was over, but a few die-hards who'd promised to clean up stayed on, and by then we were hungry again, so the five or six of us had a second round of food.

Almost three years after the celebration, Frieda and I are still so pleased we had it. We can still feel the love and support of all the womyn who were there that day. Our relationship celebration will always have a special place in our hearts.

—*Naja Sorella*

ঌ

*Frieda Feen: I am a thirty-seven-year-old working-class, Jewish Lesbian. I am a late bloomer, presently working on a master's degree in music and becoming functional in my personal life.*

*Naja Sorella: I am a thirty-eight-year-old working-class, half-Portuguese, quarter-German, quarter-other, Lesbian separatist. I have been severely disabled by immune system illnesses for the past seven years. Besides having the most wonderful lover in the world, I enjoy collecting stones of all kinds, reading, writing and painting when I have the energy.*

*Mary Ann Martin*

*&  Linda Ochs*

Linda (right) & Mary Ann (left)
photographer: Kelly Holland

*April 1, 1983*  ❧  *The Oregon Coast*

# To Wed at First Sight

How could I have known when I poured my heart out in a letter to a women's spirituality magazine ten years ago that I was taking the first step down the path to a whole new life? Linda Ochs read my letter, and—as she told me later—she was instantly smitten by Cupid's arrow. She had never been romantically involved before, but she knew in her deepest heart that she was a lesbian. I, on the other hand, thought I was a straight lady who had just had uncommonly bad luck with men. But when I got a letter from Linda, Cupid's second arrow also hit its mark.

After coming to know each other from afar through letters and long telephone conversations, Linda and I pledged our eternal love and commitment to one another on April 1, 1983. We had not met in person before that day, so many people may think April Fools' Day was highly appropriate for such a rash act. But we had been searching for each other, without knowing it, all our lives, and when, in our middle years (Linda was forty-two then, and I was forty-six), our separate wandering stars finally came into conjunction, we knew it, we felt it. We were transported by love to a level of certainty which gave us each the courage to make that wild leap of faith—into each other's arms.

I met Linda at the Eugene airport on that magical day almost eight years ago. We were scared and shy, joyful and full of wonder at the enormity of what we were about to undertake. We drove out to the coast. We each had a ring for the other's pinky finger: a turquoise, my birthstone, for Linda and an opal, her birthstone, for me. We exchanged vows high on a cliff above the wild ocean waves as night was falling and the wind was blowing in a storm.

"I will never leave you or forsake you."

"I will love you and cherish you always."

We slipped the rings on each other's fingers with Our Divine Mother and all the saints and angels as our witnesses. We poured a libation of champagne into crystal goblets and linked arms in the traditional way for our wedding toast. Then, as raindrops began pelting us like rice thrown by our invisible guests, we ran hand-in-hand to our lodging for the night, and into the beginning of our shared future.

We later chose identical wedding rings to wear on the customary finger of the left hand: delicate floral circlets of gold to proudly proclaim our union to the world. And we still celebrate the first day of each month as our own special holy day, sometimes with a gift, sometimes with a fancy meal or a bottle of champagne, and sometimes with just a smile, a kiss and "Happy Anniversary, My Love!"

*—Mary Ann Martin*

ॐ

*Mary Ann Martin (born 1935): I approach the Goddess through clay and other art forms. I build altars on the beach from whatever the tide brings in. After I finish a beach altar, I leave it for the sea to take away. I leave Goddess sculptures in odd places for other people to find. After a wretched early family life and two disastrous marriages, I have finally found out who I really am and what's important to me. I consider myself to be a very lucky person to have found that precious pearl—True Love. I look forward to a zany and productive old age, side by side with my beloved Linda.*

*Linda Ochs (born 1939): I grew up on a small farm in southwestern Washington. I was the older of two girls and was my father's helper about the farm as well as a tomboy in all environments. My mother never worked outside the home, and my father was a blue-collar factory worker. I played all sports open to girls and questioned the fairness of those not open to girls, because I could outplay any of the boys in my school. I have a bachelor's degree in health and physical education, a master's in physical education and additional work in therapeutic recreation and special education. I have taught physical education at the secondary level and college level and held a variety of administrative positions at the college level. I currently work for a behavioral research institute in Eugene, Oregon, as a research assistant and project coordinator. Mary Ann and I own our own home, which comes equipped with four bicycles, two motorcycles, one car, three beloved, although not altogether well-behaved, dogs who serve as pets and protectors, at least in theory. I hope we can retire in fifteen years and move to a small secluded farm where we can associate with additional animal friends and be closer to the land.*

# Nancy Bent

## & Barbara Burns

Barbara (left) & Nancy (right)
photographer: Bonnie Palter

*April 23, 1988* ❧ *Georgia*

# Celebrating the Journey Together

Barbara and I met in August 1980 while working at an Atlanta advertising agency. Taking a brief hiatus from her work and training as a psychotherapist, Barbara was the agency's bookkeeper. She was twenty-nine. I, at age twenty-three, was working as a secretary and trying to figure out what I wanted to do next. Neither one of us belonged. We stayed just long enough to fall in love, form an inseparable bond, then move on together to pursue our respective careers. Barbara went back to school in counseling psychology, and I set out to become an editor and writer.

Barbara first proposed having a commitment ceremony after we had been together for two years. I balked. I had never been involved with a woman before Barbara. The idea of making public something so intensely personal and so subject to criticism terrified me. I guess I was still working through my own homophobia. Barbara was six years older than I and had identified as lesbian for four years before meeting me. She was ready to celebrate what we had together. I bought some time, telling her I would be ready by our fifth anniversary.

By our fifth anniversary, we were ready for couples therapy instead. We had begun to grow apart and resented each other for the changes that were happening. That scared us both. We worked hard over the next year and a half to learn how to be both individuals and a couple. After we had weathered those difficult times, our relationship seemed better than it had ever been before. There was greater trust, and our life together seemed much richer. We had more friends, both separately and as a couple. We were both happy in our work. Yet we valued being at home together most of all. In hindsight I realized—and I think Barbara did, too—that we had made our lifetime commitment to each other before our relationship got into trouble. It took tremendous commitment to stay and work it out.

By our seventh anniversary, I was more than ready to stand in front of friends and family and affirm my love for Barbara as well as for the life we had made together. By this point, we were also planning for me to get pregnant within the next one or two years, and the ceremony seemed an appropriate prelude to such a major transition. Barbara especially wanted to have "wedding" photos to show our future children.

We spent many months planning the service and party. Although the process was filled with overwhelming details and frustration, the excitement and fun at seeing it all come together so successfully far outweighed

218

the difficulties. We rented a charming four-room historic house maintained by a local Junior League, which everyone found amusing. Fortunately, they just turned over the key upon receiving our money and had nothing further to do with the proceedings. We had the reception, which we held in the same place, catered—we went the whole nine yards with wedding cake, champagne and a sumptuous spread of hors d'oeuvres. We also discovered that we could ask our friends to help us. In fact, people considered it a gift to be included. And we were overwhelmed by their generosity. Friends helped us with the invitation, program, flowers, jewelry, music, videotaping, photography, set-up, cleanup and management of the unending details.

Planning the actual service is where most of the frustration occurred. As a writer, I wanted every word to be perfectly chosen and placed. As a therapist and great extemporaneous talker, Barbara just wanted what we said to be genuine. After many arguments, I finally let go of the need to control every element of the ceremony. Instead, Barbara and I were able to develop the program by passing the script back and forth—each making our own statements and adding our own ideas. The final script really did represent us both. And some of Barbara's ideas, which I had initially opposed, turned out to be among my favorite parts—like handing out the crystal hearts and singing "Song of the Soul" at the end.

The actual ceremony was magical. There were nearly eighty people present. And a thunderstorm that lasted just the duration of the service added drama as well as brought us all closer together. When we stepped into the room, my stage fright evaporated as I drew power from all the people I cared about gathered in one place. I was so worried I wouldn't be able to find my voice, but instead I felt completely in control, without fear, embarrassment or self-consciousness. I was not only making public my lifetime commitment to Barbara; I was also claiming pride in being lesbian. I don't think I've ever been happier or more open to love. It was a day of great triumph.

—*Nancy Bent*

❧

When I read back over our ceremony or watch the video, I am repeatedly touched by the love. Nancy and I were able to stand up in front of all those people and be completely open to each other and to others. We had finally laid down—outside somewhere—the last remnants of our shame, and we were able to rejoice.

As we planned that glorious day, there were several parts that were very important to me:

I wanted more than anything to be real and genuine in whatever we
did or said.

I wanted to have lots of fun.

I wanted to celebrate.

I wanted to be fully present, and when it was over I wanted to remember it all.

I wanted to be surrounded by all the people I love and to tell them I
loved them.

I wanted good food and good music.

I wanted lots of flowers, and I wanted to look pretty.

I wanted to sing a song, and I wanted to exchange rings.

I wanted to laugh, and I wanted to cry.

Given how much I let myself want, it is truly amazing that I got it all.

The next day, when it was all over, I just wanted to do it again. It had
been so wonderful. I said on that day and still say it today—it was the best
day of my life. The only thing I can imagine topping that day is the birth
of our first child, which is due at the end of October 1990. I feel truly
blessed.

—*Barbara Burns*

## The Ceremony

*Song:* John McCarthy sang "The Ones Who Aren't Here" by J. Calvi.

I'm thinking about
the ones who aren't here
and won't be coming in late.

Home all alone.
And the family.
And won't be coming out tonight.

Wish I could know
all the lovers and friends
kept from gathering.

I think of you now,
the ways you could go,
we're all of us refugees.

Telling myself
and the family,

my friends and the folks on the job.

One by one,
and it's never been easy,
and me and everyone changed.

The hopes and the fears
when they show you their hearts,
and some never speak again.

Every pot off the wheel
can't bear the kiln,
and every love
can't bear the pain.

So let's pass a kiss
and a happy/sad tear
and a hug the whole circle round.

For the ones who aren't here,
for the hate and the fear,
for laughter, for struggle, for life.

Let's have a song here
for me and for you
and the love that we cannot hide.

And let's have a song
for the ones who aren't here
and won't be coming out tonight.

*Nancy:* I asked my dear friend John McCarthy to open our ceremony with that song because for me it so beautifully captures how painful it can be for a woman to love a woman—or a man to love a man. And how painful it can be to hear that someone you love is lesbian or gay. We wanted to acknowledge the painful part—which is a real part—in the beginning, so we can move right past it to the joyful and fulfilling parts.

*Barbara:* This song also makes me think about some very important people who aren't here because they have died. The first is my mother. She would have been here with bells on. She loved both me and Nancy and was very supportive of our relationship. I miss her a lot today. Second is my friend Carlen. We had been friends for twenty-five years—we shared our childhood together, and I wish we could have shared today. And the last is Bob Yeakle. He should have been here. He wanted to be here. I miss him a lot, too.

*Nancy:* Finally, the song pays tribute to those who do come forward with support and love and encouragement—the ones who are here—all of you. I want to thank you for coming. Your presence here today means so much to me.

*Barbara:* It is so wonderful to look out at all of your faces. I love that you are here today with us. Thank you for your love and support.

*Nancy:* Now we'd like to share a dialogue we've written together about our journey to this day. This first part we call "Coming Together."

(We turned and faced each other.)

*Barbara:* In the very beginning I thought you were really cute. I loved your red glasses, beautiful hair, beautiful eyes and your warm smile. I laughed a lot with you. You listened to me. The very first day we met I thought, I've found a new friend.

*Nancy:* When we first met, you knocked me clear off my guard. You took such an interest in me. You were so responsive. You always made me feel worthwhile. As I opened myself up to you more, I'd study your face for signs of criticism or disapproval. But all I saw in your dear face was acceptance and even admiration.

*Barbara:* Pretty quickly I knew that I was very attracted to you and I was falling in love. But I was also afraid that I would get my heart broken. I wanted to spend all of my time with you. I was never bored or unhappy with you. I felt safe and loved.

*Nancy:* When I realized I was in love with you, I was both thrilled and terrified. I didn't share these feelings with anyone and in many ways was very lonely. But when I was with you, the fear was replaced by elation and a lot of laughter. I knew that I could be intimate and safe with you. I wasn't going to deny myself that happiness.

*Barbara:* Even though we were both afraid in the beginning, I'm so glad that we decided to plunge in and get involved. That was in October 1980. The last seven and a half years have been more than worth the risk.

*Barbara's sister, Sherry Burns:* In my lifetime there have been, of course, many memorable events—many, many of them shared with Barbara, and many shared with Barbara and Nancy. One that particularly sticks out in my mind is a weekend about twelve years ago when Barbara told my parents that she was a lesbian. It's really an understatement to say that that weekend was pure hell. Barbara and I were alternately running back and forth to the bathroom. And it was particularly traumatic for me because I wanted to support Barbara in her telling my parents, but I also wanted to support my parents in hearing something that in the beginning is very hard for parents to hear. After she told my parents, I think Barbara and I felt a great deal of relief. Like the weight of the world was lifted off of our shoulders. And it seemed to be put on my parents' shoulders. The next day my mom asked the inevitable questions: Where did we go wrong? What did we do wrong? And I really only had to think for a few minutes before I responded to her that, "Mom, yes, you did something here—you probably did have a hand in this. Somehow you taught us to love people not because they are black or white or red or purple or male or female, but because they are the right people to love." And today I think about that and I think about my parents and how did Barbara and I end up like this, when our parents were like that—we all think that of our parents. And I still don't know the reason for all of these things. But I do know that Barbara is one of the rare people that loves completely and totally. She wants and expects and sometimes demands—often demands—of herself and of the people she loves that they be the best persons they know how to be. And she has what it takes to make a relationship work. Be it a friend or sister or lover, she has what it takes.

Now Nancy—what about Nancy? That weekend is such a vivid memory in my mind, yet on the other hand I can't remember a day or a moment without Nancy in my life. I really can't remember Barbara without Nancy, and I can't remember Nancy without Barbara. And I never want to imagine it. Because Nancy is the ultimate right person to love. Their love for each other and for me and I have to say their total devotion to my son is the very best thing that exists.

*Nancy's sister, Barbara Bent:* Nancy's told me quite a few times over the past few years that it has meant a lot to her that I have been so accepting of her and her relationship. Every time she has said that I've thought, gosh, that's a really nice thing to say, but I don't feel like I ever had to put any effort forward. My sister has always meant everything in the world to me. And she, I'm so happy to say, has shaped me and helped form my character. And part of that, I'm grateful and proud to say, is that I am an accepting and open person. When she first told me about her relationship with Barbara, I was seventeen years old and we were sitting in our house that we had grown up in together. Of course, I was initially shocked. And the second thing that hit me was that she was going to have to face so much pain—it was just going to be a hard life. And then I met Barbara. And Barbara is such a wonderful person that I began to realize that those things really didn't matter. All that really mattered was that there was this wonderful, loving relationship, this positive relationship. And it's been a real inspiration for me to watch them, to watch their relationship grow and endure. I'm sure that it always will endure, and I'm really glad about that. And I'm honored and thrilled to be part of this celebration.

*Song:* Mary Liz McNamara and John McCarthy sang "Soaring" by Cris Williamson.

*Barbara:* This second part of our journey we call "Staying Together."

*Nancy:* Over our many years together, we each have changed and grown. It has been a great challenge to always be supportive of change—especially when we change at different paces. For a while now we've been on parallel tracks. But there was a time when that wasn't so, and we had to work hard to regain our grounding in the relationship. But I think these ongoing challenges are what keep our relationship alive. For me, the most rewarding challenges have been to be as honest with you as I can, to confront our problems before they become too damaging, to be generous with you—to give to you without expecting anything in return and to receive from you without feeling in debt.

*Barbara:* I feel challenged by conflict. It takes energy and concentration to create my life with you. It's been a challenge to keep at it. It's a challenge to face homophobia in you and me—to not give in to fear and depression. It's a challenge to move out of the safety of our bond and make new friends— to risk losing my connection with you in order to build other relationships. But I guess the biggest challenge is just to stay together—to keep on loving, fighting, laughing and growing old with you in a world that does not embrace us.

*Nancy:* But our life together is much more than meeting these challenges. Our life and our home is my haven, where I am nourished by the laughter and the passions and the friends that we share. I love best making us dinner at night, sitting at the dinner table telling you about my day and hearing about yours, curling up with you and Maggie and Princess in a great big family spoon, sharing all that confounds and upsets me and being soothed by you, sharing my accomplishments and joys, too. You renew me daily.

*Barbara:* I really love my life with you. You are a wonderful companion. No matter what we are doing, it feels good to be doing it with you. I feel a tremendous amount of support from you to take risks—to go after any goal that I set for myself. You nurture me, challenge me, comfort me and make me laugh. I love the home that we have created. It is my favorite place to be. I love that we create our life together—like this ceremony to-day. We make it happen for ourselves.

*Reading:* Barbara read the words to "Song of the Tao," which appeared in *Circle of Love* by Mary Porter-Chase.

*Our friends, Linda Travis and Gary Piccola, spoke.*

*Reading:* Gary read Elizabeth Barrett Browning's Sonnet 39.

*Song:* Mary Liz McNamara sang " Since You Asked" by Judy Collins.

*Nancy:* Barbara, I promise to love you,
    To remain honest and faithful to you,
    To be available for you when you are in pain or in grief,
    And when you are filled with happiness.
    I promise to challenge you always,
    To support and nurture you
    And to be receptive to the gift of your love.
    I love you with all my heart,
    And I will love you for the rest of my life.

*Barbara:* Nancy, I promise to love you,
    To remain honest and faithful to you,
    To be available for you when you are in pain or in grief,
    And when you are filled with happiness.
    I promise to challenge you always,
    To support and nurture you
    And to be receptive to the gift of your love.

    I love you with all my heart,
    And I will love you for the rest of my life.

(Michael Burns, our three-year-old nephew, brought us our rings.)

*Barbara:* Nancy, I give you this ring as a symbol of my love and commit-ment.

*Nancy:* Barbara, I give you this ring as a symbol of my love and commit-ment.

(We kissed.)

*Barbara:* Just as the rings that Nancy and I have exchanged today are a symbol of our love for each other, we have something that we want to give each of you as a symbol of our love for you. Last night Nancy and I held each of these crystal hearts and thought of each of you individually. We would like to go among you now and hand them out.

(We handed out the hearts.)

*Barbara:* Now we're all going to sing a song together. It's in your program, and it's called "Song of the Soul." John and Mary Liz will sing the first verse and the chorus by themselves. Then all of us will sing the first verse, the chorus, the second verse and the chorus together. And then we'll have the reception. Before you leave, please sign the guest book and if you want to write any comments, feel free to write whatever you want.

*Song:* We all sang "Song of the Soul" by Cris Williamson.

*Nancy Bent and Barbara Burns: Nancy is a writer who would like to move from corporate communications to journalism in the near future. Barbara works as a psychotherapist and is in her fourth year of work towards her doctorate in counseling psychology. Barbara and Nancy celebrate their tenth year together in October 1990, but have only been married for two years. They are expecting a baby at the end of October.*

*Martha*
&
*Rita*

*June 11, 1988* 🐦 *California*

# With Love's Law

*Rita:* Martha and I met in 1978, but we first got together in 1981. We were both eighteen years old then and had just graduated from high school. A couple of months after we got together, Martha was sleeping over at my house, and my parents caught us caressing.

My parents are extremely strict; they immigrated here from Mexico in the mid-fifties, and they have very old-fashioned values. When they found out what I'd been doing, they thought I was crazy. Actually, what they said was, "Are you crazy or are you possessed by the Devil?" My mom insisted that I talk to a priest and to a psychologist.

The psychologist didn't say much to me one way or the other, but when I went to confession, I asked the priest if being gay was wrong in the eyes of God. He said no. I was totally astonished; after all, this was the Catholic Church. That was an important thing for me to hear, especially at such a critical point in my life. I felt a lot better about who I was, but my parents still demanded that I end the relationship with Martha.

*Martha:* It got kind of scary when her brother came after me with his twelve-gauge shotgun.

*Rita:* The whole family thought I was crazy, and they were determined to break us up. So our relationship started right after graduation in June and was ended by my family very quickly in August.

Between 1981 and 1986, Martha and I stayed in contact. We went to college together and ended up becoming best friends. I watched her go through her relationships, and she watched me go through mine.

*Martha:* At that time we were both dating men as well as women. To be with women really means fighting society, and I think we both felt that we had to try being with men. Our more complete relationships, though, were always with women.

*Rita:* In 1986, I decided to join the California Highway Patrol (CHP). I had to go up to Sacramento for training, and Martha drove up with me in her own car. When we got up there, she wished me good luck, left me a letter she'd written, and turned around and drove back home. In the letter, she said that because of my family, our relationship had never really gotten a chance to grow. She said she had always wished we had gotten to know each other more, not just as friends.

228

I went ahead and started the training with CHP. I lasted five days: it was just too physically rigorous for me. I thought my career in law enforcement was over, and I was really upset. I called Martha, in tears. She said, "Just relax. I'll be right over." That night she came into my house for the first time in Lord knows how long. I was living with my parents, and always before she had just stayed outside. But that night she came in, and we talked and talked. After that, we started seeing each other romantically and just grew closer and closer.

*Martha:* That was after a time in my life during which I had been through quite a few relationships, the last one of which was with a man. He and I had gotten to the point of deciding to get married when I finally realized that there was no way I could marry this guy when every time we drove down the street, I'd find myself looking at women.

Taking a look back on that whole period, it seems as though I kept looking for someone who shared my values; I kept looking for someone like Rita. It had just felt right to be with her; I had shared everything with her. So when she was going up to Sacramento, I decided what the hell: every now and then you have to do something bold. So I decided to make a play for her, and it worked out. It felt so right to be together again.

In December of that same year, after we'd gotten together, I asked her to marry me. I was tired of running around, tired of going from relationship to relationship. I wanted to be committed with somebody. I loved Rita. She was the right person for me, and I wanted to spend the rest of my life with her. She'd always been right there for me, always been totally honest, totally sincere. I felt that Rita was everything I needed, everything I wanted. And I was hoping that I was the same to her.

I knew that I probably moved too quickly. I get very impulsive: when I want something, I go right out there and get it. So I guess I popped the question a little too soon, and I saw fear written all over her face. I let her know that this was where I was coming from, this was what I wanted. I said I would understand if she didn't answer the question right away, but she needed to know that I wanted to commit to a life-long relationship with her. I wanted to start a family with her.

*Rita:* I panicked. Actually what happened was that I said yes, but I really meant no. It didn't take long for me to tell her that it was just too soon for me. She said, "Well, when you're ready, let me know."

We had both just come out of pretty serious relationships, and I wanted to make sure that we were both clear that the feelings from those relationships were totally over. It took a few more months for me to feel that I had worked that through for myself. Then it became clear to me that I *did* want to make this commitment with Martha. She had never really left my heart, and I knew she never would.

I'm a very quiet person, and I don't come out with my feelings easily. Martha's helped me learn how to communicate, with myself and with others. That's been very significant for me. It just seemed right that we should be together.

So by mid-1987, I decided to say yes. Martha's the kind of person you can never surprise, but I think I got her that time.

*Martha:* I was totally shocked. Rita had taken me to a French restaurant. French food is my favorite kind of food, and I thought it was a little strange that she would take me there when it wasn't a special occasion, but I didn't really think that much of it. I can't remember exactly how it happened, but there was a perfect set-up, and she followed it right up with, "Well, I understand what you're saying, but what do you think about this?" I looked down at her hand, and there was a wedding ring. It blew me off my chair. I got so excited that I kissed her, right in the middle of this totally straight restaurant.

*Rita:* Which blew me away! We're both in law enforcement, and we're very conservative. Out of all of our friends, Martha and I are probably one of the few couples that won't hold hands in public. Given our careers, we're just not ready to come out like that. So I was pretty astonished when she leaned over and kissed me!

*Martha:* Soon after that, we began planning the ceremony. We started by thinking we'd get married at a Metropolitan Community Church and have a traditional wedding. Then we started to feel, "No, that's not us." It didn't seem very personal. We'd be going to a church we didn't really know, having someone perform it that didn't know us. It just didn't seem very warm to either one of us.

*Rita:* It seemed more like a display, a show, and we didn't want it to be that way. We have a house in Marin County, so we decided to have the ceremony at our home. We invited about sixty friends. The only relative that came was my sister. I was totally shocked that she was there; she was one of those that had thought I was possessed by the devil back in 1981. But she came, and it meant a lot to me.

We never told our parents; we just didn't think that they could really deal with it. My brother still doesn't know about the ceremony, but he knows we're together. In fact, recently he came over to the house and built us a trellis. That's something he never would have done in the past.

*Martha:* The change in his attitude towards me has been overwhelming. It's like I'm part of the family now. That's true with all of Rita's brothers and sisters, as well as her parents. I really feel that they love me. They all know that we're together, but it's just something that's not discussed.

*Rita:* I have one sister who lives in Mexico, and she came and stayed with us for a few days last year. She knows we're gay, but again, we don't really talk about it. Well, while she was here, she asked, "Have you and Martha ever thought about getting married?" It blew me away. I told her that we had had a ceremony, and I showed her the videotape of it. Boy, have we come a long way.

*Martha:* I had come out to my parents when I was eighteen, and they had been very accepting of it. They just said, "Honey, it's something you'll grow out of. Don't worry." When Rita and I got together again, I didn't tell them. My mom is no dummy, though. She'd had her suspicions for a while, so we just recently had a two-hour discussion on the phone, clearing the air. We went through just about every emotion possible, and I think in the long run she accepts us. My dad's very accepting; he'll go along with anything as long as I'm happy. My mom, on the other hand, is a lot like Rita's parents. Both of my parents are Chinese, and I'm adopted—I'm half-Chinese and half-Italian. My mom's very traditional. One thing that's made it easier, though, is that both of my parents love Rita to death.

*Rita:* Our families are both very, very important to us, and one of the biggest joys of my life was that on Christmas 1988 we were able to get my entire family and Martha's entire family here together. It was wonderful.

*Martha:* It was our first Christmas in the house, and our first Christmas after the ceremony, and we were all here together: all of my relatives and all of her relatives. Their ethnicities were different, but so many of their traditions and values were the same. If you didn't look at the faces and just heard the conversations, you would think that they were each other's relatives. My mom and Rita's mom sat next to each other during dinner and talked all night. It was something we had never dreamed would come true.

*Rita:* My family has always been extremely prejudiced. Either you associate with your own race—and I'm not talking about anybody from Central America, either, they would have to be Mexican—or you associate with Americans. So that Christmas was really a big step for them.

*Martha:* Both families had actually taught us a lot of the same things: treat others as you wish to be treated yourself; save your money; don't be too extravagant; keep your house clean; and be a good upstanding citizen. Rita and I are both like that, and being in law enforcement kind of keeps us in that mode.

*Rita:* It was wonderful to have them all together and all getting along. I felt like we had all come so far together. I still don't think either family could have handled the ceremony, though.

*Martha:* The ceremony itself came together pretty easily. We figured out our color scheme, decorations, food, flowers and entertainment. We kept it all pretty simple. We decided that the ceremony itself would be an exchange of vows and rings.

The biggest question was who was going to bring our rings to us. Rita thought maybe her best friend, Marsha, should be the one to bring them to us. But we also have this dog, Lacy, that I am totally crazy about; this dog is like my child. So we decided to take a heart-shaped satin pillow and tie our rings to it. Marsha could hold Lacy, and then when it was time we'd call Lacy and she'd bring us the pillow.

When the day came, the ceremony itself started about twenty minutes late. I kept stalling because I was so nervous: I couldn't get my heart beat to slow down. I wanted to calm down enough to at least be able to talk. Finally, one of our friends said, "Okay you two. Let's go."

*Rita:* We both walked up and stood in front of the fireplace. All our friends were sitting around us.

*Martha:* Before we started our vows, I told our friends that part of why we wanted to have this ceremony was to include all of them in the love that Rita and I share for one another. It was kind of like a little introduction. Then Rita said her vow. It was very beautiful. She hadn't written it ahead of time; it just came from her heart.

*Rita:* To this day I'm still embarrassed about it. I'm an extremely nervous person in front of people, and I found that I repeated myself a lot. I talked about wanting to take this next step with Martha; wanting her to know how happy I'd been with her; that I knew it would only get better; and that I loved her and wanted to spend the rest of my life with her.

*Martha:* Then I went ahead and said my vow. It was something that had been written on a card I'd bought. The best way for me to show what's in my heart is to find the words that other people have written, since I'm not very good at putting them together myself. So I read her this quote which talked about how relationships are never easy, but that love just grows stronger from those struggles. It talked about how each obstacle had only strengthened the love between us, and that we could now face the future with confidence. I said I looked forward to living, loving, sharing and staying with her.

*Rita:* She also said something to me in Spanish: Vida, si tuviera quatro vidas, quatro vidas serian para ti. (My love, if I had four lives to live, I'd live them all for you.)

Then we had Lacy bring us our rings. I gave Martha her ring and said, "Martha, with this ring, I thee wed. Although not lawfully, I thee wed." Then, as Martha put my ring on me, the first thing she said was, "Ditto," which got a big roar out of the room. I was thinking, "Oh, how romantic! Ditto!" Then we ended the ceremony with a kiss. Everybody came up and congratulated us, and then the two of us danced to Stevie Wonder's "A Ribbon in the Sky."

*Martha:* After toasts and cake-cutting, we had a giant party that ended at about four in the morning. One of the best things about the ceremony was actually something that we hadn't planned. Toward the end of the night, the crowd kind of died down and only about twenty-five friends stayed on. We were all in a circle, arms linked, rocking back and forth to the music. Without any planning, each of our friends, one by one, entered the middle of the circle, walked in front of us and spoke. It was so touching: people said the most beautiful things, some of them crying as they spoke. They talked about how happy they were that we were together. They wished us the best of happiness throughout our lives, and they said they would always be there for us. I'll never forget it.

*Rita:* It felt to me like the whole ceremony really completed my relationship with Martha. I'd never really trusted anybody before; I'd always had some fear that kept me from trusting fully. Martha was able to get that fear away from me. I learned how to say "I trust you" and mean it. Somehow, for me, the ceremony completed that process of trusting.

*Martha:* I feel that we're really a family now, with each other and with our extended families. When my parents come over, or her family comes over, there's a sense that together we are a family.

The ceremony also made a big difference in terms of how open I was willing to be. When I was younger, and going through a lot of different relationships, I probably would have denied being involved with a woman. I don't feel that way now. Now I feel that this who I plan on spending the rest of my life with. I'm not going to go out and tell the world, but if somebody asks, I'm not going to deny it. This is the person I love. This is my family.

*This account is based on an interview with Martha and Rita.*

ॐ

*Martha:* I am twenty-seven years old. I was born in 1963 in San Francisco and currently live in Marin County. I am of Italian-Chinese descent and was proudly adopted by pure-blooded Chinese parents. I have no siblings, but I have a cousin who has always seemed like the sister I never had. I am employed with the state of California as a police corporal and am currently working in the criminal investigation unit. I enjoy playing the piano, and I believe that life is like a piano: what you get out of it depends on how you play it.

*Rita:* I am also twenty-seven years old. I was born and raised in San Francisco. My parents came here from Mexico in the mid-fifties. I feel very lucky to speak, read and write both English and Spanish fluently. I have one brother and two sisters; I am the youngest. I am currently a deputy with the San Francisco sheriff's department.

# *Joanne Gold*

## *&  Jodie Shapiro*

Joanne (left) & Jodie (right)
photographer: Barbara Lockhart

## *June 19, 1988  ❧  Massachusetts*

# Recommitment:
## To Each Other, Our Community and the World

*Joanne:* Jodie and I had been talking about having some kind of ceremony for several years. We had both been feeling the need for public support and recognition of our relationship. I saw it as an opportunity to deepen our bond with each other and to rethink the reasons we were still together after so many years. It was also a chance to appreciate each other as individuals and to appreciate the ways in which we are able to support each other.

*Jodie:* Initially, we thought about having some kind of celebration at our ten-year mark, but the timing wasn't quite right. We were still getting settled in the Northampton area, and most of our support system was in the Bay Area and in Santa Fe, New Mexico, where we had lived for the seven years prior to our move east in 1984.

For me, the move to Northampton had begun a period of transition to a new level of adulthood: turning thirty in 1984, finishing graduate school in 1987, and buying a house with Joanne in 1988. It was also in 1988 that we decided we were ready to have what we called our "Twelfth-Year Recommitment Celebration."

We decided to have it in June, because we both love the summer and wanted an outdoor ceremony. We chose to have it at Woolman Hill, a Quaker community, because it offered the space we needed and also because of their support of gays and lesbians. Their commitment to peace and their activism around social-change issues were important to us, too.

*Joanne:* Planning for the event took many months and was exhausting. We each had a "support person," or "best woman," on whom we relied for emotional support prior to, and the day of, the ceremony. Jodie and I have both been a part of Re-evaluation Counseling, a peer counseling program, and Jodie's support person was her co-counselor. My support person was a good friend of ours who is also Jodie's flute duet partner.

We truly could not have pulled it off without all the help and support we received from our community. There were so many details to work out: designing invitations, organizing the potluck, arranging for setup and cleanup crews, arranging for photographers, getting a cake baked, choosing music and deciding what to wear!

*Jodie:* It was made more difficult by the fact that we began preparations for it right as I was studying for my comprehensive exams. We were also moving into the first house we'd bought together, and we were working on a large fundraising benefit for a local AIDS organization. What a crazy spring it was!

*Joanne:* It seems as if the most difficult problems we encountered had to do with whom to invite and whom to even tell about the ceremony. The most serious for me was the decision of whether or not to invite my blood family. Deciding not to invite them was very painful. Although my parents have come to accept my lesbian lifestyle, I realized it would be asking too much to invite them to celebrate it. And I wanted the day to be one of celebration: no holding back. I also knew I didn't want to feel that I had to take care of them emotionally. I wanted it to be totally our day. It saddened me, though, not to be able to share the richness of my commitment to Jodie with my parents.

It was also difficult not being able to share all my excitement around planning and preparing for the celebration with people at work. I am out to a few people, but I didn't feel it was safe to share the celebration with them. At about the same time, one of my co-workers (heterosexual) was preparing for her wedding. Seeing how much support she got from everyone, and not feeling free to talk about my own ceremony, left me feeling very isolated.

*Jodie:* I knew from early on that I would not be inviting my family. I would have liked to have invited my dad. He has been supportive and, I think, would have been honored to be a part of this event. My mother has had, and continues to have, a difficult time accepting my lesbianism and my relationship with Joanne. She has known Joanne for thirteen years, and even though we have had a few dialogues about lesbianism, she still does not recognize our partnership. It felt impossible for me to invite my father without also inviting my mother.

I had a difficult time at work as well. There are three other lesbians at my workplace, and they were the only ones who knew about the ceremony. There is one other worker with whom I feel very aligned, but I did not feel I could tell her about the ceremony. I am not sure if this was my own craziness of the moment, or if it was my own internalized oppression creeping up on me. I would love to take a picture from the celebration and put it on my desk at work. Maybe someday...

*Joanne:* For the ceremony itself, we drew on several traditions. We are both Jewish, although that is more important to me than it is to Jodie. There were certain Jewish rituals and customs that I felt were important to include: we had a chuppah to stand under, and we said blessings in Hebrew and English over candles, bread and wine. I changed the Hebrew blessings to reflect a feminine spirit instead of the usual masculine one. We also broke a glass at the end of the ceremony, and when the ceremony was over, our friends carried us in chairs to the sounds of klezmer music.

We also borrowed from Native American tradition by having a cedar purification ritual at the beginning of the ceremony. This aspect of the ceremony felt like a very important connection to our seven years in Santa Fe.

The rest we created ourselves, including music, poetry, and a time for people to share their feelings about commitment. We spoke at the beginning about why the ceremony was so important to us as lesbians and why we had chosen not to invite our blood families.

The last part of the ceremony we called "Our Promise of Commitment." We both had trouble with the word "vows," so we decided to rename that part ourselves. We each wrote something for the other that spoke of where we had come from and where we were going. It was incredible to share our intimate feelings in public and be so supported.

*Jodie:* We also had a table set up with paper hearts on which people could write messages. The hearts were then hung from a beautiful nearby apple tree. The messages floated in the summer breeze all day. A few of them were:

> "I hope, for both of you, acceptance from the world for your beautiful commitment and love."

> "Wishing you creative, productive lives together, full of beauty, struggle, triumphs and growth. Always make each other strong, sometimes make each other crazy and continuously make each other a home."

> "I wish you all your wishes."

Much of what I feel about that day has to do with that quote about acceptance. The recommitment celebration to me signified an acceptance of myself on a very deep and personal level. It was also a public acknowledgment of our lesbian selves and of the family Joanne and I have together. That in itself felt like a profoundly political act: to say proudly, "I love this woman," for all the people there to hear.

*Joanne:* It felt very different to me from a traditional heterosexual wedding or marriage. Perhaps it's because as a kid I didn't see many positive models of marriage. To me, "wedding" and "marriage" somehow connote two people merging into one unit. I saw our recommitment celebration as a way to come together as individuals with mutual respect and love. Neither of us has a desire to merge. I see each of us having our own separate paths, as well as our shared path. The day felt like a celebration of that. In all, it was an incredibly empowering experience for me. It was a very important act of self-love.

*—Joanne Gold and Jodie Shapiro*

## The Celebration

*Cedar Purification Ritual*

*Welcoming*

*Jodie:* Welcome. We thank you all for sharing this day with us. We want to welcome those who could not be here physically today, but who are with us in spirit. These include friends in Italy; Holland; Calcutta, India; Santa Fe, Truchas Peaks and other parts of New Mexico; the Bay Area; North Carolina; New York City and Portland, Oregon. We also want to thank the many people who have traveled long distances to be here.

As for our blood families, we have both gone through our own individual processes to arrive at the decision not to invite them. We struggle on a daily basis for acceptance, and today we want to create a safe, positive environment. We want this day to be truly a celebration of our pride in being lesbians and of our love for one another.

*Joanne:* As lesbians, we don't have any established rites of passage. There is so little support for our relationship from the outside world, and so little recognition for the longevity of our relationship and for all the the hard work it has taken, and still takes, to live as a lesbian family in this heterosexist world. We want to take in all the love and support that you, our friends, are sending our way. You are part of our family.

*Blessings*
Candles:
Baruch at shechina elohaynu malka ha olom, asher kidushanu b'mitzvoh tov, vitsivanu l'hadlik nair shel yom tov.
Blessed is the spirit of the universe who watches over us as we kindle the lights for this special day.

Baruch at shechina elohaynu malka ha olom, shehechujanu, v'keyimanu, v'heegiyanu, lazman ha zeh.
Blessed is the spirit of the universe who has brought us here and sustained

us to celebrate this day.

Kiddush—Wine:
Baruch at shechina elohaynu malka ha olom, boree pri ha goffen.
Blessed is the spirit of the universe who gives us the fruit of the vine.

Hamotzi—Bread:
Baruch at shechina elohaynu malka ha olom, ha motzi lechem min ha aretz.
Blessed is the spirit of the universe who gives us the grain from the earth.

*Commitments*
At this point we opened it up to anyone who wanted to talk about commitment: commitment to ourselves, to each other, our community and the world.

*Song:* "Into Morning," lyrics by Jodie, music by Joanne (1980)

*Our Promise of Commitment*

*Reading:* "Birthday Poem" (Joanne, 1977)

*Joanne:* Jodie, I choose to be an important person in your life just as you have been an important person in mine. I look with pride and love on you, my friend, as one who works hard to empower yourself and others; one who cares deeply not only about your friends, but also about the earth and about all people who are struggling for their equal place in the world.

I choose you to be my family, to share all of life's joys and difficulties. May we continue to grow in love and to find the wisdom and courage to struggle on our own paths, together.

We have been such stable forces in each other's lives over the years. You have given me strength and clarity when life has been muddled and unclear. Things have not always been easy, but I am continually amazed at how willing we both are to work on our issues and to be there for each other in very deep and profound ways. I hope we become old ladies together. I love you.

*Reading:* "Dancing the Shout to the True Gospel or The Song Movement Sisters Don't Want Me to Sing" by Rita Mae Brown

*Jodie:* Twelve years ago last week, we embarked on a cross-country hitch-hiking adventure together that set the stage for these twelve years. We had only been together about five months at the time.

In that summer of 1976, while we were traveling, I wrote in my journal, "Someday when we live together... existing in our own reality, society will have no check on us. We will live with the rules we make for ourselves. I feel we could be together for a long time."

When I think about the miles we have traveled and loved; how we've continued to give strength to each other; supported each other's dreams, our separate voices and chosen paths—this is indeed commitment.

Joanne, you are such a gentle friend. I have watched you continue to grow as your creative, artistic self explores the options and challenges ahead of you and seeks out ways to make changes within yourself. You have been an inspiration in flexibility and spontaneity, teaching me how to slow down and appreciate life. Your strong identification as a Jewish lesbian-feminist has set a model for my own continued political work on internalized oppression. I respect your commitment to healing the mother earth and giving back to her what you reap from her soil.

The struggles and challenges within each of us, and between us, have only made us closer and stronger. At first glance, issues that appear easy to solve have instead been rather difficult and complex. Your ability to stick with them has been unending.

I am so glad you are my family. For each piece of wisdom you share and teach me; for each time you dance freely and joyously; for each time we are truly there for one another; for each time we dream, plan and map out new adventures; for each time we make music and for each time we challenge each other, I celebrate. I love you.

ᐧ᠊

*Joanne Gold: Joanne is a thirty-five-year-old Jewish lesbian-feminist who loves wild socks and who still brings roses home even after fourteen years. She is learning to live with a hidden disability and works as a dental hygienist and a potter. She hopes to pull it all together soon.*

*Jodie Shapiro: Jodie is a thirty-five-year-old Jewish lesbian-feminist growing her hair into a tail. She delights in gazing through the skylight with her cat, Cisco, purring by her side, and she dreams of building an adobe house in New Mexico. She is a special educator/social worker who has rediscovered her childhood athletic abilities and dreams of becoming a bassist in a women's band.*

# Linda Quiring

## & Cindy Reichley

Cindy (left) & Linda (right) & daughter Kaitlin (center)
photographer: Leslie Trimble

## May 18, 1985  ❧  Pennsylvania

# Among Friends

*Linda:* Cindy and I got to know each other slowly. We had both been active in the women's movement in Philadelphia and, being that it's a small community, we had been bumping into each other for a long time. Then, about six years ago, we started dating.

What struck me about Cindy right away was that she was very strong and independent. That was a relief to me. I was tired of being a caretaker in relationships, and it was nice to find someone who would meet me halfway. We seemed to complement each other; we shared the same ideas about life and had the same sense of what kind of lifestyle we wanted. We also shared a commitment to spiritual growth, which was important to both of us.

*Cindy:* I had a sense very early on that Linda was the person I should marry. It was early in our relationship, and I wasn't ready to actually marry her yet, but I already had this deep sense that she was the one. I felt like she believed in the best parts of me, and she brought out the best parts of me. It seemed as though the same things were important to both of us. We liked going for walks in the woods together. We liked talking about herbs and plants. She was interested in living simply; she wasn't interested in a lot of flash and dazzle. We just seemed to fit well together.

I had been raised as a Mennonite until I was sixteen, at which point my family left the Mennonite Church and joined a Quaker meeting that was forming. My parents and I have been members of that same meeting ever since. So when I met Linda, I had been a Quaker for about ten years and had been active in Friends gay and lesbian issues. Linda had been raised Catholic and wasn't Quaker when we met, which was fine with me. I didn't feel at all like she had to become Quaker. I felt like what was important was what was inside her, and at that level we were very similar. I felt like she was somebody I could share the deepest parts of myself with. She did end up becoming a Friend several years after we got together, but it would have been okay if that hadn't happened.

I had been involved before with people that were different from me, but in the long term I wanted someone that shared my values. Part of what was going on with me at the time was that I was planning to have a child. It was something I had always wanted, and I felt like I was ready to go ahead with it. That does a lot to change how you enter a relationship. If you're going to be raising a child with someone, it becomes more important that you have a very solid base together. And, of course, I had to see how Linda would feel about helping to raise a child.

*Linda:* When we first talked about raising a child, I felt like it wasn't something I would necessarily have chosen for myself. Parenting is a lot of work and a lot of responsibility. And if you're a gay or lesbian couple you don't ever have children without doing it really consciously; you don't ever just happen to get pregnant. So I think we went into it very seriously. And I had apprehensions. But Kaitlin is here, and she's a wonderful child. It's a lot of work, but you take the work in stride. It's a reality; it's part of the relationship and part of the commitment.

*Cindy:* Even though I knew I wanted to have a child before I ever got involved with Linda, the two of us have been parents together. She's been there from the very beginning; she was there at all the birthing classes, and she was there when Kaitlin was born.

I think that in some ways having Kaitlin played a part in wanting to have a ceremony. We would have done it anyway, but with Kaitlin there I felt even more like I wanted us to be seen as a couple and also as a family. We'd been living together for about a year, Kaitlin was several months old, and I was really feeling as though we were a family, and I wanted some way of having that recognized.

*Linda:* It seemed important to have some kind of celebration of the relationship and of our commitment to each other. I think it was a way of holding ourselves out to our community and saying, "Yes, this is my life partner" and "Yes, we are a family." To me it meant that our relationship would be taken more seriously by the community, and that it wouldn't be seen as some phase that we were going to grow out of at some point. We had both been lesbians for many years, but sometimes it seemed as though people still thought, "Well, someday they'll each meet a man and get married." Getting married to each other was a way of validating that this was it: this was our lifestyle, and this was our commitment to each other.

*Cindy:* I knew that I wanted to spend my life with Linda, and it was important to me to make that commitment public. The traditional Quaker vow begins with, "In the presence of God and these our friends. . . . " And both parts of that felt important to me. I wanted to make that commitment before my spiritual community and before the Spirit. I wanted to publicly say, "This is the person I'm going to spend my life with. This is my family." I wanted a way of recognizing and celebrating the bond that was there.

I also wanted to have the community support our relationship. If times got rough, I wanted to have people around who would not only be concerned for each of us individually, but who would also look out for the relationship.

*Linda:* So we applied to be married under the care of meeting. I hadn't joined the meeting yet, but I had been attending regularly for a while. The meeting was a little taken aback and decided to first address the broader issue of whether they should have marriages for same-sex couples at all. That was in the fall of 1984, and they proceeded to have a series of dialogues discussing the pros and cons of having same-sex marriages.

Up until then, the meeting had been very accepting of us and our relationship. Two of our friends, a gay male couple, have been part of the meeting for years, and they had also always felt very accepted and supported. When the meeting was faced with the idea of a same-sex marriage, though, and publicly condoning that kind of relationship, it brought out a lot of people's concerns. Most of the adults in the meeting are in their thirties and older, and many of them are pretty conservative. A lot of them had a difficult time deciding to go ahead with this.

*Cindy:* Quaker decision-making is all done by consensus, so if one person says, "absolutely not," then the change can't go through. So, finally, after about six months of dialogue, they reached a point where most of the meeting agreed on going ahead with the ceremony. They didn't feel they could use the word marriage, because that connoted all the legal stuff, but they were willing to call it a celebration of commitment. So as not to make it a second-class ceremony that only gay couples have, they decided that the meeting from then on would have celebrations of commitment for heterosexual couples as well. They wouldn't call them marriages or weddings anymore.

Even with that, though, there was one couple that couldn't go along with it. One option in Quaker process is that if you can't support a decision but don't want to hold back the whole meeting, you can say, "I'm not going to go along with this, but I'm going to stand aside and let the meeting go ahead with it."

And that's what this one couple decided to do, mostly out of respect for my father. My family has been a part of this meeting almost from the beginning, and my parents have always been very actively involved. My father had also been very supportive of this particular couple at a time when they were having problems with their own children. So basically they said, "Well, if it's really important to you that your daughter have this ceremony, we'll stand aside."

My parents were both very much in favor of us having a ceremony, and it turned out that that made the real difference in helping the meeting reach consensus. When I first came out to my parents, years before, they had the typical hard time with it, and it was actually other members of the meeting that helped them come to terms with it. They did come to terms with it, and ever since then they've both been very supportive.

*Linda:* After the meeting agreed to have same-sex celebrations of commitment, the next step was to have our union approved by the Clearness Committee, which is the committee that recommends to the meeting as a whole whether or not a particular couple should be married.

It's actually a nice tradition. They sit down with you and ask you all kinds of questions like, "Do you plan to be monogamous? How are you going to raise your children? What problems do you anticipate? What about financial concerns?" They really grill you about what you're bringing to the marriage, and they decide whether or not they feel the two parties have known each other for long enough and whether it's going to be a marriage that can last. They help you, too: they don't just grill you. You get the feeling that the Clearness Committee is kind of your back-up, or your support. If you come across a rough spot or have a problem, they'll help you work it through.

*Cindy:* The process also helped us as a couple get clearer about some things. Some of the concerns they voiced had to do with the fact that it wouldn't be a legal marriage, and they encouraged us to make whatever legal provisions we could. For instance, we wrote a will saying that should anything happen to me, Linda would raise Kaitlin. And we went ahead and did powers of attorney. These were things that we had been intending to do, but the process spurred us on.

After the Clearance Committee recommended that the meeting perform the ceremony, things got very exciting. One wonderful thing about being married through Quaker meeting is that in addition to the Clearness Committee there's an Oversight Committee, which takes care of most of the arrangements for the celebration. It takes the load of organizing off the couple. It also turned out that the daughter of the woman in charge of the Oversight Committee had come out as a lesbian to her parents about a month before. In a way, getting involved in our ceremony was a way for the mother to be supportive of her own daughter as well as supportive of us.

*Linda:* The invitations we did ourselves. We ran them off on a photocopier and colored in each one. We also planned a potluck meal afterwards and asked everybody to bring a dish. It was real homespun in a lot of ways.

*Cindy:* The meeting was very supportive, once they decided to go ahead with it. A lot of people brought flowers from their gardens. Everybody brought a dish for the potluck. There were people from the meeting there, as well as our friends and family.

The ceremony itself took place as a part of a special meeting for worship. The meeting met in silence, as usual, and the two of us sat facing each other in benches at the front. Then, when we felt ready, we stood up and exchanged our vows.

*Linda:* After the vows, there's traditionally a long period of silence, and again, anyone who's moved to speak just stands up and does so. People wished us lots of luck and happiness. They talked about marriage and commitment and what it was like to see Cindy married after knowing her for so long. It felt like a very joyous celebration of what marriage is about, and there were a lot of expressions of love.

*Cindy:* In Quakerism your vows are written up on a big certificate that you sign, and everyone who's there witnessing signs as well. So after your vows and after people have spoken, you have one person designated to stand up and read the certificate at the end of the meeting. Ours was a traditional Quaker certificate that basically repeated our vows to each other:

> Whereas, Linda Marie T. Quiring and Lucinda Ann Reichley, having declared their intentions of commitment to each other at Unami monthly meeting of the Religious Society of Friends, held at Pennsburgh, Pennsylvania, their celebration was allowed by that meeting.
>
> This is to certify that for the accomplishment of their intentions on this 18th day of the fifth month of 1985, they, Linda and Lucinda, appeared in a meeting for worship held at Unami Meeting. Linda taking Lucinda by the hand, did on this solemn occasion declare that she, with great respect and love, came here to take Lucinda in the presence of God and these her friends to be to her a loving partner, a source of strength, comfort, happiness, understanding, joy, and love, as long as they both shall live.
>
> And in the same assembly, Lucinda did in like manner declare that she took Linda to be her loving partner, promising with divine assistance to be loving and faithful always, a source of strength, comfort, happiness, understanding, joy, and love to her as long as they both shall live.
>
> And then they, Linda and Lucinda, as further confirmation thereof, to this certificate set their hands. [our signatures]
>
> And we, having been present at the celebration of commitment have

as witnesses hereunto set our hands. Amen. [signatures of all present]

*Linda:* After the certificate was read, people shook hands and broke meeting in the traditional way. Cindy and I signed the certificate, then everyone else signed.

*Cindy:* Then we all had lunch and sparkling grape juice. It was in the springtime, so we all sat outside on the grass and hung out together and had a good time.

When I look back on it, I remember worrying so much about all the details: we were worrying about the weather being good; Linda was worrying about which blouse to wear; we were worried about her family finding their way there. It all becomes a blur in some ways, but it was also wonderful. There were so many people there who meant so much to us, and it was wonderful to have all of them supporting us and wishing us well. And I loved that everyone else pitched in and took care of the details and let us just be sort of fuzzy and nervous. I felt that we were very loved and cared for.

I also think that it made a big difference for our relationship. I think it made us feel that we could relax and trust that the other person was really going to be there. We have a commitment to work things through, to go the extra distance. We're committed to working through the bad times, and we intend this to be for keeps.

*Linda:* We both still wish that the meeting could call it a marriage. We've been considering going back and asking them to rethink that. That's still kind of a sore point for us, because it feels like a marriage. We consider it a marriage.

*Cindy:* My parents consider it a marriage also. Linda's like another daughter to them, and they're the classic adoring grandparents with Kaitlin. We're just another couple within the larger family. All the other grandchildren just figure that we're Kaitlin's moms. I have one brother who's very fundamentalist Christian and didn't come to the wedding. That caused some hard feelings, but he is who he is.

*Linda:* I invited my siblings to the celebration, but I never said anything to my parents. I was actually planning to, and then my mother died suddenly about a month before we were married. As a matter of fact, when she went into the hospital all my sisters called me up and said, "You didn't talk to Mom, did you? She had a heart attack!" I felt like, "Thank God, I didn't tell her." That kind of guilt I didn't need. So I never did tell her, and I haven't yet told my father, but we were married on my parents' anniversary, which somehow felt like a way to include them.

My family is funny about things, though. Even though we don't talk about it, my father considers Cindy and Kaitlin part of the family. Kaitlin calls him Grandpop Quiring, and he considers Kaitlin his granddaughter. That's just the kind of family we are. We don't talk about things, but they're silently acknowledged. As a matter of fact, when my mother did pass on, they listed Kaitlin as one of her grandchildren. That felt good to me.

*Cindy:* Since then we've concentrated on making our relationship work and raising Kaitlin. And we try to live our Quakerism. That makes a big difference. We don't make it the be all and end all, but we try to go to meeting as often as possible, and we try to be involved in Quaker issues and events, and we're very committed to making sure that Kaitlin gets a Quaker education.

*Linda:* To me it's a challenge to live Quakerism. We're human beings, and we have our shortcomings and our own biases, so it's hard. But one thing that really drew me to Quakerism is that Quakers seem to be a group of people who really try to practice what they believe. They don't just do it on Sunday and then turn around and cheat somebody in business the following day. It just seems to be something that's very solid and very basic.

The basic premise is that there is that of God in all of us and in all things. I think it's a very basic and very pure spiritual message, and one that I think is important to expose Kaitlin to: that there is that of a higher power in other people, in the earth, in the universe, in the environment, and that we need to recognize that and respect it. We need to take responsibility for caring for it in others.

*Cindy:* Quakerism also puts a lot of emphasis on each person having his or her own experience of God, or of the Spirit. You do check it out with your community, with the other Quakers around you, but essentially you have your own spiritual experience. There's a sense that the Bible, or whatever else, is not the be all and end all, but that God continues to talk to us and that we're always trying to listen.

I hope it comes through in what we teach Kaitlin. We're sort of odd Quakers in some ways. A lot of Quakers are fairly traditional Christians, which we are not. To us, Easter and Christmas and all those holidays are not really meaningful. We tend to celebrate the solstices and the equinoxes. When you're raising a child, you're more aware of developing traditions within your family. It's a challenge to try to figure out how to celebrate things. It's exciting to be able to create just what you want. We've come up with some interesting celebrations. We burn sage and have a circle to celebrate the solstice. We also bring in sweetgrass for Kaitlin to carry through the house as a blessing, and we both walk with her as she blesses each room.

*Linda:* On the winter solstice, we drew on the Celtic tradition of "bringing in the green." It's an inviting of the woodspirits into your home. It reminds me that a lot of time we're very human centered, and perhaps instead we should look at the entire earth and everything that's in it.

*Cindy:* Kaitlin's in a Quaker kindergarten now, and that's been wonderful for her. When a kid has a problem with other kids in the class, they can call a meeting. If some little kid keeps calling her a "poopihead" and won't stop, she can tell the teacher she wants to call a meeting, and they sit down and work the whole thing out instead of just slugging it out on the playground. I think she's really learning a lot about how to work out differences with other people. She's learning how to respect other people and also how to ask for that respect herself. I think in the long run that's what it's all about.

*Linda:* In a lot of ways, we're the same as any other family: when you're parents, you're parents. And even though there may be less rigidity around roles, a lot of the same issues come up: money, sex, kids, vacations, work. All of those still come up, and it takes effort to work them out. But having been with Lucinda for six years now, it seems like the effort helps the relationship grow. We learn more about each other all the time.

*Cindy:* Things have their own rhythm. We'll get caught up with the day-to-day mundane stuff: "Why aren't the dishes in the sink done?" or "Why doesn't Kaitlin go to sleep and give us some peace and quiet?" And we don't even think about the relationship really. Then all of a sudden we look at each other, and we're in love again. Sometimes I feel like we just keep falling in love with each other over and over again. So there's the steady day-to-day of being together, and then there's the suddenly seeing each other all over again and realizing what we have.

*This account is based on interviews with Linda Quiring and Cindy Reichley.*

❧

*Linda Quiring: I am one of seven children from a working-class, Irish-Catholic family. I worked my way through college and graduated with a bachelor's degree in social work. I worked as a paralegal after graduation and became active in the women's movement, gay rights and the civil rights movement. Later on I joined the carpenters' union and have been doing carpentry for ten years.*

*Cindy Reichley: I am from a small town in Pennsylvania. When I was in high school, my family left the Mennonite Church to become Quakers. I have been active in Quaker women's group and Friends for Lesbian and Gay Concerns, and I now work as a registered nurse and enjoy gardening in my spare time.*

# Patty Bralley

## & Becky Butler

Patty (left) & Becky (right)
photographer: Lucy Phenix

*October 17, 1987*  🐦  *Georgia*

# Outward Signs, Inner Blessings

*Becky:* It was April, 1986, and I was standing in front of the Tara movie theater in Atlanta, waiting to meet Patty for the first time. I remember her walking up to the theater wearing her "coat of many colors" sweater. It seemed to me that there was such light around her. We sat down to watch *Hannah and Her Sisters.* As the lights dimmed, the film opened with a white title on a black screen: "My God, she's beautiful." I didn't breathe. I felt as though through some strange and frightening miracle my thoughts were being projected in front of me. And I was trying to be so cool.

In retrospect, I see that night as the culmination of one chapter in my life and the beginning of another. The preceding ten years seem all of one piece. In 1976, when I was eighteen, I had traveled alone to Greece, intending to drink and dance my way through it. To my great surprise, after several months in a tiny village on the south coast of Crete, I instead experienced a sense of the infinite that completely changed the course of my life.

The next ten years, though filled in part by work in film and television, were characterized much more by an inner journey. Part of this involved tracing the paths of those who had left spiritual maps: Jung, Gurdjieff, Krishnamurti. I felt as though I were struggling against the limits of the physical universe, trying to part a thin veil that separated me from a constant awareness of the infinite that I'd glimpsed in Greece. At first, it seemed to me that the physical world was a distraction from a more fascinating immaterial universe. Then I began to read about Buddhism. My meditations left their busy visualizations and rested instead on the subtle in and out of my breath. I found a sense of silence and stillness and, in the "simple" task of being present for each moment, I found a path that could easily last lifetimes. It was as though I had come home. There was no longer any distance between the infinite and the manifest.

Somehow that entire journey seemed very present as Patty and I talked after the movie that first night. We were in a strange little pizza joint, neon lights buzzing and flickering above us, talking about meditation and consciousness. Patty had spent the previous fifteen years deeply involved with Transcendental Meditation, and though our paths and traditions had been different, I felt a kind of communication between us that was almost intoxicating: there was a feeling of unboundedness in our discussions. Here was someone with whom I could share the full range of my soul. It took us a while to ground our conversations, but I cherish the excitement of those early dialogues.

As we said good-bye that night, I was struck by a sense that everything would work out. The fact that I had an almost unblemished history of getting involved with unavailable people was inconsequential. I felt no urgency, or even questioning, about this relationship. For the first time, I had a wonderful faith that it would all work out in its own way and time.

*Patty:* I must have asked Becky to marry me within a week of telling her I loved her. The "Will you marry me?" seemed to rise spontaneously out of the love I felt. I think in part it came from my usual manner of saying things right out: I need to have situations clearly stated, otherwise I get confused. I think, too, the question was a way of searching for a guarantee: "You'll stay with me forever?"

Early on, I told my father of our plans. He slammed his hand down on his desk with a "Now, why do you want to do that?" He could understand living with someone, "throwing your lot in life together," but the idea of two women having a ceremony was just too much for him. All I could say was, "Why did you want to marry Mom?" To that, he replied, almost with a question, "To make an honest woman of her." I had to leave the room.

His remark, as absurd as it was at the time, has come to represent an important reason for having a ceremony: to take a step out of invisibility. Pop recently explained that he just didn't want to see us get hurt: to his way of thinking, if you're invisible, no one can hurt you. He doesn't understand that the more you're out, the less you can be hurt, because you have consciously chosen to live at the deepest level of your being.

One thing I cherish from our ceremony is the part where we say, "To deny one another is to deny God." It really defines the price of hiding. To us, losing God means losing the best part of yourself. That one little phrase from our ceremony comes up in my mind every time I want to slip by unnoticed, every time I get scared and want to hide. That one promise to Becky keeps me true to myself. It keeps me coming out. It makes me "an honest woman," in the best sense.

*Becky:* I was confused when Patty first asked me to marry her. I wasn't sure exactly what that meant. I felt a "yes" resonate deep inside me, and on some gut level I knew what it *might* mean, but there was nothing I could articulate. Images of heterosexual weddings floated through my mind. There was little in those images that appealed to me, and I knew it didn't make sense to transpose them onto a lesbian relationship. Yet there was something in this relationship that called for acknowledgment and celebration.

As we talked about the meaning of such a ceremony, the possible date for the ceremony began to be pushed further back. Just being together seemed like full-time work. We were coming together at such a deep level that it seemed as though every long-hidden hurt opened, bled and then closed again, this time more healed. I think we both felt so fully loved; the love we felt for one another seemed abundant enough, and powerful enough, to help heal the oldest of wounds.

At the same time, while once we had seemed so similar, now that we were living together we seemed diametrically opposed. Transcendental Meditation and Buddhism seemed to be completely different paths; our approaches to politics were different; the way we handled money was different; Patty's sarcasm was a far cry from my passive aggressiveness; and my love of blank walls and bare furnishings collided with Patty's thirty-odd years of collecting treasures. Every difference seemed traumatic, and each one had to be dealt with, cried over and discussed thoroughly, all before anyone could sleep.

I look back on that first year with astonishment at how quickly we moved through passion, fear, grief, anger, finally returning to passion. I can't imagine that we slept more than a few hours a night for that entire first year. We jokingly came to the agreement that all we really needed was two hours of sleep a night to take the edge off total exhaustion.

I remember sitting on the front stoop after one such night, having moved through at least three issues, one after another. As we sat there at three or four in the morning, Patty started to quietly sing, "Getting To Know You." We couldn't stop laughing. It summed up the entire year.

*Patty:* What does a ceremony mean? Episcopalian catechism defines sacrament, of which marriage is one, as "an outward and visible sign of an inner invisible grace." It's that simple. Celebrating a marriage is an outward sign of an invisible blessing. It's like singing when you're happy. It is that natural, yet it gets layered over by so many political and social issues. It involves a lot more than simply celebrating.

It means the commitment to a lifetime together, with the understanding that if it gets too destructive, you leave. That simple caveat is remarkably paradoxical to me, but no different from what heterosexuals face. For lesbians, there are additional concerns: I think for lesbians it means a whole other level of coming out.

Another part of our ceremony that I love is the reading from *The Riverhouse Stories*, which speaks of the surprising place our love takes us. Becky and I half-jokingly call it "beyond our brains." To me, that means beyond all that is familiar and beyond all childhood expectations. Very few little girls are raised with lesbian on their list of people they hope to become. Yet ever since I saw the golden beauty of Jenny Best in seventh grade, I dreamed of marrying a woman. I didn't allow myself to dwell on it though. I had no name for how I loved; I only knew I must never mention it to anyone. So I stuck all that love down inside the black pit I labeled "ugly."

If marriage is a dream come true, and I think it is, then it is a two-fold process for most lesbians. You not only have to find your dream woman, you must also awake from ignorance and fear and reclaim the light where your love can reside with honor. Such awakening takes you beyond your brain, beyond fear, into a whole new world.

There are new standards for me now. I am in school, and I think about the day I'll interview for a post-doctoral research position. Going in, I will claim Becky, just as any employee claims a spouse. It's an obligation I feel stemming from our ceremony. If I weren't in a relationship, I'd not mention anything, but it is a point of honor with me now to claim my family.

*Becky:* After our first year together, we both felt ready to go ahead with a ceremony. The traumas of the first year had subsided, leaving a much quieter, steadier love. There was no doubt in my mind but that this was the relationship of a lifetime; I wanted to honor and celebrate that, and I wanted to express my gratitude for the gift I had been given.

Our first step was to each separately write what we would like included in the ceremony. When we came back together, neither of us could believe what the other had written: "You want to say *what?*" Patty's idea of a ceremony was to "work the crowd" with a combination of high Episcopalian mass and Hindu yagya, in which a white stallion galloped round the world three times as the pipe organ pealed out crescendos upon which angels slid to earth. I wanted a ceremony that was as intimate as possible, with only our two hearts and a great and infinite stillness.

The process of combining our visions was extraordinary. It forced us to look at our relationship and see what it meant to each of us. It was a way of creating a blueprint of the relationship, a way of seeing what qualities we wanted the relationship to nurture. It became apparent to both of us that the ceremony was a way of honoring our spiritual selves and of ritually acknowledging that this relationship was aligned with our spiritual paths.

We asked our friend Carolyn Mobley to preside and to read the words which we had written. More than anyone else we know, Carolyn carries with her a sense of spirit grounded in action. In addition to being an associate pastor at an MCC, she's also a wonderful singer and activist in the lesbian community. We knew Carolyn would bring to the ceremony a combination of spirituality and joyful exuberance.

*Patty:* We made our invitations. Becky found the right card in a shop in New York and we laser-printed our announcement: "With joy and an abiding commitment to give our love its full expression, we invite you to the celebration of the joining of our lives and our exchange of vows."

Then we made the guest list. I got depressed as I realized that now that I had come out, most of my oldest and dearest friends didn't want to have a thing to do with me. It felt like a very important event to be attended by only new friends. It made me doubly aware of the new world I was entering.

Most of my family had difficulty with the ceremony, too. Mom was great. She wanted to bring the grandkids, but my brother didn't want them "confused," though he said we were welcome to visit them and have them over to our house. He wasn't sure until the last day if he'd come himself. We didn't want anyone there who felt uncomfortable. What I failed to appreciate at the time was how much I was asking from them. When I came out, I was lucky to have my heart as a guide: I knew my loving was good. Then I made an effort to re-educate my intellect so I could understand how such a heart could have been labeled as bad. But then it seemed to take forever for my stomach to feel okay. Heart, head, stomach—they each adjust in their own way at their own pace. I asked my family to make this adjustment all at once in a few months, and then I felt crushed when they didn't measure up. I wanted my brother to love me enough to make it to the ceremony—and he did, even though it was harder for him than he'd admit.

My older sister, who was in her second year of medical school, raising three kids and running a pig farm, was just too busy. I think, though, if it had been a "real" wedding, she would have made the extra push required to be there. I think in different circumstances her world would have been more understanding and would have supported her being there. It's just too inconceivable to miss your sister's wedding because you're busy. But that understanding just wasn't there, though I think she has it now.

A straight friend assured me that all families hassle you when you're planning a wedding; they never approve of this or that or the person you've chosen. She insisted that there was no difference between gay and straight weddings. I could never articulate what a huge difference there was between your family not liking your husband and your family being uncomfortable with your existence. After much debate, she declined our invitation, saying, "You and Becky might want to kiss, and that would make me sick." Since she didn't want to hold us back, she would stay away. She never saw what an incredible thing she'd said.

I regret that there was so much trauma around family issues that I was blind to the enthusiasm of the people in my lab at school. I had told my advisor of our plans, because I wanted some time off. She told the others in the lab, and the next day they were all abuzz, inviting themselves. I was so caught up in hassles elsewhere that I didn't recognize the genuine excitement these new friends felt for me. They still tease me about excluding them.

*Becky:* My background was very different from Patty's. While Patty had grown up in central Illinois, I had been brought up in a blacklisted community of screenwriters in Mexico. Little in my history gives importance to many of the norms of American life. Part of Patty's stress from this time involved losing an "all-American dream" that I simply had never had.

I had come out to my mother when I was eighteen. She'd reacted with concern about my life being more difficult but also with a complete assurance of her support and love. Ten years later, when I told her that I had fallen in love with Patty, her first question was when were we going to set up housekeeping together. In addition to family support, my background in both Buddhism and film had made for an accepting community of friends.

The day before the ceremony, my brother and one of his sons flew in from Santa Barbara, my mother from Los Angeles, one sister from Boston, another from Seattle, and friends came in from Boston and New York. I felt that the ceremony was being truly honored by both friends and family. That evening, my brother treated both families to a meal at a Japanese restaurant. Patty and I realized how rare it was to have both sets of parents willing to be present at the ceremony. We felt very lucky.

*Patty:* I guess I don't do well on the eves of weddings. The night before my sister got married, I started crying and continued until they knocked me out with a tranquilizer. I couldn't get over how that night marked the end of our eighteen years of living together. There was such a never-again quality. With Becky, I felt that for the first time in my life, I was choosing to leave my family, that I love so much, and move into a world where they could never fully go. It goes back to *The Riverhouse Stories* quote:

> It took her out of the roles she thought she would grow up to fill. It took her away from her automatic stream of pictures of what life should be and forced her to create her own version of what life could be.

It felt like a dying. I don't think heterosexuals die before they marry. I died. But that's part of a true rite of passage, because death and rebirth are how we become transformed. Actually, though we hadn't planned it, I think this eve of tears marked the beginning of our ceremony. And Becky, after comforting me, began crying herself.

*Becky:* The issues were different for me, but also potent. It had been very powerful for me to see the members of my family gather. I'm the youngest of six children, all scattered across the country. I began to mourn that we were all so far apart geographically; we rarely get together as a family. I was also struck that my mother, at age seventy, was not immortal. My father had died when I was ten, and the idea that someday I would lose my mother seemed unbearable. My family is very precious to me, and the bonds that held us together were becoming increasingly fragile. I felt that I was saying good-bye to the family of my childhood and beginning to create my own new family with Patty.

Finally, after hours of tears, we managed to stand back and see ourselves. We realized that we were two women slipping over the edge emotionally. It suddenly seemed ridiculous, and the tears shifted into laughter. We laughed ourselves into exhaustion. We had already lost all hope of a good night's rest, but we cuddled in together, now quite happy, ready to fall asleep.

*Patty:* Then we heard purring. It was Orange Pekoe climbing onto our bed. You have to understand the family traumas of our cats. Kitty Carlisle, Pekoe's kitten, had only one desire in life: to always nurse at her mother's breast. But Pekoe, pregnant again, had grown to despise her daughter. For the last month, the mere sight of Kitty Carlisle had brought a terrible hissing from Pekoe. Pekoe deserted our house to hide in the back alleys and cellars of the neighborhood. But tonight, amazingly, there was Pekoe, curled up on our bed, purring and licking Kitty Carlisle's face. Kitty Carlisle was in bliss. We "oohed." What was going on? It seemed like a miracle; as if Nature was replaying and then resolving our issues of family loss right there in front of us.

We fell asleep, feeling that Pekoe's behavior was a sign of how deeply our love echoed in the world. An hour later, we were awakened by little peeps. Pekoe was having her kittens right there on top of us. Eyes glazed, deep in some hormonally-induced mother-trance, she neatly delivered her baby to us as Kitty Carlisle watched. A profound silence permeated the room, and nestled in the middle of that silence was this birthing. Our room seemed blessed beyond any means we might have planned.

Through the night, kittens kept arriving, and in the morning we made a nest for them by our bed. And even though there were thirty people around the house, and music and laughter and talking, our bedroom felt like a chapel. No one could enter without feeling its holiness. And it was from this center that we went out to meet our guests and have our ceremony. I take those little cats as Mother Nature's gift, consecrating and blessing the vows we made that day with a power far beyond that of any government or church.

*Becky:* We woke in the morning to a glorious fall day. We had decided to have the ceremony on our back deck, and the leaves that day were brilliant orange and yellow, backlit by a low autumn sun. There was one bough in particular that swept over the wooden fence, looking like an arch leading out to the most brilliant blue sky. The day before, Patty had gone to the Farmer's Market and come home with two cartloads of roses, mums and carnations. There were flowers everywhere. Friends unable to come had also sent flowers and huge bunches of balloons.

Leaving the flower arranging to our two mothers, and the house in the hands of friends and sisters, Patty and I went out for a massage—a wedding gift from a masseuse friend. The massage lifted the anxiety of the past weeks of preparation and worry. I finally felt conscious and present. I'm still very grateful that that sense of being present lasted for the entire ceremony and celebration. I feel as though I drank that day in so completely; all concerns, all self-consciousness and all anxiety left with that morning massage. From then on I felt truly open to the wonder and extraordinary love that filled the day.

*Patty:* By the time we got back, the flowers were arranged in vases everywhere. There were so many that at the end of the day each guest took home a bunch, still leaving our house filled with flowers.

Becky had built an altar out of white pine which we had set up on our deck in back. On it was a picture of the Buddha. I wanted the Buddha there because there's a phrase in my head, "bowing to the Buddha," which comes from a story told by a therapist Becky knows about a visit she made to Buddhist temples in Japan. There is a ritual you follow in these temples to pay your respect: you sprinkle water, recite verses, then bow to a picture of a Buddha. By the end of her trip, the traveler had had her fill of recitations and bowing, but she entered one last temple before leaving. In the temple was a series of altars, and she began the now familiar routine. She sprinkled the water, said her verses, bowed to the Buddha, and moved to the next altar, repeating the sequence over and over. Finally, she reached the last altar, bowed and raised her head. She hadn't noticed that at this altar a mirror replaced the picture of Buddha. Expecting Buddha, she saw herself and, for a moment, could not see the difference. In that one instant, she'd seen God in herself. So to me, "bowing to the Buddha" means a pause. You bow to God, knowing that that's your own true nature. I wanted that to be part of our ceremony.

We also had some crystals set up on the altar: one black smoky quartz and another clear quartz which my grandfather had given me when I was a child. We had a little brass bowl of water used in Hindu pujas to purify the air and some incense for the same purpose; a bowl of fruit, as an offering of nourishment; Becky's tree-of-life candelabra from Mexico; bouquets of flowers; and Tibetan chimes given to us by a friend that morning.

People started to arrive in the early afternoon. A friend of my mother's had invited herself when she first heard that Becky and I were having a ceremony. Her son had died of AIDS, asking her to keep the cause of his death secret. I felt that our ceremony was in some way a healing to her as she saw gay love celebrated and saw the happiness that she would have wished for her son. I felt very privileged to have her there.

*Becky:* While Patty and I were still inside, the ceremony began outside with music from Ray Lynch's *The Sky of Mind* and a meditation. Everything became still, while two roses held our seats in the semi-circle of chairs.

*Patty:* Waiting to go out, Becky and I sat on the side of our bed, holding hands. I began to hyperventilate and thought I might "spin out." But Becky put her arm around me and said, "Stay with me, hon. Stay with me." And then we walked out together.

❧

*Song:* "Sarah's Circle," by Carole Etzler (Sung by Carolyn with all joining in)

*Welcome:* (Carolyn)

We gather today as a community to acknowledge and to celebrate a new life: the life Becky and Patty have created from the union of their own individual lives.

This joining has already taken place, the new life already launched. But as their love and commitment has deepened, there has been born a desire for ceremonial acknowledgment and a blessing of this love.

As individuals, they have both, for many years, been on separate paths to God, or Goddess. They have each been blessed with their own vision of, and understanding of, the sacred and transcendent unity we call God.

Now they have been graced with a love which has made of their two lives one union. Today we gather to give thanks for this love and the new life it has created. Thanks to God and to each of you—friends, sisters, brothers and, above all, parents, Jean, Jim and Rusty—for allowing your love to shine so brightly.

We also gather today as a symbol of Becky and Patty's commitment and willingness to create of their life together, one that is aligned with God. We ask that they be blessed with the wisdom to find the path upon which they both may travel, the courage to overcome any obstacles that may lie along the way and clear vision to keep sight of the grace which surrounds them.

We pray that they may continue to make of this love, one that is clearly and truly a reflection of the infinite love which embraces us all.

*Readings:* From *The Dream of a Common Language* by Adrienne Rich (Read by Becky's sister, Debbie Butler Spiegelman):

> The rules break like a thermometer
> quicksilver spills across the charted systems
> we're out in a country that has no language
> no laws, we're chasing the raven and the wren
> through gorges unexplored since dawn
> whatever we do is pure invention
> the maps they gave us were out of date by years...
> > —From "Twenty-One Love Poems: XIII"

> *I am the lover and the loved,*
> *home and wanderer, she who splits*
> *firewood and she who knocks, a stranger*
> *in the storm,* two women, eye to eye
> measuring each other's spirit, each other's
> limitless desire,
> > a whole new poetry beginning here.
> > > —From "Transcendental Etude"

From *The Riverhouse Stories* by Andrea Carlisle (Read by our friend, Maria Papacostaki):

> [She] loved loving her. Out past the edges of the world's agreement, beyond... the rules of her childhood, beyond even her own mind, she loved her and loved loving her. The loving brought forth in her all of her courage as well as her limitations, all of her blind desire to be like the others, to melt in, to be invisible. It took her out of the roles she thought she would grow up to fill. It took her away from her automatic stream of pictures of what life should be and forced her to create her own version of what life could be. And beyond all of that was the woman she loved, living a life made from nothing more than her own imagination, and she was beautiful.

Selection from *New Seeds of Contemplation* by Thomas Merton (Chosen and read by Becky's sister, Susan Butler).

*Charge to Witnesses:* (Carolyn)

We are here today because Becky and Patty have asked you to bear witness to their love; realizing the promises they make intend a life and a lifetime; realizing the difficulties they face as well as the joys.

We are here today, in part, to name this love. Naming is a curiously social phenomenon in which the consciousness of community acknowledges the newly sprouted seed, and this acknowledgment and respect allows the nascent life to become full and strong.

Your support and sharing of their love and life will make their journey together easier and certainly much fuller.

*Charge to Couple:* (Carolyn)

Becky and Patty, for two people to create a life together is both difficult and miraculous. It evokes the deepest fears as well as most luminous devotion. An enduring union is always an odyssey of repeated deaths and births, each birth making the dying worthwhile, forging deeper understanding, more tender devotion, spirits more healed and whole.

To do this with the blessing of God requires that you honor the divine in each other and in yourselves; that you recognize that spirit is made manifest in a multitude of ways, all equal in holiness; that you honor the many voices of the soul—the joys, the delights, the love, as well as the anger, the fear, the illness and the unhealed wounds; that you allow each other and yourselves complete dignity and wholeness; that you not ask your life partner to be any less than the fully powerful woman that she is; that you embrace her in her complexity—in her longings and in her delights, in the fullness of her dreams, in her relationship to God.

Know that the world will ask you to deny her a million times. Know also that denial of your love for her, or of any part of either soul, is a denial of God.

This is both God's blessing and charge to you: to live together with honor, courage and honesty. Do you agree?

(Yes, I do . . . Yes, I do.)

*Exchange of Vows & Rings:* (Becky & Patty)

Asking God's blessing, and giving my own, I give you this ring as a symbol of my love, and join you in heart, soul and body.

*Blessing by Prayer:* (Carolyn)

Most loving God/Goddess, eternal Mother/Father of us all, we thank you for the joining of these our sisters, Becky and Patty, and we acknowledge now your blessing upon them and ask that your loving spirit may abide with them always, sustaining their love and life throughout their journey on this plane, and even into the next. Amen.

ðŸ‚

*Becky:* After the prayer, our friend Peggy put on a tape of music we had made ahead of time. "Song of the Soul" by Cris Williamson was first. I felt as though my heart were about to burst. The sun was still streaming through the trees in the back yard, and I felt as blessed as I could be. I think everyone was hugging everyone. At one point I let out a whoop and a holler to release the joy that was bursting my heart open.

*Patty:* Everyone was crying. We have an angelic picture of Becky's brother Michael. She'd never seen him cry before, but there he was, tears running down his face. I think people were crying because they felt that we had all done something brave and true and good. It seemed very rare. What was it that we had done? Said yes to our love? I think so.

*Becky:* We had also proclaimed the goodness and the holiness of our love.

*Patty:* There doesn't seem to be such a sense of triumph in heterosexual weddings, maybe because they are such a part of the expected. Recently my sister Sandy told me that she'd mentioned to a friend that I was lesbian. Her friend was shocked and asked her, "How'd you deal with that?" Sandy just replied, "Becky is the best thing that ever happened to Patty." She's right.

—Patty Bralley and Becky Butler

ðŸ‚

*Patty Bralley: As I write this, I'm just about forty days into being forty years old. I spend my time working on my Ph.D. in molecular genetics, studying how a virus makes decisions. I'm also trying to translate DNA into music and am exploring the swamps, mountains and woods of the Southeast with Becky.*

*Becky Butler: I'm thirty-two and, after ten years of working in film and television, have gone back to school to get a master's degree in social work. I practice vipassana meditation and am interested in the union of psychotherapy and meditation. I love canoeing along the winding waterways of the Okefenokee Swamp, am currently learning about shade-gardening, and have recently discovered the wonder of woodworking.*

# Kwambe Omdahda

## & Patricia Omdahda

Kwambe (left) & Patricia (right) & daughter Kashiko (center)
photographer: H. L. Keller

*August 19, 1989* ❧ *California*

# Building a Family: Together We Soar

Patricia and I met in 1981 in law school. I was the only Black lesbian there until Patricia arrived, and we sort of gravitated toward each other. We didn't really hang around much together, but we talked a lot and considered each other a friend. Then Patricia withdrew from school, and I didn't see her again until about two years ago, when I ran into her at a dance. I was so glad to see her. She was someone I liked a lot, and I'd always had a lot of respect for her. I hadn't really thought of her romantically, but I had held her in my heart all that time. During that long period when we hadn't seen each other, we had talked once on the phone. I had asked her to go out with me, and then I'd called back later to cancel because I had to go out of town. So when we finally saw each other two years ago, I said, "Well, you owe me a date. Let me take you out next weekend."

To me, it was just a casual thing. I've always dated heavily, so I didn't give it much thought. As a matter of fact, I had another date earlier that evening, so I arranged to take Patricia out later. Well, it turned out to be a serious date. We talked about what had happened during all the years we hadn't seen each other, what had happened between us the last time we had seen each other, and then progressed on to what was currently going on with each of us. I picked her up at nine o'clock, and we talked until about four in the morning. Finally, she said, "You know, you're not going to spend the night. I don't spend the night with women that I've just gone on one date with." And I thought, "I like this woman." Most women usually let me spend the night. There was something in her statement that attracted me.

At that time, Patricia also had a two-year-old daughter, Kashiko. When I arrived that first night, I peeked into her bedroom and there she was, asleep. She was this beautiful little bitty girl. She had the prettiest skin coloring. I was just hooked on this baby the moment I looked at her. I just thought, "My God, what a beautiful little child."

In the past, I had always stayed away from women with children; I liked life in the fast lane too much. It was okay with me if a woman had other partners, but not children. Then slowly I had begun to be really attracted to women that did have children. It got to the point that I would see a pregnant woman and I'd try to date her. That led to very strange relationships. Somehow, they would still be straight and I would still be dating them. It was always a mess. Anyway, it was a real plus for me that Patricia had this little girl.

There were other conditions that seemed right, too. We had both gone from sort of a wild life toward more spirituality and wanting family unity. Patricia told me about the church she was involved with, and it was just the kind of church I'd been looking for. She asked me if I wanted to go with her the following Sunday, and I said, "Sure!" She was really taken by that, because most people were ridiculing her for embracing spirituality. But it was just right for me. All the conditions between us seemed right.

I came back the day after that first date, and that was when I met Kashiko. She and I hit it off so well. She's a remarkable little girl. When I came in the house that day, there was all this tension, because Patricia was breaking up with a lover, and the lover was still living there. I came in, and neither Patricia nor this other woman said much to me. Then Kashiko said, "Hi. Sit down. Take off your coat. You want some water or something to drink?" I couldn't believe it; she was only two years old. The baby came back in the room with this glass of water, and Patricia said, "Where'd you get that water?" She was too little to get to the faucet, and Patricia was worried that maybe she'd gotten it out of the toilet. But it was okay. I took it and said, "Thanks, baby. This is all right." Then the baby climbed up on the couch and began to make conversation. She just won my heart over.

I had been quite a runaround before that, but from the moment that Patricia and I went out together, I became monogamous, even though we weren't together sexually. She acted like, "Why would you want to do that so soon?" I was thinking totally the opposite. I was thinking, "This is bizarre. I'm here again and *still* not having sex." Patricia is a very intelligent woman. She doesn't jump into things; she thinks about them. She kept the physical thing out of it so I had to focus on her as a person. I had to slow down and actually listen. I started to lose all the surliness that I'd had. There had always been a little swagger about me, which just dissipated when I got together with Patricia. You run into the truth, and all your shields disappear. I could see right away that she was someone I wanted to be with. I said to myself, "Uh oh, this is serious stuff. I like this too much."

By the middle of May, I told her that I was really feeling serious about her. She said, "You want to be really committed and that type of thing?" I said, "Yeah, I really do." She told me she needed more time to think about it, so I said, "Let's go to Reno for the weekend, and during that weekend tell me what your decision is." So we waited until July, and we went away together. She was a little hesitant, but during that weekend she told me yes, she wanted to be with me. I said I wanted to live with her; I wanted to move in. She said, "Now that's fine, but I don't want you to live with me without commitment. I want a real commitment, not just some words."

Never in my life had I been monogamous, so all of this was really new for me. I had never created mutual goals with a person. I'd had lovers that I'd lived with, but we'd always kept everything very separate. And even when I'd lived with a lover, I'd always seen other people also, like satellites around that relationship. This time, I wanted to be totally monogamous. I wanted to really focus on the relationship; I wanted us to build something together.

Patricia explained that she wanted to build a solid base for her daughter and did not want a lot of drama. She didn't want a lot of telephone calls and didn't want to be jumping up and running out in the night because some friend was distressed somewhere. She didn't go for people moving in and out of her life. She also said, "You can move in, but I have to have a ring."

What she didn't tell me was that she wasn't ready for me to move in right then. Well, I ran out and bought these really expensive rings. I took her out to dinner, showed her the rings, and she gave me hers right back! I was shocked. I took the rings back to my condo. I was so confused; I had paid something like two thousand dollars for these rings. I thought that was what she wanted. I still had absolutely no desire to date anyone else. I just wanted to be with her. Usually I'll obsess a little bit about someone until I party it out with them, and then I go to the next person. But with her, it wasn't obsession; I just felt a very strong sense of satisfaction being with her. I was just so satisfied sitting there and talking with her and being with her. The sex was also very moving; it was the first time I'd had sex with someone I had a lot of deep feelings for. I decided to put the rings in the drawer and wait it out.

Finally, in October of 1988, she said "You know, you're here all the time. You may as well move in." I figured I would finally be able to give her the rings, but she said, "First of all, those rings are too expensive. It's ridiculous to spend a lot of money on rings. A gold band would be fine. In the second place, I want to pick my own ring." So I kept one of the rings for myself, and she picked a different ring for herself.

It was very strange that first year. We had very different approaches to family holidays. In my family, holidays were something you embraced. You cooked up a lot of food, and you had a wonderful time. In her family, there wasn't necessarily a big celebration. I wondered why I was doing all this holiday stuff when Patricia was just kicking back and reading or watching TV. I kept thinking that we were supposed to get excited because it was a holiday. So she and I had strong adjustments to make around holidays and birthdays. We had to talk with each other a lot, but we made it through the holidays, and then by April 1989 Patricia said that she would like to have a ceremony to acknowledge our commitment.

Every once in a while in the past, I had run into someone who'd had a trysting, and I had always thought that it was ridiculous. I always thought that if I said I wanted to be with someone, that should be enough. I'd always felt that doing that kind of ceremony meant pigeonholing ourselves and following a heterosexual pattern. We were women of our word, and if we said we were committed, then we were: we didn't need a ceremony. But when Patricia said she wanted a ceremony, it made perfect sense to me. I said, "Yes. I would really like to do that."

It seemed important for a couple of reasons. First, she was so embraced in my heart, and I was so committed; I wanted to declare her as the woman in my life in front of all the people that I really cared about. I wanted to openly proclaim to them that this is what it's like when you are with someone that you really love. As Black women here in Oakland, and as lesbians in general, we'd been through a lot together; we'd always rallied and supported each other in times of crisis. This time, I wanted to stand up in front of them all, all the women who love me, and I wanted to show them Kwambe at her happiest moment. I wanted to say words that would show them how wonderful life was for me. I also wanted to say that my relationship with this woman was a very serious thing. It's a very long road and a road that I embraced with wonder and delight. I wanted the world to know it. I also wanted to give Kashiko a feeling of foundation, a feeling of security in her home.

The ceremony was important for Patricia because she wanted the feeling that the family was being solidified. She wanted to know that she and I would stand together, no matter what happened. And she wanted to know that if anything happened to her, Kashiko had someone to take care of her.

When we were planning the ceremony, I called my mother, who's in her late seventies. I said, "Mom, I am with this woman now, and this is serious business. She has this little daughter, and I want you to come out and meet both of them." So Mom came out and met them. I also called my sisters. I have seven sisters; I am the eighth girl. I called several of them and said, "This woman is talking about a ceremony and it feels like it's something I should do, but it's also something I've always ridiculed." One sister said something very interesting. She said, "What she's really saying to you, Kwambe, is that it's time to face up. Do you and your word really stand together? Either you have to say no, they do not, because I want this little door left open so I can dart out, or you have to stand up and say yes." What Shirley said was absolutely right; it was time either to stand up and be counted or to sit down and shut up and stop acting like I wanted to be counted.

So we went ahead with our planning, and we found a Presbyterian minister to perform the ceremony. One thing the minister said was that she wouldn't just show up on the day of the ceremony and say the right words. She said we'd have to spend some time with her and discuss what it was we wanted out of the relationship and see what our challenges and our compatibilities were. We went to see her about four times, and she gave us a lot of homework in between. She gave us wonderful questionnaires that we each filled out separately and then brought back to her, and she went through them with us. We found out a lot during those sessions. We found out that money was going to be our big issue, but we also discovered that we were extremely compatible in terms of raising a child together. Neither of us believes in spanking. My mother spanked a lot; she'd come at you in the name of the Lord and beat the shit out of you. Both Patricia and I agreed that we didn't want Kashiko spanked. We both believe in building her self-esteem by not eroding what she naturally has going for herself. We don't call her names. We give her a lot of leeway in her thinking; she has choices and she knows there are consequences to them. It was really through the minister's counseling that we found out that we agreed on these things, and it was also through her that we started recognizing the things that were going to be hard for us, like money issues.

Next, we sent out invitations. I wrote the invitations myself. Patricia had said, "Kwambe, we are not going to find words already written for us. There is nothing written already that says what we feel." So I sat down, and I wrote about the depth of our love and how we wanted a ceremony to reflect that love. It was all very moving and pretty, I must say. Once we sent the invitations, though, a very terrible thing happened with my family; my family went crazy. They suddenly turned on us. They were very angry. They didn't want to see it. They didn't want to be a part of it.

I got a call from one of my sisters who said that she and Mom were very upset, and how could I bring this kind of trauma on my mother. I said, "Wait a minute. Excuse me. As I recall, I am forty years old, and I first told Mom about all this when I was twenty." This is the same mother that used to say that I was the only one of her daughters with any sense because the rest of them were "penile worshippers." For twenty years, my mother had been meeting my lovers, pushing twin beds together so I could sleep beside the women I was bringing home. Fifteen years ago, she called me and said, "Honey," in her soft-spoken Christian voice, "I'm curious. What exactly do you do with these women? I've heard that women have sex with each other." I said, "Mom, yes, of course that's what we do." She said, "You mean you're not with men at all?" I said, "Business-wise, I stand with men. But Mom, when it comes to my heart, I give it to women." She said, "Fine." I told her what lesbian meant, and she said okay, she had it all straight. But then it was like the whole family went crazy.

I asked them what was going on. I said that I had already talked to them about it earlier and there hadn't been a problem. Mom had even said she'd come out here for it. My sisters said that she hadn't wanted to tell me what was really going on because she didn't want to hurt my feelings. They said that she was afraid I was going to burn in hell forever. Mom is almost eighty, and she does get into quite a fever about Christianity. All her life she's been in a tizzy about it, but now it's a fever. My sisters said that she had gotten every Bible out, and that she was working herself into a frenzy. They were afraid I was going to give her a heart attack and kill her.

I think what happened is that I crossed over the line with them. They had been able to tolerate who I was because I hadn't been with anyone in a serious, monogamous situation. While I would talk about the person I was with, I never before had really talked about the relationship itself. Then I sent them an invitation that put the relationship right up in their faces. I think it challenged their own feelings about their world being right. They felt like there had to be a right and wrong, and I was going to have to be wrong.

I was so furious with them that I stopped all communication. I didn't answer any letters, I didn't acknowledge anything. I just stopped. I took every picture I had of them and threw it in the trash. I was furious. I was finished with the whole group of them, except Mom; I kept her picture. She's heading towards eighty, and you can't throw a picture away if that's all you have. But I was through with those other rascals. I figured the best way to punish them was not to say anything to them at all, just to go about my happy life.

The only one of my sisters who was okay with it was my youngest sister, who lives out here. She's married to a very nice man, and she and he were part of our ceremony. So we had our ceremony with only my youngest sister and her husband present from my side of the family. Patricia's mother, who was very supportive, was there as Patricia's side of the family. The rest of the people there were really good friends.

In the early planning, we had been debating whether or not to have Kashiko present at the ceremony. We were thinking that maybe we would just make other arrangements for her during the actual event. However, she soon got wind of it on her own, and one day she asked, "Are you guys going to get married?" We wanted her to know about it but not be overwhelmed by it. I said that her mommy and I wanted to have family commitment. I wanted to say what I felt, and Mommy wanted to say what she felt. Kashiko said, "I want to say what I feel. I want to be in this holy union thing." So she became the flower girl for the ceremony.

At first, Patricia and I were just going to stand up and say how we felt. It was going to be simple. Then I told our friends what we were going to do, and they got all moony-eyed and excited and took over the planning of the whole ceremony. They came over, they had meetings, they brought wedding books, and they planned this elaborate event. They decided that we needed a flower girl, and a ring bearer, and that we had to come down this long aisle, and that people had to sit on this side or on that side. There were all these rules that I had never known. I hadn't been to all that many weddings, and I don't think that Patricia had either, so we had no inkling that so much was involved. But my friends knew, so they got everything organized. It ended up being a big ceremony at the Oakland Rose Gardens.

We also went through the ordeal of what to wear. I wear pants or I wear nothing, and since I knew I couldn't get away with wearing nothing, I wore pants. I ended up wearing a tuxedo with full tails. I'm a large woman, and I was worried about how I'd look in tails, but I think I ended up looking quite fetching. Then Ayanna, a friend who is like a sister to me, took Patricia shopping. Patricia is not a gown-wearer; she's not the swooping Loretta Young type. But for this, she wanted to wear a flowing-in-the-wind type of dress. What she ended up with was a beautiful traditional wedding gown. I was so surprised. My friends hadn't let us see each other dressed up until the ceremony, so the first time I saw her in her gown was at the Rose Garden. She was so beautiful, she took my breath away.

Then there was the reception to plan. Patricia had decided that she wanted to have the reception at our house. We have a nice house, but I don't think it's the kind of house where you have a formal gathering. But I said, "Okay, we'll do it." Well, we ended up with all of this elaborate silver everywhere. There were even fountains. It was bizarre, yet wonderful. Between planning the wedding and organizing the reception, though, my nerves were ruined. Everybody at work said it was going to turn out all right, but I could hardly do my job. I was so stressed that friends truly did have to take over; I was not in control at all. Fortunately, my youngest sister and my best friend were there, and they just carried it through. It turned out to be a really wonderful event. At the end of the ceremony, we cut loose seventy-five silver and rose helium ballons, all of which had written on them:

Patricia, Kashiko, Kwambe
We Soar.
8/19/89

Kashiko still talks about our day. We called it a holy union; I didn't want to call it a marriage or a wedding, because I didn't want Kashiko to be confused. I knew she was going to talk about this to her friends, and I didn't want people to say "No, two women cannot do that." She was having a lot of questions anyway, "Mommy, can two women get married? Can two men?" I told her that people have choices. They can do whatever they want. The law may not say it's okay, but you have to think through for yourself what you can do without hurting other people's feelings.

We have pictures all over the house of us on our big day. When Kashiko's friends come over, she shows them all the photos. She's really proud: "Look at me in my beautiful dress. These are my mommies. We had a holy union and the whole family was together." She really embraces this family, though she says it causes a problem on Mother's Day; she has to make two cards, and everybody else only has to make one. She and I have this joke; we call it putting the breathe on things. You go, "Whooeee," puckering your lips and blowing. She said, "Mommy, I have really got to put the breathe on these cards. They work me so hard." I said, "You poor thing. Just don't make me one." She said, "No. I have to because you are my mommy, and you have to make a card for your mommy if you love her. So I have to make you one."

For me, in my heart, the ceremony didn't really make any difference in how I feel about Patricia or Kashiko; I'm committed with or without symbols. But I think our holy union made a big difference in Kashiko's life; she stands grounded in what our relationship is now. I wanted to give her that foundation and let her carry it on from there. Patricia and I are also thinking about having another child, so I think our family will probably expand. But we'll see. We're still exploring.

*This account is based on an interview with Kwambe Omdahda.*

੨ৱ

*Kwambe Omdahda: Kwambe is from the Midwest, and she proudly retains that unique regional humor. She is a committed health care professional who has served the geriatric community for many years as a registered nurse. She plans to combine her experience in nursing with her law degree to achieve progressive health care laws. Kwambe continues to create an environment of love and stability for her family. Her secret fantasy is to raise five daughters.*

*Patricia Omdahda: Patricia grew up in Harlem, New York. She is an engineering student who will one day build environmentally-sensitive structures. Her vision is of a long line of Omdahdas who will live their time on this planet as gentle and humane beings, guided by their hearts as well as their minds.*

*Atimah*
*&*

  *Aylana*

    *December 21, 1986* ❧ *Texas*

# With the Guidance of Dreams

*Atimah:* Some pretty amazing things happened at the beginning of our coming together. I had a solstice ceremony one year and invited Aylana, along with about fifty other friends. I had built a medicine wheel in my backyard, and we did a medicine wheel ceremony around the solstice fire, followed by a feast and celebration. It was all in line with the Native American religion, or the Nature spirit way. Afterward, Aylana stayed, and we talked late into the night, just as friends. This was before any thought of intimacy ever opened between us. For one thing, Aylana had never been involved with a woman before, and I had made a strict vow of no relationships. That night, after everyone had gone home, we sat outside under a full moon and talked and watched the fire die. Finally, when the fire was dead, I covered it with some dirt where the coals had glowed, just to make sure that nothing could ignite. Having been a camper for many years, I'm very careful about making sure fires are completely out.

The next day Aylana came over to show me a crystal ball she had bought. We stepped out on the back porch to look at it in the sunlight. We were standing there talking for about two or three minutes when I looked over in the direction of where the fire had been the night before. This was one or two the next afternoon and, of course, the fire was dead. There was even a spider building its nest in it, which it wouldn't have done if there had been any heat left at all. As we stood there talking, smoke started to come up from what had been dead coals. Within a matter of maybe three minutes, to our amazement, this dead fire began to reignite.

*Aylana:* We went into shock. All of this time there was this energy charge going between us, and both of us were trying to ignore it. I certainly was trying to ignore it. I had known for some time that I was attracted to Atimah, and then I'd had a dream the night of the get-together that had told me that I needed to tell her. I've learned to follow my dreams, so I was prepared to humiliate myself and tell this woman I was attracted to her just to follow my dream and get it out of the way, because I knew it wasn't reciprocated. I would just do what I had to do, get it over with and go my merry way.

Meanwhile we were looking at this fire, absolutely in shock, sitting around it with our mouths gaping, neither of us quite believing it.

So we talked for a while, and then I got up my courage, and being very shy, I just sort of said, "Well, you know, I have to admit that I'm attracted to you. . . mumble mumble." I think I had to repeat it three times before I could get the words out. And much to my surprise, she said that she was attracted to me, too! Then we decided that that was interesting and we were going to ignore it.

*Atimah:* We decided that it was a nice attraction, but we had a good friendship and a good partnership in terms of healing. I do dream analysis and Aylana is a psychotherapist, and we'd done some healing work together with people. We had a good relationship, and we weren't going to complicate it.

*Aylana:* We had both been in prior relationships, and so we were both thinking, "Oh God, do I want to trust again? Do I really want to try this again at all?" I was thirty-four at the time and Atimah was forty-six, so it wasn't like we were nineteen or twenty-three, with any starry-eyed illusions. We had both been through a couple of messy breakups; the kind where you wonder if you'll ever trust anybody again. I think it was also hard for Atimah because she had made a decision not to have children and I have an eight-year-old daughter. So it not only meant becoming a couple, it meant becoming a family.

*Atimah:* I simply had decided that I had done all the learning that I wanted and needed to do, thank you very much, through relationships. I had decided that that was the end of that particular mode of growth, at least in regard to one-on-one primary relationships.

Well, that was in December, and we didn't truly get involved intimately until May.

*Aylana:* For both of us it was a challenge, because the relationship had a level of intensity that neither of us had ever experienced before, and intensity is often frightening. We had to go through a lot of fear around that.

*Atimah:* My fear was also fear of commitment. That's a big one for me. I had been in relationships before, including a three-year marriage to a man, but I had never encountered someone who really touched those deep, deep places in me. I had always been a bit of a loner in a lot of ways. But it gradually became clear to both of us that we were involved in a relationship that was bonded by a deep and intense love and that we wanted to nurture it and take it as far as it would go.

*Aylana:* That's really how we viewed the ceremony—as a gathering of the Light forces. We did it at the winter solstice because that's the returning of the light. It was a bringing in of all the positive energies to nurture the relationship and to help heal what needed healing. We regarded it as a wedding, and everything that that means—a marriage.

I had been married before, to a man, and it was interesting to see the differences between my first marriage ceremony and my ceremony with Atimah. When you do a traditional "wedding," it's sort of something that just happens to you. After all, the basic structure is already laid out for you. In our ceremony, there was no pre-existing basic structure, so we had to decide on each element. Everything we included we included for a very conscious reason. It was a conscious decision to sit down and say this is what we want to do. This is what we're bringing in. It was a conscious desire to cement and commemorate and make a binding commitment to a relationship that we certainly want to last for the rest of our lives.

*Atimah:* I think a wedding and marriage represent the joining together of two individual paths and a shared path. A sharing of growth and of learning. Of healing. And loving and fun, and laughter. But it also represents a bonding that is only possible, I think, if you recognize the spiritual dimension of the relationship which you share. This relationship was something that I felt comfortable with in regard to my spiritual path, and for both of us that comes first. So finding a way to make this relationship a part of my path, and to honor that in a sacred way, was something I felt very much at home with.

*Aylana:* For much of our ceremony, we drew upon Native American traditions; Atimah's grandfather was a Shoshone medicine man, and I have some Iroquois-Seneca heritage.

A lot of the ceremony also came to Atimah through her dreams. For literally months before we did it, Atimah would wake up in the morning and say, "Guess what. . . I dreamed this and this and this. . . . " And she would write it all down. It was wonderful to see how it all came together. She's been working with her dreams for twenty-five years and has a clear communion with them. She's able to get very clear messages.

*Atimah:* I had a number of dreaming experiences, and they came, it seemed, almost always after I had gone through a tremor of questioning and pulling back, or Aylana had gone through one of her silent periods.

*Aylana:* We suffered many attacks of "Oh, what am I doing?"

*Atimah:* I often rely on my subconscious to let me know what my conscious may not be seeing, and I was asking for inner guidance on whether or not this was right, whether or not this was supported by my higher self and by her higher self. So I stayed tuned to that and periodically this flurry of dream activity would come through. They talked to me a lot during that period. And they led me very strongly toward the ceremony.

*Aylana:* I'm just really happy that we did it. I'm happy that we got through all of our fears about doing it, and while I guess the fears were probably uppermost, they were also balanced by a whole lot of joy and happiness. The ceremony itself was a very important milestone, but so also was the process of getting to it. As painful as it was, the process of moving towards that with somebody was really wonderful. God, we worked through a lot of stuff, and it's great to have it worked through.

*Atimah:* And it will never ever rear its head again! Ha! Ha!

## The Ceremony

We started with a large solstice fire, and we asked everybody to bring something to burn—something old that they were letting go of. It's a way of symbolically letting go of all that old garbage, sort of a ritual cleansing and purification. Aylana had just been to visit her parents for the first time in eight years, so she burned a lot of family stuff in the fire as well as some things from old relationships. Atimah burned some poems and photos that symbolized her fear of commitment.

The guests brought all kinds of things. Gerry, a friend, burned something that symbolized his wandering eye. He's been married for some time, but he still tends to look around a lot. Some people with health problems burned their disease. Some people burned things silently, but most spoke and said what it was that they were getting rid of.

Then we had smudging, using sage and cedar sticks from New Mexico. Smudging is a purification ceremony. It involves the concept that smoke is an agent, a medium, that carries prayers to heaven. Sage and cedar are sacred herbs in the Native American religion. They represent the male and female powers in the grandmother and grandfather. The smoke of the sage and cedar is much akin to the frankincense and myrrh of the Middle East, Egyptian and African cultures. It raises the vibration and purifies the energy field of the surrounding environment.

As the stick is burning, you start at someone's feet and use a feather to blow the smoke over them. Everyone was smudged. That's also Native American tradition. You want everybody coming into a ceremony to be ceremonially cleared. You don't want a whole lot of junk being brought in.

After the smudging, we went up to the living room. On the living room floor, we had spread a king-sized bedspread, and underneath the bedspread was a ceremonial rug which served as our foundation. On the bedspread, we had built a circle of crystals. It was a large circle, about twelve feet in diameter, with each of the four directions marked by a large crystal cluster. The clusters were probably a foot in diameter. Then between the clusters were smaller crystals. Inside that circle, right up against the crystals, was a circle of twelve candles. Twelve is a symbol of wholeness of the tribe and numerologically it signifies the complete circle.

In the center of this large crystal circle was a round piece of oak, on top of which was placed a round mirror, and then on top of the mirror was a perfectly round clear bowl. In that bowl was water from both the Atlantic and the Pacific oceans. On the water were eight floating candles, so the fire and water were together. The number eight represents the grandmother, the earth element, the feminine principle at its highest level of vibration. It would be the green abundant time.

The floating candles, reflected in this beautiful clear bowl and again in the mirror, were just gorgeous. The room was lit only by candlelight.

After meditating and lighting the candles, we entered the circle. We sat on opposite sides of the central bowl: Aylana sat on the west side, Atimah on the east. To the left of each of us was our own crystal ball arrangement. We each had a large crystal ball five inches in diameter, and each had eight smaller crystal balls. The large crystal ball was in the center, with the smaller crystal balls set around it. Those represented our personal medicine wheels, crystal medicine wheels.

Then to the right of each of us was a small bamboo tray on which was placed a dish of almonds, a Japanese cup and a little Japanese sake pitcher filled with pomegranate juice. Pomegranates are very ancient symbols of the feminine principle, associated with love and also with lushness and richness. Pomegranate juice is considered a very rich blessing, besides which it's delicious. The almonds are considered the seed of life. The trays represented that which we wanted to give one another, what we came bringing as gifts to give one another. We each had a tray, and later in the ceremony, we would pour one another the juice and offer almonds from our own tray, offering each other communion.

We also had some very beautiful chimes and several singing crystal bowls. When we were ready, we played the crystal bowls, which was the sign for everyone to come in from outside. People sat in a large circle. In front of them was the crystal circle, then the circle of candles, and then we were in the center of the circle.

Amanda started with a movement prayer. A movement prayer is like a dance that is done as a spiritual offering. Then she spoke some words to each of the four directions and to the spirit above and below. Then Rick announced the purpose for the gathering, and did an incantation calling on the powers of light and love to bless the gathering:

Today on this day of solstice, we
gather to witness and bless
a joining of two life paths
in One Spiritual Light!
We call upon the powers of
Heaven and Earth; the
Ancestors and Angels of Light; and
the keepers of the Sacred
fire to give truth, Life,
Love and Light to this Union!
*Ramahesh*

*Ramahesh* is a word that came to Atimah in a dream many years ago
and it wasn't until ten years later that she confirmed the meaning with a
Hindu professor; it's a Sanskrit word meaning basically to be one with
God. It's a very powerful blessing.

Then, after some recorded flute music, our friend Ellen did a drum
beat for us. It was the heartbeat of a drum—very low and soft, and while
that was going on another friend, Heloise, read "The Ancient River,"
which is a poem that came to Atimah in a dream.

"The Ancient River" just came flowing out of dream state. It was
during a period when Atimah was really wrestling with her fear about going through with this, and going any further with the relationship. She
was in a lucid state, and yet not quite awake. She heard a voice speak these
words, and since she wasn't yet awake enough to write them down, she re-
played them in her head until she felt they were captured:

Over many eons and through many forms, our souls have come together. Yet, through all the forms, our hearts have never failed to
recognize one another. Through the many lives, pleasures and pains,
through all the various roles we have played in each other's unfolding story, one constant has remained. Like a river of Light, a powerful Love has flowed in, around and through our history of being together. It is the flow of that river which brings us together again.
Once again we plunge joyfully into the powerful currents of Love.
We come together in Light and in the company of our friends and
family to celebrate the river of our Love and to affirm our commitment to forging the river together. We ask your blessings and support, that we may swim easily and well. That we may know when to
let the current carry us and when to stroke for all we're worth. And,
most importantly, that we keep the river clear and sweet so its pure

waters can nourish the growth and well-being of all Life, especially those who live near the banks.

The drum beat continued while Heloise read "The Ancient River." As she finished, the drumbeat stopped and the chimes were rung once, and then, after a pause, another friend, Jenny, read a poem of Atimah's called "All."

> All anyone truly wants is Love.
> All anyone can truly give is Love.
> And, if in a single lifetime one is blessed
> to be able to give and receive Love.
> Then one has truly Lived.

The chimes were rung again, and then everybody played the crystal bowls. There must have been about six or seven bowls. They were incredible. They are similar to the Tibetan cast-bronze meditation bowls, but they have the sound of clear quartz crystal. Imagine a huge wine glass of pure quartz crystal being played, with the kind of pure clear note that only crystal can give. But the tone is so much fuller than that of a single glass, because these bowls are huge. One stands twenty inches deep and eighteen inches in diameter. Another is twelve inches in diameter and twelve inches deep.

While everybody was playing the bowls, we took our large crystal balls from the center of the smaller crystal balls and formed an energy ring. We each looked through our crystal ball at the other, forming an energy bond between us.

This is basically a visual meditation whereby we draw on the energy of the crystal to help amplify our intent, and the intent is then projected to an energy field that moves in a circle. It's like an energy ring that goes through us, through the ball and cycles between us.

When we put our crystal balls back, people gradually stopped playing the bowls. Then four poems were read. Terry read one from a book of poems on Native American themes called *Many Winters,* by Nancy Woods. The second poem was "Gebo" from *The Book of Runes,* read by our friend John. The third one was one we call "Song of Summer," again from *Many Winters.* The fourth one was read by Rich, also from *The Book of Runes.* It was the rune of "Wunjo."

Then, after a silence, the music which we had recorded earlier was played as a background for the offering we performed.

We each had a little bit of sage we had collected from sacred land in New Mexico, which we lit in small smudge pots in front of us. We started by pouring a little bit of pomegranate juice into the cup. Before offering it to each other, we held it over the sage smoke, and then over the bowl of candles and sea water, giving a blessing to it. The same was done with the dish of almonds. So the almonds and juice were blessed as they passed between us.

Then we blessed each other by pouring frankincense oil on our hands, then dipping them in sea water, and then touching them to each other's third eye and heart chakra. This connected the higher self to the love center so that that which flowed between us would lead us to a higher form of love.

Then the large crystal bowl was struck once. After the vibration faded to silence, the Sun and the Moon speakers entered the circle. These were friends each of us had chosen to speak for us.

One of the themes that played throughout the ceremony was that Aylana is Leo with a lot of sun energy, and Atimah is Cancer with a lot of moon and water, but to look at us you would never know that. Aylana appears to be much more of a water person, with a quieter energy, and Atimah is the more fiery one. Aylana has a moon in Scorpio, Atimah has Aries rising, with Mars in Aries.

So then the Sun and Moon speakers entered the circle. Their words, again, had come to Atimah in a dream. They each stood behind us and read. Glee, the Moon speaker, stood behind Atimah:

> I was born in the time of the Moon—and yet that luminous serenity of a quiet inner light eludes me. This I see in you—and seek, not to live through you, but to learn through you the gentle ways of the Moon. I offer in return that which comes without effort to me: the passionate powers of the Sun! I offer also my love and my commitment to keep it alive with honesty, laughter and the spiritual life which we share.

Atimah then said "Yes." "Yes" was the only thing either of us said in the whole ceremony. It was very much a desire that the only words spoken would be "Yes," holding in our own hearts the full knowledge and energy of what was being said, with "Yes" being the only word necessary. Full affirmation. This was seen in the dream.

Then a woman named Bobbi, the Sun speaker, read, standing behind Aylana:

> I was born in the time of the Sun—and yet, that radiant exuberance of a confident outer light eludes me. This I see in you—and seek, not to live through you, but to learn through you the passionate ways of the Sun. I offer in return that which comes without effort to me: the gentle ways of the Moon! I offer also my love and my commitment

to keep it alive with honesty, laughter and the spiritual life which we share.

And then Aylana said "Yes."

After that we exchanged pendants and rings. We had found the perfect pendants: a small quartz crystal ball enclosed in a silver moon that hung on a chain, and a small quartz crystal surrounded in a gold spiral, with the crystal pointing out. They're symbols of the moon and the sun. At the beginning of the ceremony, Aylana was wearing the moon and Atimah the sun, because that's what's home to each of us, and then we traded them. Aylana gave Atimah her moon energy, and Atimah gave Aylana her sun energy.

We also had rings of turquoise—the sacred stone to many Native American tribes. In terms of cultural tradition, the finger we wear them on is the traditional wedding finger, but for us it's the finger of Apollo. Apollo is the god of love and beauty and grace in life.

Then we did a coming together ritual. We were on our knees, with our hands palms down. Then our hands rose very slowly up in front of us, palms outward, and we rose with them, very slowly, until our hands were facing one another, about a quarter of an inch apart. We looked into each other's eyes, and we paused for about five seconds. The energy shooting between our hands was beautiful. Then we very slowly brought our palms together, leaned forward over the bowl of light and kissed.

Then everybody chanted "Om" three times, and our friend Metis entered the circle and performed the blessing prayer, "On the Path":

> Great Spirit travel with
> them and make their way
> light.
> Keep their hearts open through
> the long cynical night.
> Let the river of love flow
> through their souls. . .
> And the fire of courage
> keep them from the cold.
> Great Spirit travel with
> them and make their way
> light.
> *Ho!*

Then the drum was struck with three powerful strokes and another friend, Jerry, read another poem that Atimah had channeled, called "Passion":

Keep your passion alive—
it will warm you when the
world around you grows cold.
It will not allow comfortable
familiarity to rob you of that
special glow that comes with
loving deeply. It can lift
you over stone walls of anger
and carry you across vast
deserts of alienation. But its
greatest gift is that of touch—
for passion cannot dwell in
solitude—it thrives best in
loving embrace. So keep your
passion alive—hold one
another as a tree holds the
Earth and your love will
bear the fruit of many,
many seasons!
*Ho!*

We had a ringing of the crystal bowls while Aylana's daughter, Andrea, came into the circle with a basket of rose petals and corn and threw them all over us. It smelled wonderful, and the rose petals fell in the water. Andy had a great time. When she went back to sit down, she just put her hand on her chest and said, "Oh my!" She hadn't expected to have so much fun!

After that, with everybody laughing and in good humor, Rick and Amanda entered the circle and wrapped us in a wedding blanket, which is another Native American custom.

Then, as the ending, Rick read a pronouncement of union:

We speak for the Circle—
for the spirit of love in each
heart gathered round you, seen
and unseen. With the power
of Life invested in us—we
pronounce you joined
together as partners in
Life, Love and the
Spiritual Path of Light!
*Ho!*

*This account is based on interviews with Atimah and Aylana.*

કે

*Atimah:* I am of African, Native American and Irish heritage. My life and work are focused on personal and spiritual development, and I incorporate ceremony as an expression of my beliefs. I perfom ceremonies, including weddings, as rites of passage for others.

*Aylana:* I find balancing a career (psychotherapy), marriage and motherhood (a daughter, age ten) a daily challenge and joy. I survived growing up in a military family. My life today reflects my spiritual and political beliefs.

*Rosanne Leipzig*

*&    Judy Mable*

Rosanne (left) & Judy (right)
photographer: Joan I. Heller

*March 20, 1988*  ❧  *New York*

# Tikkun Olam—Healing of the World

*From every human being there rises*
*a light that reaches straight to heaven.*
*And when two souls that are destined to be together*
*find each other, their streams of light flow together,*
*and a single brighter light goes forth from their*
*united being.*

—Baal Shem Tov

*Rosanne:* When Judy and I got together, we both felt overwhelming joy at having found each other. For us, a ceremony was a way to celebrate our relationship and to share that joy with people we cared about. We also wanted to announce to the world that we were together. We wanted to have our relationship fully acknowledged in a public way and in a way that would bring together the various parts of our lives.

*Judy:* Initially we had no concept of what type of ceremony to have. We were both very involved in the gay synagogue, and the more we talked, the clearer it became that we wanted a Jewish ceremony. So we bought a book called *The New Jewish Wedding.* Every night we read a chapter together. I had never thought it would ever be possible for me to have, for lack of a better word, a wedding. So for me, even thinking about being able to have such a ceremony was exciting.

*Rosanne:* One important aspect of preparing for it was that the process really emboldened us to come out. For me it started when we sat down to put together a guest list. I kept feeling that had I done this as a heterosexual wedding years before, when my parents were alive, there were many relatives that I would have invited. When I sat down to make this guest list, I realized that because I was gay I had really distanced myself from many members of my family. I have a very large extended family, and I had no idea how they felt about me or how they would feel about this ceremony. I had always just gone under the assumption that since my mother had had difficulty with my being gay, the rest of the family would, too. But when we started to figure out whom to invite, I said, "I have no reality check on this at all. Let's just see."

What we did was to send out a postcard to everyone we wanted to invite early on, before the details were set, just letting them know to save the date. And then, to the family members to whom I wasn't out, I sent a cover letter that said:

> Judy and I have decided to share our lives together and will be having a Brit Ahavah [the Hebrew term we coined for this, meaning, literally, a covenant of love.]

> I'm sorry I haven't spoken directly with you about this before. Over the years my fears of rejection have kept me from being open and close with many people who mean a great deal to me. Now, to my delight, my own personal growth and my relationship with Judy have helped me arrive at a comfortable place where I can share this important step with the people I care about the most.

> I hope you will be able to share our simcha [happy event] with us, but if not, I hope we stay more closely in touch.

We sent this out to about sixty people, and we presumed that out of that sixty we would hear from twenty and three would come. Well, were we surprised. We got back the most beautiful letters from almost everyone we'd written. Thirty of these people ended up coming, all from out of town, including seventy-year-old cousins and aunts.

*Judy:* Rosanne's family also sent wonderful material for the chuppah, which is the canopy under which Jewish weddings are held. We had decided to make our own chuppah, so on the postcard we requested fabric from all of our friends and family members; we asked for any piece of fabric that was significant to them. Then, after the mailman had lugged up seventy or eighty packages of material for us, we sewed it all together. It contained everything from babies' blankets to wedding dresses to pieces of fabric designed especially for the chuppah.

*Rosanne:* Much of what we got back from members of my family were items that had belonged to my late parents or to my grandparents. It was really very moving. The whole process lifted this weight from me. That was never the intent of having the ceremony, but it certainly was a benefit.

*Judy:* That was true for my family as well. I have a much smaller family. My father is alive; my mother is dead. I have a sister, a niece and a nephew. My sister has been married twice, and both her current husband and her ex-husband came, which was interesting! My family had not been together since my mom died thirteen years ago, so this was very special. My aunt from Vermont, whom I hadn't seen in thirteen years, also came.

The most amazing thing for me was having my father there. He had been a career Navy officer for thirty years and had always been a rigid man.

When he learned I was gay, he was not too pleased, to say the least. For him to witness this event was extraordinary. He spent a good part of the time reflecting on how he had behaved when I was growing up. He began to realize what a tyrant he had been. He also cried, wishing my mother could have been there. Most extraordinary for me, though, was the fact that he was there, and that he has accepted Rosanne and been supportive of the relationship. I think he has grown with us, and, at sixty-eight, he's changed. It felt like a miracle to have him share that day with me.

*Rosanne:* The other part of the chuppah story is bittersweet. When we first told our friends, Shelly and Jay, that we wanted to have this ceremony, Shelly looked at us skeptically and said, "What do you want to do something like that for?" He started saying the old stuff about aping heterosexual tradition, and so on. Then, as the four of us sat and talked about it, he got more and more enthused about the idea. We talked about how much we wanted to celebrate our love with the people we cared about. Finally we got to the part about wanting to make the chuppah, and he said he wanted to embroider the center piece for us using our Hebrew names.

It turned out that while he was still working on it he was hospitalized with AIDS. He worked feverishly and finally finished it. It has our Hebrew names, and then on the bottom it says, "With love from Shelly and Jay." The day after he finished embroidering it, he lost the use of his right hand. He regained use for a very short time and signed our ketubah, which is the document stating the contract of the wedding. The next day he lost the use of his right hand again, this time permanently. It was amazing. He was very ill, but he still made it to the wedding. He died a few months later.

*Judy:* The embroidery was just beautiful, and there it was above us. The chuppah is like a tent of peace, or a tent of love; it's supposed to symbolize the home we're making together. It was wonderful to feel like all of our friends and family were enveloping us, protecting us.

*Rosanne:* We used many of the traditional symbols from a Jewish wedding, sometimes modifying them for our purposes. We commissioned an artist to make our ketubah. The wording of the ketubah has been greatly modified over the years. The more egalitarian ones are really quite lovely. In addition to being contracts of marriage, they are also works of art.

*Judy:* We went to a Hebrew arts fair and saw some that we really liked, one of which had a circle of people dancing around the bride and groom. It was a beautiful paper cut on a silk background. So we decided we would ask this woman if she would make a ketubah for us. Twenty minutes later, we were still pacing around, passing her again and again: "Should we? Shouldn't we? No, yes."

*Rosanne:* Finally we went up to her, and I said, "I think you've probably never been asked this question before, but would you do a ketubah for two women?" About two seconds passed, and she looked at us and said, "Is it a Jewish ceremony?" We said,"Yes!" It was interesting. She was initially reluctant to use the term ketubah, because she said that to her that term was specific to a heterosexual ceremony. That made us uncomfortable, and for a while we weren't sure we wanted her to do it, as we didn't want to work with someone who wasn't completely supportive. Then we went to her studio to re-open the discussion. You could see her grappling with issues that she had really never dealt with before. Within half an hour, she was calling it a ketubah.

In planning our Brit Ahavah, we met and dealt with people who had never thought of gays and lesbians as human beings with the same needs and wants as other people. Most of them began to relate to us as a couple in love, lesbians in love. There's a term in Hebrew, tikkun olam, which means trying to mend or repair the world. We began to have the feeling that by doing all this we were starting to participate in that process of healing. People who had never before recognized their encounters with gay people began to see gays as living, breathing human beings.

*Judy:* Sometimes, of course, we weren't sure that people knew what was going on even after a transaction. For instance, we had told the woman who designed our rings that we wanted to have them engraved in Hebrew. She lives in Connecticut, but she said that the engraving would have to be done by the Chassidic men in the jewelry district in New York. We were a little concerned about how these Orthodox Jewish men would deal with all this, but we went ahead and sent her the inscription, which read: Ahoovot Chaiim [beloveds for life] 3/20/88.

Rosanne wrote the inscription in Hebrew, exactly the way we wanted it. Soon the designer called to tell us there was a big problem. She had taken the rings to New York, and the engraver had told her that, "Whoever wrote this inscription does not know Hebrew." All Hebrew nouns have a specific gender, and to the engraver it was impossible that we would want both rings inscribed with the female form of beloveds for life. I told her to tell him to engrave it exactly the way it was written. So it ended up being done correctly, but I don't think it ever occurred to him that the rings were really for two women. I bet he's still convinced that someone made a mistake.

We were also concerned when we ordered the yarmulkes (skullcaps).

The people that run these stores are generally very Orthodox and reactionary; they're the same people that kept New York from having a gay rights law for fifteen years. So when we went in, we hemmed and hawed trying to decide whether or not we should have our names and the date stamped on them. Finally we decided to go for broke. So Rosanne wrote out: Brit Ahavah, Judy and Rosanne, 3/20/88. The salesman read it and said, "Oh we'll have to make up a new stamp. This isn't a Bar Mitzvah." And we said, "No, it's not a Bar Mitzvah." We had written Judy and Rosanne, and we were waiting for him to ask what this Brit Ahavah was all about. He never asked. We went ahead and ordered the yarmulkes. As we were leaving, he said to Rosanne, "So, it's your son that's having the Bar Mitzvah?"

So I called up the following day, because I really didn't want Bar Mitzvah written on all these yarmulkes. I made him find the order. He kept saying, "Lady, don't bother me. You're being crazy." I kept saying, "Just get the order. We have to talk. Just get it and read it back to me." He said, "Don't worry. They'll be right." Finally I got him to read the inscription back to me, and he read it back exactly the way we'd written it. He still didn't ask what it was. He never asked. He assumed, though, that we were having a huge event. In our synagogue both men and women wear yarmulkes; traditionally only men wear them. So since we were ordering 150, he assumed that 300 people would be attending the event. When we went to pick them up, another customer asked him what they were for. All he said was, "Oh they're for a big affair. A very big affair." That was it. I remember walking out of that store and beginning to laugh uncontrollably. We were hysterical for blocks. It was like, "Well, we did that. Let's see what we can do next."

We also worked with straight people who knew exactly what was going on and who were incredibly supportive. We had a wonderful bandleader, a straight woman, who kept calling us up and asking, "Did you get your dresses yet? What did you decide to wear?" She was just really excited and concerned. She was great. It all kept making us bolder and bolder.

*Rosanne:* Actually the biggest challenge we faced was to get the initial approval to have the ceremony at our synagogue. Congregation Beth Simchat Torah, New York's gay and lesbian synagogue, was founded in 1973. During its early years, it was decided that commitment ceremonies would not take place at the synagogue. I think that decision was both a product of the times ("as gay people we do not want to mimic the oppressive heterosexual institution of marriage") and internalized homophobia ("How will we be able to control this? Some people will be with a different partner every other week!"). We had to lobby both the synagogue board and the religious committee. It was interesting that some of their concerns were not all that different from those expressed above, but there was an overall understanding of our desire to have our Brit Ahavah at our spiritual home. We finally prevailed, and so became the first couple to have a commitment ceremony at the synagogue in its then fifteen-year history.

*Judy:* Our next task was to find a rabbi. Although our synagogue has many rabbis as members, we do not have a rabbi for the synagogue. The rabbi we really wanted was Helene Ferris. She was the rabbi who had sponsored my conversion the previous year. I had been raised as a Catholic but had never really connected with the Catholic church. I had been attending the gay synagogue for about ten years and had wanted to convert for a long time. I finally met Helene. We worked together, and I converted in May 1987. I had a wonderful connection to this woman, and to have her officiate at another rite of passage felt very appropriate.

*Rosanne:* We also chose her because she and Balfour Brickner, the other rabbi with whom she works, have been actively involved in trying to integrate the gay and lesbian Jewish community into the mainstream Jewish community. At their synagogue they have a written policy welcoming gay and lesbian Jews into their community.

*Judy:* When I was converting, we had asked her theoretically whether she would feel comfortable participating at such a ritual, and she had said then that she was comfortable with the idea, but she wasn't sure if she could do it. She's so busy that she usually doesn't deal with anything that doesn't have to do with her own temple's congregants. So we really didn't expect her to officiate. When we called her up, she was so excited; we were shocked. She said, "Of course I'll do it." She was so supportive. We worked with her to create new terms, in Hebrew and English, for ourselves and for who we were to each other. We certainly weren't the bride and groom! We discussed the structure of the ceremony, as we didn't want to ape a heterosexual wedding. Finally I remember her saying, "What's the matter if you want a wedding? If you want a wedding, then have a wedding. It's okay. It's fine." What we ended up with was something which was unique but which was also a very traditional Jewish wedding.

*Rosanne:* It meant a lot to me to have a traditional Jewish ceremony. I had been very involved with Judaism growing up, but I had distanced myself from it with coming out. I used to say that there was no place for a single woman in Judaism let alone a gay woman. When my mother died, I wanted to follow the tradition and say the Mourner's Kaddish daily, for eleven months, in a synagogue. But I never found a synagogue where I felt comfortable. People would ask, "Who are you? You're not married? Would you like to go out with my son?" And as soon as you said "No," the openness and conversation ended. When I moved to New York and found the gay synagogue I felt as if I'd come home. It was the first time I had ever been able to combine these integral but completely separate parts of my life. So for me the ceremony was a celebration of our relationship, our spirituality and my return to Judaism.

*Judy:* The ceremony itself was wonderful. We have a good friend who was the cantor and also played the clarinet at the beginning of the ceremony. As people entered, we played some taped Jewish music to set the mood and the tenor. First the rabbi and our family and friends who were carrying the chuppah came in. Then they lifted the chuppah up, to create the tent. We had wrapped myrtle around the poles; we found out that we're both allergic to it, but we didn't mind the itchy eyes. Rosanne was carrying a bouquet of heather and dill, and I had heather and parsley. That's not traditional at all, but we wanted to have herbs there to symbolize our love for nature. There was a table next to the chuppah, and when we got there we put our heather and herbs into a vase on the table, joining them together. Candles and cups for the wine were also on the table.

*Rosanne:* The ceremony consisted of many of the traditional parts of a Jewish wedding. There were a couple of cups of wine, the talk by the rabbi, our vows, the exchange of rings, and then the Shevah Brachot, which are seven blessings. It was a really beautiful ceremony. Many people said it was the most Jewish wedding they'd ever been to.

*Judy:* After the ceremony we had a small Kiddush at the synagogue and then a large reception several blocks away. This is New York, and you can't get anywhere easily. We figured it would be hard to get people in cabs, and it's impossible to park, so we hired a bus to transport people back and forth. It was a lot of fun. You know what it's like when you're on a bus with lots of people; it's like camp. Everyone was singing and really getting into it.

*Rosanne:* By the time we got to the reception, which was probably an hour after it started, the mixing was absolutely amazing. We walked in and couldn't believe what was happening. The band said they had never been to anything where people were so incredibly high. The dance floor was unbelievable. Everyone was dancing with everyone: gay, straight, men, women, young, old.

It was also incredible to have all of these people from different parts of our lives in one room at the same time. It was very therapeutic, after having kept these parts of our lives separate from each other for so long. Not only was my family there, along with all of my gay friends, but everyone from my work life as well. I'm a doctor, and I'm on the faculty at a medical school. I had invited my whole division, and every single one of them showed up. The same thing happened with Judy's colleagues.

*Judy:* We have this one picture of my boss, who has snow white hair, dancing with his wife. They were both scared to death to come to our ceremony, but they wanted to be supportive. In the center of this one picture, the two of them are dancing. All around them are men dancing with men, and women dancing with women. The two of them ended up having a great time and telling all their friends about it. Here were all these different kinds of people having a wonderful time together. My aunt who lives in Vermont was there, along with the dairy farmer she's dating. The woman I had my first little love affair with in sixth grade was there. All the parts of my life were there.

*Rosanne:* Besides eating and dancing, we had a candle-lighting ceremony at the reception. We asked people from different parts of our lives to come up and light candles for us. We had the band play specific music for each group of people that came up. My brother started it off by making a toast which left everyone in tears. He said that he felt that our parents were with us that day, at the ceremony and the celebration.

*Judy:* Our bosses lit a candle. My boss is someone I've known for twenty years. He's a real wise-guy, and I never trust him when he opens his mouth. Well, when he got up there, he took the microphone. We didn't know what was going to happen. He said, "Judy didn't know when she invited me up here that I was going to speak." The look on my face on the video is priceless. It's like, "Oh, my God!" And then he said, "Judy has been like a third daughter to me, and today's she fulfilling my fantasy." I was thinking, "Oh, Lord." I didn't know what to expect. "One daughter got married last year, one's getting married later this year, but Judy is the only one to snare a Jewish doctor." It brought the house down. People were roaring with laughter.

*Rosanne:* Then we lit the last candle with Shelly and Jay, and we said the Shehechlanu, the prayer that thanks God for letting us live until this point in time. It was very emotional. Everyone knew that Shelly was very ill. It was amazing that he had been able to get to the ceremony.

Everyone danced, and they lifted us up in chairs, decorated us, and danced us around. We had no idea that was going to happen. It was wonderful. I have always had trouble with the idea that I need to have outside forces or other people validate my lifestyle or my relationship, yet there was something so incredibly high about having all of these people affirm our being together. To have them there while we danced together, while we slow danced together.

We've also both been aware of the effect that the ceremony has had on our relationship. It's a cementing, in a very positive sense. It has to change a relationship when you can call a cousin, with whom you had been very vague and distant for several years, and immediately are asked, "How's Judy? How's she doing? Will she be there, too?" Being able to be open and accepted allows us to enlarge our world and our visions.

*Judy:* If we could afford to, we'd do it again! Neither of us drink, but the high from that day was incredible. I don't think there's anything that can describe it. I wish we could bottle the elation and joy from that day and use it every once in a while when we need it.

*Rosanne:* I was raised in a family where it was expected that you would get married immediately after college. So much so, that at one point during college I told my mother I was going to drop out; I knew I wasn't going to get married, and I figured if I didn't graduate I wouldn't have to worry about it. I kept feeling the pressure to get married everywhere, and it seemed as though the pressure just increased as I got older. I know heterosexual couples that have wonderful relationships, but I've also known people to get married for reasons totally other than love. So it was strange to me when people in our community talked about commitment ceremonies as mocking heterosexual experience, because for me the creation of our Brit Ahavah was so different from a heterosexual wedding. The fact that gays and lesbians do this against all odds makes the whole process completely different.

It took many years for me to find the right person to live my life with. When I finally found her, it felt completely right and natural to have this kind of a celebration. It put weddings in an entirely different context for me. People kept asking, "Aren't you nervous? Aren't you scared?" Why would I be scared? I had waited a lifetime for this.

*This account is based on an interview with Rosanne Leipzig and Judy Mable.*

## Brit Ahavah

*Rabbi Ferris:* Blessed are all of you who come here in the name of G-d. We bless you here in this house of G-d.

Our G-d and the G-d of our ancestors, Creator of love and companionship, joy and gladness, the hearts of Rosanne and Judy are filled with gratitude today, as they stand under Your protective chuppah, pieced together with tokens of love from all of their friends. They are here to affirm and celebrate their love. They thank You for each other and for all the influences which have led them to each other. Help them constantly to be worthy of each other. May their life together be illumined by your light. May they be ever faithful to the finest within themselves, to each other and to You. Let us say together: Amen.

We join together now in the blessing of thanks for having reached this sacred time:

Baruch ata Adonoi, Eloheynu melech ha-olam, she-heh-cheh-yanu, v'kiy'manu, v'higi-anu, la-z'man ha-zeh.
Praised are you, Adonai our G-d, Ruler of the universe, for giving us life, for sustaining us and for bringing us to this joyous moment.

*First Cup*
This cup of wine is symbolic of the cup of life. As you share this one cup of wine, may life be that much sweeter because you share it, and if there is any bitterness within your lives together, may the bitterness be that much less bitter also because you share. Let us say together:

Baruch ata Adonoi, Eloheynu melech ha-olam, bo-rei p'ri hagofen.
Blessed are You, Adonai our G-d, Ruler of the universe, creator of the fruit of the vine.

*Personal Vows* (music: Iti M'lvanon)
(Adapted from the "Song of Songs")

Together:  For the winter is past, the rain is over and gone, the flowers appear on the earth—the time of singing has come, and the voice of the dove can be heard in our land.

The fig tree is bearing fruit, and the vines are fragrant. So arise, my love—let me see your face, let me hear your voice—for your face is sweet, and your voice lovely...

Rosanne:  I am a rose of the meadow; you are a lily of the valley;

Judy:  You are a fountain of gardens; I am a well of living waters.

Together:  We are streams flowing from the mountains...
Before I was aware my soul set me searching for you.

Rosanne:  Who else could I spend my life with?

You've changed my world from black and white into techni-color, given names to the flowers, fragrances to the spices and music to my soul.

Judy:    Who else could I spend my life with?

You've transformed my dormant spirit into a vibrant rainbow of light; made the luna moth immortal; arranged a fragmented rock into a beautiful mosaic; and given harmonious melody to my previously silent soul.

Together:    With whom else could we listen to Roumania and Phillip Glass, Liz Story and Holly Near, Vivaldi and Judy Garland?

With whom else could we sing "You are My Sunshine," Broadway tunes or trope?

Judy:    With whom else would I light candles every Friday night, and on Saturday night look to the sky for the three stars to make a distinction between Shabbat and the rest of the week?

Rosanne:    Who else would wake up with me at 5:30 every morning— cuddling and laughing?

Together:    Before I was aware, my soul set me searching for you.

*Judy and Rosanne* (each with own candle):

As we bring together the two candles of our lives up until this moment, we ask that our bond be as vibrant and as illuminating as this new flame, that it continually be renewed by the strengths of our individual selves, and that, like this powerful flame, our life together radiate light and warmth.

Baruch ata Adonoi, Eloheynu melech ha-olam, bo-rey m'orey ha-aish. Holy one of Blessing, Your presence fills creation forming the lights of fire.

*Rabbi's Talk*

Rosanne and Judy, I do not think it a coincidence that you are here in this place at a most important time of the Jewish year. As you stand on the threshold of a new life together, the Jewish people stand at the threshold of the celebration of our freedom—the celebration of Passover. There is a link between these two events. Heinrich Heine said that ever since the Exodus, freedom has always spoken with a Hebrew accent. Throughout the millennia, Jews have always been in the forefront of the struggles for free-dom, knowing that the cause of freedom and the cause of peace are bound together.

All of us here today know that our world is far from shalom—far from wholeness, oneness, peace. Not only because there are wars, and physical suffering and injustice, but also because so-called free people are not really free. There is an all-pervasive slavery of the mind of a different sort—intolerance and bigotry, prejudice and oppression. Your standing here to-day symbolizes the struggle of our people to escape the oppression of Egyptian slavery and the cruelties of oppression throughout our long his-tory. We have survived much cruelty because brave people have stood up for us as you stand up here today for your freedom. Great risks must be taken for great causes. Our people risked their lives when they escaped from Egypt; but throughout all of their history they survived all the cruel-ties inflicted upon them. They survived and all kinds of Jews will continue to survive. Our ancestors survived because they had each other—and they had a great vision.

You two have taken risks to be here today. You have each other—and a great vision. I greatly admire what you have done to bring us all to this very special day. You vowed to bring light and service to our people. I pray that the joy and the love that you share in your lifetime will not keep you from your life's mission—the mission of all Jews: to work for that day when all shall sit under the vines and their fig trees and none shall make them afraid—afraid for their body or their soul.

I pray that your life together will take on new meaning each day; that as your love and blessings increase, so will your commitment to your world. I pray that you will understand the cosmic meaning of your mortal lives; that you will understand the imperative of Israel—to struggle with G-d in all the ways that you can.

A midrash tells us that the angels were jealous of G-d's giving the Torah to Israel; they wanted it for themselves! G-d asked them, "Did you go down to Egypt? Were you enslaved to Pharaoh? Why should the Torah be yours?" The rabbis teach us by this midrash that only those who have known hardship and oppression can fully appreciate the moral mandate of G-d's commandments.

Judy and Rosanne—I thank you with all my heart and soul for the privi-lege of being here with you this day. May you go forth in your new life to-gether bringing greater joy and peace to our world because of the great joy and peace that you will share with each other. Amen.

*Ring Service*

In keeping with the sacred commitment you have made, you will each give and receive a ring. They are a symbol of your unity and the unbroken circle of your love.

Rosanne, as you place the ring on Judy's finger, say to her these words of commitment:

Haray at m'kudeshet li b'taba'at zo l'fnai elohim v'ha-adim ha-aleh.
Judy, you are consecrated to me with this ring before G-d and these witnesses.

(same for Judy)

Join hands and say:

Zot dodati, zot ra-ayati.
This is my beloved; this is my friend.

*Reading of the Ketubah*

And now I will read a part of the permanent record of Judy and Rosanne's commitment to each other.

(First paragraph read in Hebrew, the whole ketubah in English)

On the first day toward Shabbat, the second day of Nisan, the beginning of the flowering of spring, in the year five thousand seven hundred and forty eight since the creation of the world as we count here in the city of New York, Rosanne Mira Leipzig, daughter of Ellen Terry and Bill, and Judith Mable, daughter of Catherine and Earl, in the presence of our dear families and friends, stood under the chuppah exchanged rings, and entered into this Brit Ahavah with each other.

We promise to be ever open to one another while cherishing each other's uniqueness; to nourish, comfort and challenge each other through life's sorrow and joy; to share our intuition and insight with one another; and above all to do everything within our power to permit each of us to become the persons we are yet to be.

Our home will be open to the spiritual potential in all life; a home wherein the flow of the seasons and the passages of life are celebrated according to our Jewish heritage; a home filled with reverence for learning, loving and generosity; a home in which we resonate to ancient melodies; in which candles and Kiddush wine sanctify the table; a home that is linked to the community of Israel and the people of Israel.

This covenant, sealed with our mutual love, will be a foundation for our shared lives as we are joined together today as Ahoovot Chaiim, beloveds for life.

### Sheva Brachot

Now we will hear chanted the traditional Sheva Brachot. The number seven holds a very special place in our tradition. The number seven forms a basis for our calendar, and for our celebrations. It is the days of the week—the six days of creation and the seventh day, a day of rest. These blessings thank G-d for creation, for wine, for the creation of humankind, for the creation of the capacity for reproduction, for life, love, joy, peace and friendship.

(The cantor chants the Sheva Brachot)

*Rabbi Ferris:* Judy and Rosanne have chosen seven blessings also to share with you.
(from Rabbi Stacy Ofner)

1) Blessed are You O G-d, for creating that wonder which is our world: the mountains, the oceans, the deserts, the forests and the fields. All is full of life.

2) Blessed are You O G-d, for the creation of all people.

3) Blessed are You O G-d, for creating all people in Your image. Each person reflects the wonder of creation. All people are sacred, creators of life.

4) May the joyous hope of a better world
   Inspire all people to work together
   For justice and thus for peace,
   So that the homeless will have homes,
   The hungry will be fed,
   The persecuted and oppressed will be free,
   And all people will learn
   To live in peace with each other
   And in harmony with their environment.

5) We surround this couple with our love.
   May they be for each other lovers and friends.
   May their individual gifts help them
   To create new worlds together.

6) Blessed are You O G-d, Creator of joy and gladness,

Song, laughter, good luck, hope,
Love, happiness,
Peace and Friendship.
May we all witness the day
When the dominant sounds
In Jerusalem
And throughout the world
Will be these sounds of happiness:
The voices of lovers,
The sounds of feasting and singing,
And the songs of peace.
May these beloved companions rejoice together!

7) And now with wine, our symbol of joy, we give thanks to the Eternal
Source of creation that gives us the fruit of the vine, symbol of our
rejoicing.

Baruch ata Adonoi, Eloheynu melech ha-olam, bo-rey p'ri hagofen.

In the presence of this company as witness you, Judith Mable and
Rosanne Leipzig, have spoken the words and performed the rites which
unite your lives. Therefore, I, along with all those here, recognize you as
ahoovot chaiim, beloveds for life.

At this time I ask you, and all of you people gathered here, to take a
few moments to pray silently, so that your prayers may ascend on high,
prayers that wish you everything you deserve.

### Birkat Hakohanim

Thousands and thousands of years ago, according to our tradition, the
priests used the words that I will use to bless the congregation, to bless all
of the people who deserved blessing among our people. Although these
words have been used throughout the millennia, and they are known to us
and seem to be words that aren't so special because they are used so much,
to me they are very special because they are used so much. And they're special every time I use them because of the people who are blessed by them. I
consider it an honor to be using these ancient words to bless you.

(Rabbi Ferris takes her hands and cups them, one on the outside of Judy's
head, the other on the outside of Rosanne's, and draws their heads):

May G-d bless you and keep you.
May G-d's countenance always shine upon you and be gracious unto you.
May G-d's countenance always be lifted upon you and your loved ones,

and may you be granted that most precious gift—the gift of shalom: wholeness, completeness, oneness, peace—in a world of peace. Amen.

*Break one glass together*

*Kiss*

*Leave to simun tov und mazel tov.*

ᔊ

*Rosanne Leipzig: Rosanne is a thirty-eight-year-old physician originally from Syracuse, New York, who specializes in geriatrics and psychopharmacology. She participates as a service leader and cantor at the New York City gay and lesbian synagogue, Congregation Beth Simchat Torah. Along with Judy, music is the love of her life—singing, listening and playing.*

*Judy Mable: Judy is a forty-two-year-old vascular laboratory clinician who has lived in New York City for over twenty years. She designs jewelry, collects socks and enjoys cooking and birdwatching. Together, Judy and Rosanne play raquetball, take advantage of the cultural aspects of New York, and are members of a gay and lesbian spiritual group, Chavurah Aliza.*

Chris Lahowitch

Becky Butler was born in Mexico City and spent her early years in Mexico and Italy. Her parents, Jean Rouverol and Hugo Butler, were both screenwriters blacklisted during the McCarthy era. Having taken refuge outside the country during the fifties and early sixties, the family finally returned to the United States, settling in Los Angeles.

After getting a degree in filmmaking from Harvard/Radcliffe, Becky spent ten years working on documentary and feature films. In 1988, she left the field of film in order to devote more time to this anthology and also to pursue a master's degree in clinical social work. She is currently the clinical director of a treatment facility and has a private psychotherapy practice. She lives in Atlanta with her partner, with whom she had a ceremony of commitment in 1987.

# Selected Titles from Seal Press

LESBIAN COUPLES: *Creating Healthy Relationships for the 90s* by D. Merilee Clunis and G. Dorsey Green. $12.95, 1-878067-37-0. The definitive guide for lesbians that describes the pleasures and challenges of being part of a couple. Also available on audiocassette, $9.95, 0-931188-85-7.

THE LESBIAN PARENTING BOOK: *A Guide to Creating Families and Raising Children* by D. Merilee Clunis and G. Dorsey Green. $16.95, 1-878067-68-0. This practical and readable book, filled with humor and wisdom, covers a wide range of parenting topics as well as issues specifically relevant to lesbian families. Information on each child development stage is also provided.

THE ME IN THE MIRROR by Connie Panzarino. $12.95, 1-878067-45-1. The memoir of writer, lesbian and disability rights activist and artist Connie Panzarino, who has been living with a rare muscular disease since birth.

SWEAT: *Stories and a Novella* by Lucy Jane Bledsoe. $10.95, 1-878067-64-8. The elusive sanctity of sport. The exquisite rewards of risk. The adventure that is contemporary lesbian life. These are the themes that resonate in this refreshing first collection by Lucy Jane Bledsoe.

ALMA ROSE by Edith Forbes. $10.95, 1-878067-33-8. A brilliant lesbian novel filled with unforgettable characters and the vibrant spirit of the West.

OUT OF TIME by Paula Martinac. $9.95, 0-931188-91-1. A delightful and thoughtful novel about lesbian history and the power of memory. *Winner of the 1990 Lambda Literary Award for Best Lesbian Fiction*.

MARGINS by Terri de la Peña. $10.95, 1-878067-19-2. An insightful story about family relationships and lesbian passion.

LATIN SATINS by Terri de la Peña. $10.95, 1-878067-52-4. This second novel by the prize-winning lesbian author tells the lives and loves of a group of young Chicana singers.

LOVERS' CHOICE by Becky Birtha. $10.95, 1-878067-41-9. Provocative stories charting the course of women's lives by an important Black lesbian feminist writer.

**Ordering Information**
Individuals: If you are unable to obtain a Seal Press title from a bookstore, please order from us directly. Enclose payment with your order and 16.5% of the book total for shipping and handling. Washington residents should add 8.2% sales tax. Checks, MasterCard and Visa accepted. If ordering with a credit card, don't forget to include your name as it appears on the card, the expiration date and your signature.

Seal Press, 3131 Western Avenue, Suite 410, Seattle, Washington 98121.
1-800-754-0271 orders only
(206) 283-7844 / (206) 285-9410 fax
sealprss@scn.org

Visit our website at http://www.sealpress.com